G000057553

Britain Can Work

Inflation is unjust and deflation is inexpedient.

J. M. Keynes

I see no dignity in persevering in error.

Sir Robert Peel

IAN GILMOUR

Britain Can Work

Martin Robertson · Oxford

© Ian Gilmour, 1983

First published in 1983 by
Martin Robertson & Company Ltd.,
108 Cowley Road, Oxford OX4 1JF.

All rights reserved. No part of this publication may be
reproduced, stored in a retrieval system, or transmitted,
in any form or by any means, electronic, mechanical,
photocopying, recording or otherwise, without the
prior written permission of the copyright holder

British Library Cataloguing in Publication Data

Gilmour, Ian
    Britain can work.
    1. Monetary policy—Great Britain
    2. Great Britain—Economic conditions—1945-
    I. Title
    332.4'491   HG39.5

    ISBN 0-85520-571-7

Typeset by System 4 Associates Limited, Gerrards Cross
Printed and bound in Great Britain by
T. J. Press (Padstow) Ltd

Contents

Preface and Acknowledgements

This book attempts to set out what I believe to be the traditional Tory approach to economics and politics. Such an approach is at present unfashionable but it provides, I think, the best hope of rebuilding the country. Britain would be governed best by a moderate Tory administration.

Critics of the present Government's economic policy, and of the ideology which has occasionally nourished it, have been challenged over and over again by Treasury and other Ministers to say what alternative they would favour. Here is one answer to that challenge. In putting forward the Tory approach I have not tried to avoid knocking down other ideas which seem to me mistaken. But that was not my main purpose. My aim is to restate some of the traditional views of my party and in so doing help it to evolve policies which will enable the Conservative Party to meet challenges possibly more difficult than any it has faced before.

But this book does not offer a 'system' to replace that in which some monetarists evidently believe. It offers no panaceas or all-embracing solutions. Toryism is distrustful of all elixirs and of all allegedly simple answers to very complex problems. What it does offer is, first, the suggestion that we would have done better if we had not fallen prey to a virulent strain of monetarism; secondly, that we stand little chance of sustained recovery from our present condition unless we abandon the prejudices which have determined too much economic policy in the last few years; and, thirdly, that there are some changes, political and economic, which we should make if we are to prevent the continuance of the pretty abysmal record of the last decade.

Of the many people who have helped me, I am indebted above all to Phyllis Deane, Professor of Economic History at Cambridge, for scrutinizing my manuscript and saving me from a number of errors. That was an act of great generosity. Dermot Gleeson has made many stimulating suggestions during the writing of the book, as well as reading the manuscript and making many useful criticisms. Christopher Patten has once again read a manuscript of mine and has given me a great deal of valuable advice. I am enormously grateful to all of them for considerably improving the book.

Sir William Rees-Mogg kindly lent me Keynes's *Tract on Monetary Reform*, without my having asked for it. Reading it was one of the things which prompted me to write this book. He will not think that his benevolence has been well repaid. I am deeply grateful to George Edwards, Brian Outhwaite, Robert Franklin and Richard Needham for valuable help and expert advice on particular points. I am grateful, too, to John Patten for suggesting the book, and to David Knox, Leonard Stone and Bruce Anderson. My wife and family all helped in various ways. Naturally, the errors and the opinions are mine and mine alone.

The superb library of the House of Commons as always met every request as soon as it was made. I am especially grateful to the Economics and Statistical Sections and to the head of the Economics Section, Christopher Barclay, most of all. My secretary, Jane Gore-Booth, made innumerable inquiries on my behalf and decoded my handwriting and typed and endlessly retyped the manuscript with a speed, skill and cheerfulness which well disguised the difficulties and tiresomeness of the task. I owe her my warm thanks.

I have used fragments of articles I have contributed to *Government and Opposition*, the *London Review of Books*, *The Times*, the *Guardian*, the *Daily Telegraph* and *Crossbow*, and also some bits of recent speeches. And I have reproduced, with only minor alterations, two passages from *Inside Right* and one from *The Body Politic.*

Finally, I should like to thank Michael Hay of Martin Robertson for his friendly help and understanding and for publishing the book so quickly.

Ian Gilmour
November 1982

1

Unemployment

For there is a perennial nobleness, and even sacredness in work....In idleness alone is there perpetual despair.

Thomas Carlyle[1]

Economics is what economists do.

Jacob Viner[2]

It is only so far as poverty is abolished that freedom is increased.

Harold Macmillan[3]

At the beginning of *Bleak House* Dickens describes a London fog: 'Fog everywhere, fog up the river...fog down the river...fog on the Essex marshes, fog on the Kentish heights...fog in the eyes and throats, fog all round...and the dense fog is densest near...Temple Bar.' In *Bleak House* Dickens was using fog as an allegory of the law and legal system. Today the fog is in economics and the British economy. It has seeped into every nook and cranny of British life. It affects, for the worse, every policy from defence to social security. This economic fog gets into not the eyes and throats but the brain. There is fog in the Treasury and in the Cabinet, fog in Whitehall and in the City, fog in Fleet Street and in Westminster.

And, like Dickens's fog, much of this economic fog is artificial. It has been self-induced. Plainly, this book is not going to dispel it. It is not capable of creating, as it were, a smokeless zone stretching a mile in every direction from Temple Bar. Yet economic theories and doctrines seem to me to have greatly intensified the fog, and it is this book's contention that if we avoided the liturgy and preaching of the current economic fashion and returned to the real world, visibility would be much improved.

In a free society economic problems cannot be solved purely by economics, and Britain's economic troubles are not solely economic. Economics is not a self-contained science: indeed, it is neither self-contained nor a science. Economics and its objectives are the means to wider ends. Hence an economic policy does not stand by itself. It cannot be separated from its political and moral context. This is, of course, a reassertion of the Tory tradition and a rejection of the notion that economics is a combination of iron laws and mathematical formulae, the former beyond human control, the latter beyond human understanding. Nevertheless, much of economics is now incomprehensible except to the specialist and the cleverest layman, and much of it is irrelevant except to other specialists.

Yet though Britain's problems are not solely economic, they would be more easily solved if economics were not in a state of profound disarray and confusion. Jeremy Bentham once defined jurisprudence as 'the art of being methodically ignorant of what everyone knows'. Today he would have substituted economics for jurisprudence. Many economists have attainments at least as high as those in any other discipline. Yet over the years much of the economics profession has used a body of doctrine which glosses over a number of important features in the economy. The recent Nobel prize winner, Professor Stigler, wrote not long ago 'Today the concept of perfect competition is being used more widely by the profession in its theoretical work than at any time in the past.'[4] And Professor Deane has written that it remains 'the standard, basic model of microeconomic analysis'.[5] The existence of unions and large corporations is not denied but largely ignored.[6] Too often the fact of unemployment is not recognized. Markets are cleared, and the economy tends towards equilibrium. In general what is described has more to do with the nineteenth than with the twentieth century. And human beings in economic affairs are assumed to be always 'maximizing' and to have 'unique, stable and well behaved desires and preferences'.[7]

'Everybody knows' that none of this is true, but economics remains 'methodically ignorant' of this everyday knowledge, and many economists go on propounding the false certainties that comforted a bygone age. It is as though, in politics, professors were telling their students that the British political system was based on the divine right of kings, or teachers of physics were behaving as though Einstein and Niels Bohr had never lived, or the professors of mechanical engineering were expounding the glories of the steam engine while ignoring such tiresome complications as the internal combustion engine and electric power.

In Samuel Butler's *Erewhon* the professors 'seemed to devote themselves to the avoidance of every opinion with which they were not perfectly familiar, and regarded their own brains as a sort of sanctuary, to which if an opinion had once resorted, none other was to attack it'.[8] Some economists today have gone further than the professors of *Erewhon*. They have not merely safeguarded their own ideas and brains; they have made economics itself a sanctuary from which the pressures and facts of the real world are rigidly excluded. But if economics is thus safe from the world, the world is not similarly safe from economics. Instead of remaining quietly in their sanctuary, some of these professors periodically emerge into the world to tell it how to run its affairs. As they make no allowance for the vast differences between the world of the sanctuary and the real world of economic policy, their advice is at best irrelevant and at the worst disastrous. Of course, many economists do live in the real world. Unfortunately, it is the economists of the sanctuary who at present enjoy influence. And it is in their attitude to unemployment that their remoteness from the real world is starkly revealed.

The scourge of unemployment illustrates not only the fog of economics, but also the helplessness or insensitivity of politicians and the fears and ignorance of other people as well. There are some who think that unemployment is mainly the fault of the unemployed themselves. They believe that the unemployed could find work if they really tried, and that they do not really try either because they are better off on the dole or because they prefer idleness to work even if it involves some small financial penalty. This belief is usually based on anecdotal 'evidence' that X knows lots of such people and Y has been trying for ages to find a worker to do something without success. The same sort of beliefs were current in the 1930s. George Orwell recorded a typical conversation: 'My dear, I don't *believe* in all this nonsense about unemployment. Why only last week we wanted a man to weed the garden, and we simply couldn't get one. They don't *want* to work, that's all it is.'[9] Anecdotes may have their interest, but they cannot stand up to hard figures. We now have well over 3 million unemployed and only 100,000 vacancies. Three million into 100,000 won't go. And even if we multiply the number of vacancies by three, as we are told to do because only about a third of the number of vacancies are notified, the answer is little different.

This common-sense conclusion, that mass unemployment is caused not by the unemployed not wanting to take jobs but by there being no jobs available for them to take, is supported by a wealth of evidence. All the factual evidence shows that the great majority of the unemployed want to find work. People feel devalued and degraded by not being at work, and until they become discouraged and demoralized by frequent and long-standing failure to land a job, they make great efforts to get back into employment. And that applies even to many of the small minority who, because they have many children and no skills, do get more money when they are on social security than when they are working.[10] A PSI study found that 'there is no evidence that benefits reduce the incentive to find work; on the contrary those receiving higher than average benefits make greater efforts to find work than those receiving lower than average benefits....'[11] A study by the Manpower Services Commission came to a similar conclusion, as did researchers from the Department of Health and Social Security.[12]

In any case, since 1976–7 the benefits that the unemployed receive have declined quite sharply in relation to average earnings.[13] Yet since that time unemployment has much more than doubled. That surely disproves the theory that it is higher benefits which have stopped people seeking work. As the Supplementary Benefits Commission put it, 'the huge increase in unemployment is a consequence of more fundamental economic forces, not of changes in attitude to work brought about by over-generous benefits.'[14] The benefits are, in fact, far from generous; they are decidedly niggardly, and are appreciably lower than those of other comparable countries.[15] But it is not just the need for money that drives people to seek work. Research has shown — to most people this would be obvious anyway — that pride, the desire for status, self-respect, the satisfaction and comradeship which are derived from work are all important in urging those who have lost their jobs to seek employment.[16]

This evidence, together with common sense, would be enough, it might be thought, to convince the economists. Unfortunately, many economists are not guided by empirical evidence. They make certain assumptions which have little to do with the real world, and on these assumptions they build models and complicated theories. Usually their assumptions start not with a real flesh-and-blood individual, such as somebody who actually is unemployed, but with a construct of their own, who has been called 'economic man'. This creature is analogous to Pavlov's dogs except that he has not been trained and he does not exist. But he acts in the way economists expect him to act; he responds only to economic pains and pleasures; and he behaves as no real person does.

Armed with 'economic man' and much theory, one monetarist school of economists believes that unemployment is largely voluntary. Professor Patrick Minford of Liverpool University and Mr David Peel have therefore suggested that over the three years 1982–4 real social security benefits should be reduced by 15 per cent and the money thus saved used to cut income tax on lower-income taxpayers 'in order to reinforce the incentive effect of reducing benefits'. 'Those who remain unemployed will be worse off,' say Minford and Peel (which is obvious enough), 'but their decision to remain unemployed will be a voluntary one...' (which is breathtaking).[17] Had these gentlemen not been lost in the mist of their own assumptions, they would have discovered that incentives to work are useless unless there are opportunities to work. 'To increase incentives while unemployment accelerates upwards', in the words of the Supplementary Benefits Commission, 'is like trying to encourage somebody to jump into a swimming pool while the water is drained out.'[18] But for such economists to accept these obvious truths would mean their leaving the world of economic theory and entering the world of fact.

Whatever Liverpool economists may think, 'our business', as Canning once told his Liverpool constituents, 'is with fact.' And the fact is that so far from the unemployed being volunteers, they have been press-ganged. As the former Deputy Chairman of the Supplementary Benefits Commission put it, those out of work have been unwillingly conscripted into a growing army of the unemployed.[19]

And their numbers go on growing. The press-gang is still on the prowl. With well over 3 million unemployed (according to the official figures; the true figure is probably 4 million),[20] the annual cost to the Exchequer in lost taxes and the payment of unemployment and supplementary benefit has been estimated by the All-Party Select Committee of the House of Lords in its very useful Report on Unemployment to be more than £15 billion, or about £5,000 per person.[21] It would be difficult to persuade the Treasury to spend one-tenth of that vast sum on improving our economic prospects. Yet it prefers to spend £15 billion to pay people to do nothing rather than act to make the payment of such a sum unnecessary. Even Lord Liverpool's Government in 1817 thought it had a duty to try to provide work for the unemployed,[22] and Castlereagh, no advanced economist, thought it better that the poor should 'live on their own labour' even if it meant employing them 'to dig a hole one day and make them fill it up again the next'.[23]

The costs of unemployment extend far beyond the direct Exchequer costs. As one would expect, the health of the unemployed and of their spouses and children often deteriorates.[24] High unemployment is acknowledged to be bad for racial harmony. And since among blacks the proportion out of work is much higher than it is in the population as a whole, racialism and hostility to society are inevitably fostered. 'How can Britain's youth', asks Mr Kapo in *A Savage Culture*, giving a black British view, 'relate to leaders who are an experience and two classes removed? They have every reason to rebel, with no jobs, no prospects but a guaranteed place in the Great Britain dole queue?'[25] The causes of crime are notoriously difficult to pin down. After all, crime increased during the days of full employment. But it would be rash to deny that there is a link between unemployment and crime or between unemployment and rioting.[26] As an unemployed man told Mr Seabrook: 'My mother always said the devil finds work for idle hands. It's true of idle minds, I can tell you.'[27] The House of Lords Committee concluded that the social costs of unemployment were an additional charge to the Exchequer of 'at least some hundreds of pounds for every person unemployed'.[28]

But mass unemployment entails not just a cost to the Exchequer. It leads to a deterioration in the work force. Many skilled workers who lose their jobs and do not emigrate are driven into less skilled jobs. And many of them prefer the relative security of their new occupation to the proved insecurity of the old. In such circumstances, too, many firms cut their training programmes. That is why even in periods of high unemployment there are frequent complaints of shortages of skilled workmen. And when the recovery comes the skills will either not be available or they will have deteriorated. What the Pilgrim Trust study found in 1938 is no less true today: those out of work 'are not simply units of employability who can, through the medium of the dole, be put in cold storage and taken out again immediately they are needed. While they are in cold storage, things are likely to happen to them.'[29] Some people seem to think that whatever its other disadvantages, mass unemployment does at least help the economy. In fact, not only does human 'capital' deteriorate; factories close and there is a sharp decline in investment. Future prospects are therefore diminished. So unemployment damages the economy along with everything else.

Last and most important is the misery of many of the workless. Certainly, the unemployed are not as badly off as they were in the 1930s. Equally, as Professor Sinfield has observed, the poverty of the 1930s was not as bad as that suffered before the 1914 war, and the poverty of those days was not as grinding as that of the 'hungry forties' in the nineteenth century.[30] And rather than deriving great comfort from the fact that those out of work, like nearly everybody else, are better off than they were in the 1930s, we should be wise to remember Burke's remark about there coming a time when men would not suffer bad things merely because their ancestors had suffered worse.

Judging by the number of attempts at definition, it is difficult to define poverty. So perhaps it is better not to try. But the unemployed who are married with children tend to be the poorest of all those who are living on supplementary benefit,[31] who in turn are by definition the poorest people in the country. Leaving out child benefit in both cases, average male earnings are now about £160 a week, and from November 1982 unemployment benefit was £41.05 a week for a family with two children, £25 for the man, £15.45 for his wife and 30p a week for each child.* No

* Many of these families would be entitled to supplementary benefit.

wonder that the Minister for Social Security accepted in 1980 that 'the provision for children under the Supplementary Benefit scheme is not good enough, has never been good enough, and will not be good enough'[32] following the proposed changes. No wonder, too, that economic hardship, together with the loss of dignity and self-esteem caused by unemployment, leads to a progressive demoralization of the jobless and their families. Mass unemployment is not only an evil now; it is also storing up evil for the future.

The personal, social, economic and political consequences of unemployment are grievous and far-reaching. The unemployed tend to come from the poorest segments of our society, and their loss of employment is not their fault. In these circumstances Governments might be expected to make the most strenuous efforts to treat the unemployed well rather than punitively, and to do everything in their power to reduce their number. Yet under successive Governments nothing of the sort has happened. In Britain both parties have treated the unemployed less well than those who are poor for other reasons, and both have responded to the doubling of unemployment during their term of office with rhetoric rather than action.*

* To achieve the barest minimum of fair treatment, two things need to be done immediately. In 1980 the Government abated the uprating in unemployment benefit by 5 per cent in lieu of taxation. From July 1981 unemployment benefit became taxable, yet the 5 per cent was not restored, even though restoration would have cost only one-tenth of what the Government had gained by the taxation of the benefits. The failure to restore the 5 per cent was inexcusable and should now be rectified.

The second minimum requirement is that the unemployed should be entitled to the long-term rate of supplementary benefit. The unemployed receive unemployment benefit for only a year. That, too, is wrong. There are no grounds for ending unemployment benefit after a year. However, the more urgent need is that when it does end and the unemployed have to rely solely on supplementary benefit, they should be allowed the long-term rate. For no discernible reason, successive Governments have confined them to the short-term rate, which is some 20 per cent lower. Once again, this discrimination is inexcusable. The long-term unemployed 'include many people who are unskilled' and who have suffered 'poverty and damage to their confidence. They include many people who are physically weak or suffer from minor disabilities. They include, above all, people on whom society's demands place a heavy strain at any time.'[33] As there are now more than 1 million people who have been out of work for more than a year, the 'wholly unjust' denial of the long-term rate to the unemployed[34] is a matter of ever-growing importance. The Government has accepted the case 'in principle'. But that does not help the unemployed. They need the money, and they should be given it now. Even then, the unemployed would be receiving worse treatment here than in other countries. Still, it is important to make a start. The best way to help the unemployed is, of course, to see that there are enough jobs available for all. But that will take time. Meanwhile, as Coleridge wrote, 'Let us palliate where we cannot cure, comfort where we cannot relieve'.[35]

Even more astonishing than our inadequate response to the needs of the out-of-work is our failure to tackle the problem of unemployment itself. The Labour Government started a number of special employment and training schemes, and the Conservative Government has carried them on and has produced an imaginative plan for the training of the young unemployed. Nearly £2,000 million per annum is now spent on the various schemes. That is a sizeable sum, and these measures are very much better than nothing. Yet mass unemployment should have been treated as a major problem in its own right, like, say, reconstruction after a war or the creation of a modern transport system. Instead it has been treated as a by-product of other problems, or still worse, as a way of solving the problem of inflation. That attitude is objectionable because it is in defiance of the Disraelian tradition of One Nation. It is indefensible in that it flouts an even more fundamental Conservative tradition by treating millions of our fellow countrymen as things or means and as not ends in themselves — with all the appalling consequences that we have just noted.* To say that unemployment is something that the country has to suffer is no defence. First, 'the country' does not suffer it; the unemployed do, and they come largely from a particularly poor section of the community. And, second, neither the country nor the unemployed need have suffered the current level of unemployment. That has been made unnecessarily high by the policies of successive Governments.

The Prime Minister, when in opposition, stigmatized Labour, in a striking phrase, as 'the natural party of unemployment'. That, taken together with her speech at Birmingham during the election when she said that there was 'nothing inevitable about rising unemployment',[37] seemed to imply that the Conservatives would be more effective than Labour in dealing with the problem. Instead, if Labour is the natural party of unemployment, the Conservatives have become the party of natural unemployment. The Conservative Government now seems to believe that unemployment is merely the result of natural or market forces. According to this view, there

---

* Coleridge stated the principle in these words 'a person can never, but by his own fault, become a thing, or without a grievous wrong be treated as such: and the distinction consisting in this, that a thing may be used altogether and merely as the means to an end; but a person must always be included in the end....'[36]

is nothing the Government can or should do about it. Government action would be unnatural and self-defeating.

This conviction is a defiance of common sense. Unemployment has been caused among other things by the world recession, by competition from the industrial countries of Asia which demands structural changes in industry in this country, by the pace of technological change, by the activities of the trade unions and by the policies of Governments in the United Kingdom since 1974. The attempts by Governments of both parties to deal with the crisis of inflation has exacerbated the unemployment crisis. Governments have sought to bring down inflation by increasing unemployment. And they have done so because they have believed that only increased unemployment would prevent intolerable inflation. In consequence, they have produced intolerable unemployment. But it is not only Governments which have done this. The trade unions must bear their share of the blame for insisting on wage settlements far in excess of anything which could be paid for by increased productivity — that is to say, without increased unemployment or increased inflation or both.

Most of the causes of unemployment cannot be dealt with if the Government stands aside; with the resources at its disposal, the Government can promote industrial change. And the policies of the Government are certainly no more 'natural' than other policies which could have been adopted. Besides, it is those policies themselves, not merely natural forces, which have increased unemployment.

No one suggests that the problem of unemployment can be easily solved. We have only to look around the world to see that. It is a European problem and almost a worldwide one. Certainly, no country could fully solve it on its own. But the difficulty of a problem should not preclude attempts to solve it. Many proposals for reducing unemployment have been put forward. These will be discussed later in this book. Meanwhile virtually nothing has been done, and more people than ever are out of work. To the unemployed, the Government has behaved like a Lewis Carroll character: 'I can do nothing for you, my dear. I cannot, of course, do nothing at this precise moment, but I do hope to be able to do nothing for you very soon.'[38]

Treasury Ministers occasionally seek to justify their policy by saying that it is the only route to the creation of 'real jobs'. The difference between a job and a 'real job' has not been made clear. Sometimes it seems that a 'real job' is one which has not yet been destroyed by the Treasury. But since many more jobs have been destroyed in the private sector than in the public, that would suggest there were more 'real jobs' in the public sector than in the private sector, which seems unlikely. In any case the unemployed would undoubtedly prefer a job now to a 'real job', whatever that may be, in the very distant future.

'The solution of the unemployment problem', Ramsay MacDonald wrote in 1907, 'is the beginning of the socialist state.'[39] The truth is, of course, the opposite: if a non-socialist Government solves the unemployment problem, there will not be a socialist state. What MacDonald should have said is, 'The failure to solve the unemployment problem will be the beginning of the socialist state.' The doubling of unemployment under the last Labour Government has reduced the credibility of socialist claims to have a solution to the problem, but the redoubling of unemployment under the Conservative Government may help to blot out the socialist failure.

In any case, high unemployment is more damaging to those who believe in a free society. The strongest reason for a free or mixed economy is that it is the prime safeguard of individual freedom. But if the free economy does not provide jobs, it becomes not a buttress of liberty but a threat to it. Hyper-unemployment undermines people's faith in a mixed economy, as well as undermining the economy itself, and it gives encouragement to Marxists who wish to see our present arrangements swept away and a fully socialist state erected in their place. There are, therefore, great risks in what the Government is attempting. Even without the Marxist threat there are great dangers. Nobody knows for how long there can be mass unemployment in a free society without the political and social cohesion of that society being destroyed. If the state shows little consideration for millions of its citizens, they are unlikely to feel great affection in return. The unemployed are the innocent casualties of the battle against inflation, and the least well-off people in the country are having to bear the main brunt of the Government's policies. Yet nothing has been done to ease their lot; rather the reverse.

That humane and intelligent people should have conceived and then stuck to policies which involve manifest injustices, dramatic drawbacks and a variety of dangers can be explained largely by the fog of economic theory that I referred to at the beginning of the chapter. Otherwise the existence of well over 3 million unemployed and a badly damaged economy could not be regarded as an outcome of a rational policy. From every point of view, except that of a particular theory, it is violently irrational. And the Conservative Party has habitually treated theory as subordinate to practice and has traditionally had a far greater liking for facts than for doctrine.* But for the fog, therefore, the results of the policy would surely have been found wanting, and the theory would have been quietly abandoned. Even if the claim were true that unemployment is all the fault of union leaders, the unemployed themselves, the world recession, all previous governments, indeed the fault of everybody but the present Government — which in view of the timing and the extent of the rise in unemployment is improbable — a Conservative Government should still have regarded mass unemployment as an affront to a civilized society and a challenge to itself. Clearly, it would not have been able entirely to solve the problem. But it could have made an attempt, and in the meantime it could have treated the unemployed better, not worse.

When, after all, a badly injured man is admitted to hospital, the surgeons do not engage in abstruse technical argument about various complicated diagnoses; they act to ensure that the patient stays alive. Similarly, however stimulating the doctrines of von Clausewitz or Liddell Hart, a military commander pays more attention to the terrain over which he is going to fight and to the strengths and weaknesses of his own forces and those of the enemy than to the doctrines of those eminent strategists. Not so, unfortunately, with economics. There, currently, doctrine is the arbiter. If it were otherwise, there would surely be agreement that it is, for example, better to pay people for working than for not working, and better to have factories in existence and available for future use than closed down and stripped of equipment.

Yet the fog of economic theory and the blindness and damage

---

* The Conservative Prime Minister, Salisbury, summarized the Tory attitude when he wrote of the younger Pitt that he was 'far too practical a politician to be given to abstract theories, universal doctrines, watchwords, or shibboleths of any kind....He always preferred to sacrifice any amount of theory rather than make for his proposals a single needless enemy.'[40]

that it causes are nothing new; fog has long been a promiment element in the economic weather. In order to discover how we got into our present fog-bound condition, it is necessary to look at earlier stages of the economic debate before returning to the controversies of the present day.

2

Political Economy

Under a system of perfectly free commerce, each country naturally devotes its capital and labour to such employments as are most beneficial to each. This pursuit of individual advantage is admirably connected with the universal good of the whole. By stimulating industry, by rewarding ingenuity, and by using most efficaciously the peculiar powers bestowed by nature, it distributes labour most effectively and most economically: while, by increasing the general mass of production, it diffuses general benefit, and binds together, by one common tie of interest and intercourse, the universal society of nations throughout the civilised world.

Ricardo[1]

The condition of England…is justly regarded as one of the most ominous, and withal one of the strangest ever seen in this world. England is full of wealth, of multifarious produce, supply for human want in every kind; yet England is dying of inanition….There are scenes of woe and destitution and desolation, such as, one may hope, the sun never saw before in the most barbarious regions where men dwelt.

Carlyle in 1843[2]

To acquire, to accumulate, to plunder each other by virtue of philosophic phrases, to propose a utopia to consist only of WEALTH and TOIL, this has been the breathless business of enfranchised England for the last twelve years until we are startled from our voracious strife by the wail of intolerable serfage.

Disraeli in 1845[3]

Take the science of Political Economy — no two professors
understand each other....

Coleridge[4]

Ricardo, the greatest of the political economists after Adam
Smith, published his *Principles of Economy and Taxation* in 1817.
Not long afterwards, the writer Harriet Martineau complained that
Members of Parliament were more interested in playing billiards
than in studying Ricardo.[5] Ideally, perhaps, they should have
done both. A single-minded concentration on Ricardo would not
have made them better fitted to deal with the real world than a
singleminded devotion to billiards. Ricardo's book, nevertheless,
became the authorized version of the new economic wisdom.

The political or classical economists were utilitarians, and they
saw enlightened self-interest as the proper arbiter of the affairs of
the world. Enlightened self-interest thus took over the function
previously performed by Divine Providence, or perhaps self-interest
was its delegate. 'Economic man' was completely selfish, and it
was in the interest of every individual to acquire by his own labour
as much wealth as possible. Each man was the best judge of his
own interests. He should, therefore, be free to choose, and free to
make the best bargain he could. The division of labour and his
assessment of where his interests lay would lead him to the most
advantageous employment, which, because it would secure his
greatest productivity, would be best for society as well as himself.

Provided the law prevented or punished violence, contracts were
kept, and rights of property were secure, the division of labour
and the market would together produce the optimum economic
result. There was a natural harmony of economic interests, and so
the whole economic system, production, distribution, exchange and
foreign trade, should be left to individual choice, free competition
and natural forces. Because of this harmony, not only private
interests but also the public good would be promoted. Hence any
interference with the laws of supply and demand was unjustified
and injurious. The Poor Laws, under which the poor were supported by the parish, were an example of such interference and should
be abolished. Although order was important and government had
duties to perform in other spheres, the state should cease to meddle
in economic affairs. *Laissez-faire* should rule even if, for many, the

results would continue to be disastrous. *Laissez-faire* was for better or worse. Either way, the state should not intervene. If things were going well, state intervention would be damaging. If things seemed to be going badly, this was because of inexorable economic laws, and once again state intervention would only make matters worse.

This doctrine was denounced by Bernard Shaw, in his Preface to *Back to Methuselah* at the beginning of the twentieth century, as a determined attempt to convince the world that all progress depended

> on an unrestrained conflict for food and money, on the suppression and elimination of the weak by the strong.... In short on 'doing the other fellow down' with impunity, all interference by a guiding government, all organization except police organization to protect legalized fraud against fisticuffs, all attempt to introduce human purpose and design and forethought into the industrial welter being 'contrary to the laws of political economy'.

There was characteristic Shavian exaggeration in this and some unfairness. The classical economists were high-minded men, whose outlook and sympathies were far more humane and benevolent than those of most of the people who put their doctrines into practice. Moreover, they did not wish to expel the state completely. In *The Wealth of Nations* Adam Smith included among the duties of government not only defence and the enforcement of law but also the provision of public works and institutions, such as roads, bridges, canals, and harbours, which private individuals or groups could not maintain with profit; some seventy years later, in J. S. Mill's *Principles of Political Economy*, the area unsuitable for *laissez-faire* had increased, and it grew larger with each edition of the book. And the political economists were not necessarily opposed to attempts by government to improve social conditions; McCulloch, for instance, supported Shaftesbury over the Factory Acts, and Nassau Senior thought that the laws of supply and demand should apply to the relief of the poor.

But if the classical economists did not fully deserve Shaw's strictures, they were open to the criticism that what they were saying bore little relation to the real world. Adam Smith should be largely excepted. As his great book makes clear, he had doubts about the natural harmony of interests. The idea was plausible when he was talking about individuals, though it would only be true if there was equal access for all to tools and raw materials, which there was not. But it was scarcely credible when he was dealing with the three economic classes of labourers, capitalists and landowners. Besides, *The Wealth of Nations* was published in 1776, at the onset of the Industrial Revolution, which he did not foresee. Machines play a small part in his system. If the natural identity of interests was imaginary even in 1776, it was much less implausible then than it was twenty or forty years later. Finally, as Halévy conjectures, government in Smith's time was probably as weak as it has ever been.[6] Though there was a good deal of irrelevant and purposeless intervention, this was usually so ineffective that *laissez-faire* was often the practice even before Adam Smith supplied the theory.

Such excuses are not available to Adam Smith's successors. As not infrequently happens, the followers became increasingly dogmatic: Malthus on population, Ricardo on the law of wages, James Mill on everything. Although they sometimes disagreed on other matters, they were consistent in deprecating the ability of the state to intervene to improve the economic conditions of the poor. The evidence of destitution both in the towns and in the country was all around them. It testified, wrote Cobbett in 1826, to 'the worst used labouring people upon the face of the earth. Dogs and hogs and horses are treated with more civility, and as to food and lodging, how gladly would the labourers change with them.'[7] It was not the fault of the classical economists that England did not explode into riot, rapine and bloodshed. Unquestionably, they fostered the complacent belief that the evils of industrialism were inevitable and that, therefore, no remediable measures were necessary or possible. As the Tory radical Oastler and others pointed out, conditions for some people in England were worse than they were for slaves in the West Indies, yet most of those who campaigned energetically for the abolition of slavery remained quiescent in the face of worse horrors at home. The classical economists must have known what was going on, but they did not allow it to affect their findings. They were, after all, discovering and promulgating eternal truths. The sufferings of the poor could not be permitted to interfere with such an important pursuit.

In the year following the publication of Ricardo's book, Sismondi, a Swiss historian and economist, visited England and was shocked by what he saw. Far from finding an economic system working smoothly and harmoniously in accordance with classical principles, he saw 'production increasing while enjoyments were diminishing'. He found economic chaos, great poverty and workmen dying of hunger. 'The people of England', he wrote, 'are destitute of comfort now, and of security for the future.' Instead of ideas to deal with this crisis, he found merely belief in the non-intervention of the Government, a belief which was induced by a supposed economic science 'so speculative that it seemed divorced from all practice'.[8]

It was not only a Swiss visitor who had such thoughts. Some Englishmen and Scotsmen who were far removed from the commercial and industrial scene also found the doctrines of the political economists unreal and pernicious. Prominent among such people were some of the country's leading poets and novelists. 'God's justice is requiting,' wrote Sir Walter Scott of the industrialists who were creating misery and slums in the large cities, 'and will yet further requite those who have built up this country into a state of insubstantial opulence at the expense of the health and morals of the lower classes.'[9] In the year that Ricardo's book appeared, Scott suggested a tax on manufacturers to provide aid for workmen who had lost their jobs because of the recession. He thought any injury to the manufacturers caused by the tax would be deserved, since they had 'degraded and demoralized' the poor. It was fair, therefore, that they and not the nation should pay.[10] Scott also favoured a restoration of the income tax to pay for public works and free education for poor children. But he did not confine himself to commination and legislative proposals. He carried out a 'one-man public works programme'[11] to provide employment for those out of work near Abbotsford. 'I have kept about thirty of the labourers in my neighbourhood in constant employment this winter,' he wrote to Southey in May 1817. Scott did not claim that this was charity, since the work benefited him, but he was putting himself to inconvenience by incurring several years' expenditure at once, and his motive was certainly bene-volent.[12]

Unlike Scott, the Lake Poets, Coleridge, Southey and Words-worth, were all radicals in their youth, but when they became Tories, their views on social matters and on political economy were similar to his. Coleridge rejected the doctrines of political economy, which he thought could never be a pure science,[13] and was as a result called 'an arrant driveller'[14] by John Stuart Mill. Yet Coleridge's views were more profound and have lasted much better than the opinions of those whom he called 'the colder-hearted men' who studied 'political economy'.[15]

Coleridge's basic political belief was that no man should be treated as 'a thing' or used 'merely as the means to an end'.[16] And that, in his view, was just what 'the sect of economists' did. They worshipped, he thought, a 'kind of non-entity' which was the economists' economic man, and they made bloody sacrifices to it. Real people were rendered 'diseased and vicious' by a system of policy that made them lose 'all those virtues which made them happy and estimable as individuals'.[17]

As this system was not tolerable, the state should intervene. He pointed out that every Canal Bill showed that the legislature had the right to control every 'species of property...as soon as the right of the individuals is shown to be disproportionately injurious to the community'.[18] This was clearly true of the manufacturing system. Manufacturers, therefore, 'must consent to regulations'.[19] It was not uncommon, Coleridge wrote, for 100,000 people to be out of work in the cotton districts and to be 'dependent upon hard-hearted taskmasters for food'. Instead of relying on short-term and ignoble expedients, the Government and manufacturers should pay attention to principle and to 'enlarged systems of action' and should listen to 'the true and unerring impulses' of their nature.[20] Property was a trust and entailed duties; and just as the conditions in the factories must be improved, so the coun-try gentry should see to the education of their dependents and those who lived on their land.[21]

Coleridge had some hard things to say about political economy. The little of it that was true was obvious to every man of common sense. 'An abstract conclusion in a matter of political economy', he wrote, 'the premises of which neither exist now, nor ever will

exist within the range of the wildest imagination, is not a truth
but a chimera — a practical falsehood.' Economists should start
with the real world and real problems and try to decide 'how to
do so-and-so with them'. But instead of dealing with problems,
the political economists concentrated on theory. They deserted
reality and 'common probability' and ignored all of human nature
that did not fit in with their theories.[22] Coleridge's comments
apply equally well to most of the economics of later generations.

Coleridge's greatest economic insight, as a non-professional,
lay in perceiving the business cycle, though he did not name it.
He wrote of the periodical 'revolutions of credit' which lead to
booms and slumps, or in his more apocalyptic language: 'Disease,
I say, and vice, while the wheels are in full motion; but at the
first stop the magic wealth-machine is converted into an intolerable weight of pauperism!' He seems to have thought that taxation
might mitigate the 'great fluctuations' caused by 'the spirit of
commerce'.[23] Southey, too, described the over-production caused
by the increased investment and growing competition. In time
trade declined, men lost their jobs and 'every return of this cold
fit is more violent than the former'.[24] He thought that one of the
best ways of promoting the nation's prosperity was to spend
liberally on public works. If the nation could spend large sums
of money on war, it could do much good in peacetime by spending money on such things as making roads, building harbours,
reclaiming fens and building schools, colleges and churches.[25]

Southey was eloquent on the sufferings of the poor, the iniqui-
tous game laws, the abominable state of the prisons and much
else besides. In the manufacturing districts, he wrote in 1823,

> where the wages of the adults are at a starvation rate and
> their children are literally worked to death — murdered by
> inches...there is a dreadful reality of oppression, a dreadful
> sense of injustice, of intolerable misery, of intolerable wrongs,
> more formidable than any causes which have ever moved a
> people to insurrection.[26]

The children employed in factories were 'white slaves' and the boy
chimney-sweepers were 'the British negroes'.[27]

In contrast to the political economists Southey was sure that society's evils were not inevitable. A great deal could be done by good laws, good institutions and good governments.[28] Southey helped Shaftesbury over factory legislation and he himself proposed a long series of reforms which would certainly have greatly improved society had there been a government good enough to carry them out. Southey was mercilessly satirized by Byron and attacked as a renegade by many radicals. Yet even his political opponent, Hazlitt, conceded him to be 'once a philanthropist, always a philanthropist'.[29] He had an acute dislike of dogmas and of systems; accordingly, he regarded political economy as a 'pseudo-science' whose practitioners saw things not as they were but 'through the delusive medium of their own theories and prepossessions'.[30]

Wordsworth's view of political economy was not as fully formed as Southey's, but he wrote of the factory system in *The Excursion*:

> An unnatural light
> Prepared for never resting labour's eyes
> Breaks from a many-windowed fabric huge;
> And at the appointed hour a bell is heard....
> A local summons to unceasing toil!
> Disgorged are now the ministers of day;
> And, as they issue from the illumined pile,
> A fresh band meets them at the crowded door....
> Men, maidens, youths,
> Mothers and little children, boys and girls,
> Enter, and each the wonted tasks resumes
> Within this temple, where is offered up
> To gain, the master idol of the realm,
> Perpetual Sacrifice.[31]

Wordsworth's views were similar to Scott's, though not as far-reaching and, in his prose at least, less felicitously expressed. 'For upwards of thirty years,' he wrote in 1818, 'the lower orders have been accumulating in pestilential masses of ignorant population.'[32] He favoured government regulation and inspection of factories, and he was bitterly critical of that monument to utilitarianism, the new Poor Law of 1834. Contradicting Malthus, he thought that it was not the fault of the poor that they were indigent; 'the poor who cannot find employment have a right to support by law.'[33]

'Poets', the great Whig lawyer Cockburn said of Scott, 'may be excused for being bad political economists.'[34] Scott, Wordsworth, Coleridge and Southey would rightly have taken that sneer as a compliment. Indeed, Southey might well be considered a better economist than poet.

All four men were Tories as well as poets. Dickens was a Liberal and a novelist. He shared the views of Wordsworth on the new Poor Law and exposed its workings in *Oliver Twist*. Later in *Bleak House*, in his passages about Tom-all-Alone's, he described the squalor of the London slums and in *Hard Times* the conditions in industrial Preston, where there were 'tall chimneys rising up into the air like competing Towers of Babel'. In the same novel he satirized the systemists, who believed that buying in the cheapest market and selling in the dearest was 'the whole duty of man', and he referred to 'the little mouldy rations of political economy'. If we did not get to heaven by bargaining across a counter every inch of the way from birth to death, heaven was 'not a politico-economical place, and we had no business there'. 'God gave him', the Tory philanthropist Shaftesbury said of Dickens, 'a general retainer against all suffering and oppression.'[35] *

Another novelist, Disraeli, in an early novel, *Popanilla* (published in 1827), pilloried the attitude of the political economists to the Poor Laws. The eponymous hero, accosted by a crippled beggar who has a wife and twelve small children, is about to give him some money:

> but his companion repressed his unphilosophical facility. 'By no means!' said his friend, who turning round to the beggar, advised him, in a mild voice, to *work*; calmly adding, that if he presumed to ask charity again, he should certainly have him bastinadoed. Then they walked on.†

---

* Dickens was less generous. He described Shaftesbury as 'a kind of amiable bull in a china shop of good intentions'.[36]
† Ricardo, who was personally benevolent, would have behaved like Popanilla, but his doctrines tended to promote the behaviour of Popanilla's friend.

And in his later novel, *Sybil*, Disraeli offered a picture of the life of the working classes in the industrial north that was even starker and more sympathetic than anything in Dickens.

These six men, five of them Tories, had in common a very Tory dislike of systems, knowing that a system, which will necessarily be based on abstract thinking, will exclude facts that do not fit in with it. It will, therefore, be false and often dangerous as well. The facts that did not fit into the system of political economy were particularly important ones. The poets could see them plainly and so reacted strongly against political economy. Poets may be expected to be ahead of their time but not necessarily far ahead of the alleged experts in a particular field. Yet Coleridge, Southey and Scott, all of them writing mainly on other subjects and living in rural areas, discerned the damaging effects of the business cycle more clearly than did the classical economists who often lived in large cities and wrote about economics. The contrast is sharp. And that was not their only achievement. The amateurs were seeking to deal with the economic issues that concerned the country and the people. The professionals concentrated mostly on theoretical matters and on concocting so-called laws; real issues were left to the 'invisible hand'. Moreover, the poets were not only able to see and prescribe remedies for the evils that were endorsed or ignored by the political economists; they were also able to detect the faults of method in political economy itself.

So the attitude of the classical economists to the conditions of the poor was far from inevitable. There were people (whose immediate interests lay in other fields) who were better informed than those who claimed to have mastered the subject and to have discovered the laws which governed it. Well might Coleridge talk of 'the reputed masters of Political Economy' and accuse them of 'presumption, temerity, and hardness of heart'.[37]

In defence of the classical economists it can be said that the problems they faced were vast, and that in the century after *The Wealth of Nations* Britain enjoyed unprecedented expansion and prosperity. If the Industrial Revolution was not invented by the classical economists, at least they did nothing to hinder it. Indeed, by providing a justifying doctrine for the 'millocrats', they greatly hastened it. But their doctrines did more than that. However great the initial misery, the market economy secured far greater benefits for man than any other. An economy which allows scope for individual initiative has brought technical progress and material prosperity never previously dreamed of. Competition and a free market have proved to be vastly more dynamic and efficient methods of producing and allocating resources than direction and coercion by government. More fundamentally, political freedom cannot exist without economic freedom. There has never been a free state which has not had a free or mixed economy. Up till now, at least, that really has been an economic or political 'law'. Admittedly, there was no danger of a dictatorship's arising in early nineteenth-century England, still less of an authoritarian or state-directed economy. Indeed, probably the only risk of authoritarianism at that time was a revolution caused by a revulsion against the doctrines of political economy. Nevertheless, both then and later the influence of the classical economists, which has been enormous, has given an impetus to liberty, good as well as bad. And as Lord Robbins has rather wearily reiterated, they did not preach '*laissez-faire* all round'.[38]

Finally, even without the excuse that their writings gave for inaction, government activity to mitigate the hardship caused by the Industrial Revolution would not have been highly effective. The rudimentary machinery of government was not adequate to do what was necessary. Had the classical economists confined themselves to pointing this out and to drawing the conclusion that, for the time being at least, it would be better for governments to intervene as little as possible and to let the individual get on with his own affairs, they would have left less room for argument. But gathering the available information and then basing their argument on that information is not what they did. Instead, infatuated with their new 'science', they preferred to lay down general laws, which they reached by way of *a priori* reasoning and which they believed to be true for all conditions in all times and all places.

Hence the classical economists cannot escape the charge of being massively dogmatic and, on occasion, dogmatically wrong. Adam Smith's belief that the individual's 'study of his own advantage naturally, or rather necessarily, leads him to prefer that employment which is most advantageous to the society'[39] was extravagantly optimistic; Ruskin, who strongly disapproved of

Smith, was much nearer the mark in saying that most people's work was 'generally fixed by necessity or authority'.[40] The argument of Malthus, one of the few wholly non-utopian economists, that the living conditions of the mass of people could never be improved, since any improvement would lead to an increase in population which would outrun subsistence, was extravagantly pessimistic; people, as Hazlitt in his attack on Malthus rightly suspected,[41] do not necessarily have more children if they become better off. Ricardo's rent is an abstraction, and his theory of it is true only under certain conditions; his labour theory of value, that the value of anything is determined by the amount of labour needed to produce it, was vastly influential, but it ignored the influence of demand and was anyway inconsistent with his theory of rent. His 'iron law' of wages — the phrase was Lassalle's not Ricardo's — applied his labour theory of value to labour itself and was doubly wrong. Ricardo claimed that 'the natural price of labour is that price which is necessary to enable the labourers...to subsist and to perpetuate their race without either increase or diminution', and that therefore 'wages should be left to the free and fair competition of the market and should never be controlled by the interference of the legislature.'[42]

This was not true even in Ricardo's time, since many workers were paid more than a subsistence wage; and the 'free competition' of the market was often far from 'fair'. As Adam Smith had earlier recognized, 'in disputes with their workmen, masters must generally have the advantage.'[43] There is still less to be said for the wages fund theory. Although there were germs of this in Adam Smith and Malthus, and although it was formulated by James Mill and McCulloch, the theory was stated most simply by Nassau Senior. Wages, said Senior, 'depend on the extent of the fund for the maintenance of labourers to be maintained'.[44] The idea that there was in the country a fixed fund, which could not be increased, for the payment of wages reached the ultimate of absurdity. But it was believed by nearly everybody from the 1830s until the late 1860s, and it was useful for discouraging labourers from trying to raise their wages. The theory was only destroyed when J. S. Mill, who had formerly believed it, recanted in a famous book review. 'The price of labour,' wrote

Mill, 'instead of being determined by the division of the proceeds between the employer and the labourers, determines it.'[45]

Say's Law (believed with reservations by Jean-Baptiste Say himself and without reservations by James Mill, Ricardo and others) that supply creates its own demand and that, therefore, there cannot be a shortage of demand, continued to be believed almost until the present day. Indeed, its influence still seems to be with us. But that does not make it true.*

The belief of the political economists that, once Britain had adopted free trade, all other states would follow was not borne out by events. The American 'Tory' Alexander Hamilton, who profoundly disagreed with Adam Smith and *laissez-faire*,[47] had already shown in his great *Report on Manufactures* in 1791 how a tariff and other governmental measures would help the economy of a young country, and the progress of the American economy had fulfilled his expectations. The classical economists ignored American experience. Free trade, said Cobden, was the 'international law of the Almighty'.[48] He should have said it was the 'law of the mighty'. Free trade suited Britain because Britain was economically the strongest country in the world. The classical economists refused to see that for that very reason free trade was unlikely to commend itself to all other countries. Finally the general belief that *laissez-faire* would solve all problems turned out to be wrong.

Politicians should not be quick to complain that other people get things wrong. They make their share of mistakes, after all. Indeed, everybody makes mistakes, and big men make big mistakes. The justification for harping on the errors of the classical economists is that many of their errors have been accepted and perpetuated by their successors. 'Ricardo conquered England', wrote Keynes, 'as completely as the Holy Inquisition conquered Spain.'[49] And much of the classical system has continued to prevail even though its foundations have crumbled. In very different circumstances the basic notion of a harmony of interests, in its more modern forms of a natural equilibrium or of a natural tendency towards full employment, has lingered on. Hence, once

---

* Sismondi was the first economist to impugn Say's Law and to suggest that generalized over-production could occur.[46]

again, the argument is that Governments should not interfere: if they do, they will substitute discord for harmony.

Like their errors, the approach of the classical economists to their subject has ever since had an immense influence on economics. They derived some of their views from observation. Unfortunately, this was combined with a great deal of abstract reasoning. As good utilitarians, the classical economists believed they were scientists discovering laws. This might not have mattered had they adopted what are now regarded as proper scientific methods. For they might then have realized that economics is not a science, at least in their sense of the word. But even the most empirical of them, Adam Smith, confessed that he had 'no great faith in political arithmetic',[50] and even he wanted to 'account for all appearances from as few principles as possible'.[51] They preferred the establishing of 'scientific' laws to the amassing of evidence and statistics which might have demolished those laws.

Had they concentrated on observation, they could not have failed to see what Sismondi and others saw without difficulty. But they were shielded from the facts by their utilitarian preconceptions and by their search for laws. And by their writings they shielded many others from the facts and gave manufacturers, politicians and the well-off a comfortable excuse for glossing over them. 'The world,' wrote Carlyle, 'with its wealth of nations, supply-and-demand and suchlike, has of late days been terribly inattentive to that question of work and wages.'[52]

In other words, economics was abstracted from life in the real world. Ricardo 'had one of the most abstract minds the world has ever seen'.[53] The political economists, being utilitarians, saw society as completely atomistic; it was merely an aggregate of isolated individuals, who were wholly rational, wholly selfish, and wholly free economically.[54] For this society they constructed a model in which economic man, whether capitalist, landowner or labourer, pursued his self-interest in a rational manner in free competition, selling under free contract in the most expensive market, and buying in the cheapest one, all the time guided by his selfishness by an 'invisible hand' to promote the good of all. A 'grand governing law of human nature', according to James Mill, is the 'desire of that power which is necessary to render the persons and properties of human beings subservient to our pleasures'.[55]

Man is certainly an acquisitive animal. But to picture everybody
in England as having the characteristics and desires of an oriental
potentate or as being Roman emperors *manqués* seems a little
far-fetched. Some of the troubles of the British economy since the
war surely stem from the fact that many Englishmen have a
deficit rather than a surplus of entrepreneurial desires. Moreover,
Coleridge refuted the idea at the time: the most skilful artisans
who were able to earn high wages were, in his view, 'constantly
in the habit of working but a few days in the week, and of idling
the rest'. 'I believe', he added, 'St Monday is very well kept by
workmen in London. The love of indolence is universal or next to
it.'[56] Thus the economics of the political economists, their psychology and the society they wrote about were all unreal. They
bore little relation to human life either then or later. Man is not
just what Ruskin contemptuously called 'a covetous machine'
for producing wealth.[57]

Like other thinkers, the political economists were vulgarized
by others, and they cannot be held responsible for everything
that was done in their name. But they were responsible for their
methods and approach, which were an unhappy mixture of faith
and pseudo-science. It was arguable that the economic affairs of
the country would be best transacted by adherence to *laissez-
faire*. But reason stopped there. The belief that this would produce
a millennium of concord and plenty was based on faith and
nothing else. It was mere speculation 'divorced from all practice'.[58]
This is not to suggest that they should have proceeded by pure
induction, which had received some annihilating blows from
Hume, but that they should have tested their theories against the
facts and heeded what was going on around them. The economic
system of the political economists was built largely by abstractions
and deductive logic and not by the process of argument from
careful observation. As a result, the political economists by
an act of faith (not science) ended up in utopia, while many of
their fellow citizens remained in something like hell. As Shelley
put it:

Hell is a city much like London —
A populous and a smoky city...
Small justice shown, and still less pity.[59]

The classical economists were not alone in thinking that economics was a science. Many of their successors, with far less excuse, have made the same mistake. But physics would not be a science if the first law of thermodynamics operated only in alternate years, or if Archimedes had not been sure that every time he got into his bath the water would be displaced in the same way. And because 'economic man' does not exist, because man has many feelings and appetites and motives that are not economic, and because the environment in which he lives is continually changing and his reactions to it are changing too, economic behaviour is not predictable for long. Hence economics is not and never will be a science like the natural sciences. An economist can at the most exclaim: 'Eureka — for the time being.' Economics could, of course, be a science in a sense, if scientific methods were used. But such methods were not used by the classical economists, and they have not often been used since.

The doctrines of the political economists provided an armour of self-justification for energetic and thrusting industrialists. Yet the political economists became increasingly detached from that world. Political economy, which was given that title because the 'science' was meant to provide guidance for political action, became increasingly divorced from politics because its practitioners thought that, as a science, it should not be sullied by such a connection. Thus Cairnes (called by J. S. Mill 'My friend, Professor Cairnes, one of the most scientific of living political economists')[60] complained that 'considerations of equity and expediency' had invaded political economy. That was contrary to science. Political economy, he maintained, should be 'neutral between competing social schemes', just as chemistry was 'neutral between competing plans of sanitary improvement' and physiology was 'neutral between opposing systems of medicine'. The fallacy, of course, was to suppose economics to be akin to either chemistry or physiology. But 'Economic Science', thought Cairnes, 'has no more connection with our present industrial system than the science of mechanics has with our present system of railways.'[61] Regrettably, that was largely true, but, contrary to Cairnes's belief, it was not a matter for rejoicing. It was so much the worse for 'economic science'.

Naussau Senior also thought the role of the economists was to study. But that was just the role they did not perform. They did not study the facts; the tyranny of theory prevented them doing so. What Carlyle called 'this actual England'[62] was alien to them and their system, so instead they preferred to study what he called 'unfacts'.[63] And the divorce between politics and economics has persisted.

It is a remarkable affirmation of the power of the dead hand of doctrine that the influence of the political economists survives to this day. In economics, 'old doctrines', said Sir Alexander Gray, 'never die';[64] unfortunately, they don't even fade away. Sometimes they fade into the doctrines of the next generation. More often they do not fade at all but emerge some years later even more spruce and confident than before, with memories of earlier débâcles carefully expunged. But though politicians may often be escapists, their electorates are not. Hence most politicians have for most of the time to live in the real world. They may retain their economic fantasies; fortunately, they can seldom act on them. So while they may believe in the natural identity of interests, as politicians they must act on the other and contrary part of utilitarianism, which is to seek an artificial identity of interests by political means. The politician has to call in the real world of politics to redress the artificial world of the economists. Meanwhile, economics is still suffering from the hangover bequeathed to it by the heady mixtures of political economy.

Laissez-faire was the thesis. The misery and destitution of the nineteenth century produced its antithesis: Marxism. Not surprisingly, since Marx gained many of his ideas from Ricardo and others of that school, Karl Marx's economics at the opposite pole suffered from the same defects as did those of the political economists. Marx and Engels mercilessly analysed and denounced the evils of the capitalist system, but they, too, thought they were being scientific. They, too, constructed economic laws, most of which were soon broken. And their favoured system — the socialist — was every bit as unreal as the capitalist system described by the political economists. There was going to be a revolution, and there was going to be socialism, and then everybody would live happily ever afterwards, even if nobody knew how this would happen. This, again, was economics as fairy story to match that of the classical economists.

3

The Socialist Antithesis

One day I walked with one of these middle-class gentlemen into Manchester. I spoke to him about the disgraceful unhealthy slums and drew his attention to the disgusting condition of that part of town in which the factory workers lived. I declared that I had never seen so badly built a town in my life. He listened patiently and at the corner of the street at which we parted company, he remarked: 'And yet there is a great deal of money made here. Good morning, Sir!'

Engels[1]

No prudent man, however sure of his principles, dares prophesy concerning any event, or foretell the remote consequence of things.

Hume[2]

The intellectuals have brought a hundred times more harm than good to the people's lives.

Tolstoy[3]

The Marxian system was based on a combination of German philosophy and English political economy, and though Marx turned both of them upside-down, they remained an unfortunate parentage. Nevertheless, their offspring, Marxism, has had a greater influence on the world than any other theory, and the first volume of *Capital* constituted, in the words of Sir Isaiah Berlin, 'the most formidable, sustained and elaborate indictment ever delivered against an entire social order'.[4]

In this denunciation of *laissez-faire* capitalism much of what Marx said was true. He was justified in saying that in a free labour market with a surplus of workers ('the industrial reserve army', as he called it) wages would be starvation wages and that this with other unchecked developments of capitalism would lead to increasing misery.[5] He noticed, as many other economists did not, that high unemployment occurred frequently, and he was right in noting the importance of the trade cycle. Like Sismondi and Malthus, he was right in thinking that capitalism was unstable and not self-adjusting, while Say, James Mill, Ricardo and a long line of ideologues down to our own day persisted in believing that it was. He was correct, too, in believing that the business cycle was one of the factors which made capitalism unstable, and that the cycle and the power of the trade unions would lead to the end of *laissez-faire*.[6]

Although he came to conclusions very different from those of the political economists, Marx used many of their premises, and he took over Ricardo's framework. He even called Adam Smith 'the Luther of Political Economy'.[7] But he found their procedure faulty. For them, he thought, there were only two kinds of institution, 'artificial and natural'. In this they were like the theologians, for whom

> every religion which is not theirs is an invention of men, while their own is an emanation from God. When the economists say that...the relations of bourgeois production are natural, they imply that these are the relations in which wealth is created and productive forces developed in conformity with the laws of nature. Those relations, therefore, are themselves natural laws independent of the influence of time. They are eternal laws which must always govern society. Thus there has been history, but there is no longer any.[8]

That was sound criticism; unfortunately, Marx went on to make much the same sort of mistake himself. History caught up with him too.

Engels found the whole of Marx and the whole of socialism contained in the materialist conception of history and in the doctrines of surplus value.[9] The inconsistencies between volume 1 and volume 3 of *Capital*, the questions of what Marx meant by value and surplus value, what he *really* meant, or whether he knew what he meant happily do not concern us. In any case, Marx's labour theory of value, derived from Ricardo and the classical economists, has little relevance to modern economic theory.

But the materialist conception of history does concern us because it explains partially one of the most remarkable features of Marxism: although Marx devoted an enormous amount of time and space to attacking and analysing capitalism, he said virtually nothing about socialism. The great socialist economist wrote exhaustively about capitalist economics but entirely neglected socialist economics. He also said nothing at all about politics in the coming socialist era. This was as though Luther and Calvin had sought to propagate their versions of Protestantism by writing exclusively about the 'scarlet woman' of Rome. Had they done so, it is unlikely that Protestantism would have prospered. Despite the materialist conception of history's central place in Marxism — Marx said that it served as a guiding thread for his studies[10] — the doctrine is nowhere systematically expounded. That is not necessarily a disadvantage. Marx wrote hundreds of pages on value and surplus value which have led to much confusion; there are only fragments of the materialist conception of history, but their meaning is fairly clear.

In any society, Marx and Engels believed, it is the condition of material production that counts. On that foundation the economic and social system is built. And on top of the economic and social system is erected a superstructure which consists of, among other things, the state, the laws and the religious, moral, political and artistic ideas of the time. Now, since the conditions of production will be completely different under socialism from what they are under capitalism, the economic and social system will also be completely different, and so will the superstructure. It is, therefore, futile to speculate about what life will be like under socialism.

Yet socialism will certainly come. The internal contradictions of capitalism will see to that. All recorded history is the history of class struggle. Under capitalism, the rich will get progressively richer and the poor progressively poorer. This will lead to revolution and the destruction of capitalism. Just as the bourgeoisie has succeeded the feudal landowners, the workers will succeed the capitalists. The triumph of the capitalists has produced the bourgeois state; the triumph of the workers will produce the socialist state. But since the state is merely the instrument of the dominant class, and since the triumph of the workers will mean that there is no longer a class struggle, a state apparatus will not be needed. The state will 'wither away'.

This was 'scientific' socialism as opposed to the 'utopian' socialism of Marx's predecessors and contemporaries. These 'utopian' socialists were, to Marx, simpletons who believed that socialism could be achieved by working within the existing political system and that they could envisage what should and would happen when socialism was established. The 'scientific' socialism of Marx and Engels, on the other hand, laid down that it was economics which was all important. Politics had only a walk-on part to play, and the revolution could take place only when the economic conditions were ripe. Men could not shape their own destiny; that was pre-determined. Thus while the classical economists believed that the state and the politicians should not interfere with capitalism, Marxism proclaimed that they could not interfere. They were virtually powerless.

Hence Marxism provided no instruction as to what socialists should actually do other than hasten the revolution: they did not need further instructions because history was going to do their work for them. And it provided no guidance as to what would happen when socialism had been achieved. Such guidance would necessarily be influenced by the superstructure of the bourgeois state and would, therefore, be erroneous, 'utopian' and 'unscientific'. Indeed, according to Bernstein, Marx once said that 'the man who draws up a programme for the future is a reactionary.'[11] Whatever else the materialist conception of history did, therefore, it provided Marx with a brilliant excuse for not discoursing about socialist economics.*

Thus when the leaders of the Paris Commune attempted no

---

* In a passage in an early work, *The German Ideology*, which he wished to be published but which did not appear until after the Russian Revolution, Marx did once rashly allow himself a brief look at the idyllic socialist future. That one glimpse of utopia under communism suggests that he was wise to remain firmly in the capitalist world for the rest of his writings. 'In communist society,' he wrote, 'where nobody has one exclusive sphere of activity but each can be accomplished in any branch he wishes, society regulates [who society was and how it was going to do the regulating Marx did not make clear] the general production and thus makes it possible for me to do one thing today and another

socialist measures, they attracted the praise, not the censure of Marx.

> The working class [he wrote] did not expect miracles from the Commune. They have no ready-made utopias.... They know that in order to work out their own emancipation, and along with it that higher form to which present society is irresistibly tending, by its own economical agencies, they will have to pass through long struggles, through a series of historic processes, transforming circumstances and men. They have no ideals to realize, but to set free the elements of the new society with which the old collapsing bourgeois society itself is pregnant.[12]

The time had not yet come, and the workers had just got to go on struggling. It was Engels, not Marx, who wrote, 'Look at the Paris Commune. That was the Dictatorship of the Proletariat.'[13] Marx never applied the famous phrase to the Commune; and in fact the Communards showed an un-Marxist and un-Leninist liking for free elections and more than one party.

Half a century later, Stalin and other good Marxists were considerably perplexed by the Russian Revolution of February 1917. Things were not happening as Marx had said they would. The socialist revolution was supposed to take place in the advanced economies of the West, not in the backward economy of Russia, which had not even had its bourgeois revolution. So how could this possibly be a socialist one? Stalin and the other revolutionaries believed that it must indeed be a bourgeois revolution and that it would last some time.[14] Hence their confusion and their inability to see how the protagonists of a proletarian revolution should act during a bourgeois one.

Lenin was troubled by no such hesitations. When he arrived in

---

tomorrow, to hunt in the morning, fish in the afternoon, rear cattle in the evening, criticize after dinner, just as I have a mind without ever becoming hunter, fisherman, shepherd or critic.' Thus Marx's morning and afternoon activities would have attracted adverse notice from the League against Cruel Sports, while his early-evening activity would have engaged the attention of the RSPCA, who would be unlikely to consider the occasional evening devoted to the rearing of cattle to be good and humane husbandry. But perhaps under communism such bodies would not exist, and cattle might be able to rear themselves.

Leningrad in April 1917 he immediately announced at the Finland Station, in defiance both of Marx and of the facts: 'The dawn of the worldwide Socialist Revolution has risen....our Russian Revolution marks its beginning and has opened a new era.'[15] And, having brushed aside the theoretical doubts of his followers, Lenin got down to the practical work of revolution. But even Lenin, like Marx, once strayed from the true path of scientific socialism. In hiding in Finland in the summer of 1917, he wrote *The State and Revolution*, possibly the most utopian socialist work ever written.

In it he wrote that 'the proletarian state would begin to die away immediately after its victory.' There would be equal reward for all. 'Technicians, managers and bookkeepers as well as all officials shall receive salaries not higher than "a worker's wages".' There would be no difficulty about running society. That was a simple matter; anybody could do it. Under socialism, therefore, the division of labour would be abolished; 'Under socialism all will take part in the work of government in turn and will soon become accustomed to no one governing at all.' Lenin ended his pamphlet by saying in a postscript that it was 'more pleasant and profitable to go through the experience of revolution than to write about it'. And having gone through the experience of the revolution in October 1917, Lenin paid no attention whatever to what he had just written.

Yet Lenin's actions were as far away from Marx's theories as they were from the utopian fantasies of *The State and Revolution*. In contradiction to the materialist conception of history, a political revolution was carried out in Europe's most backward industrial country, and the means of production were altered from private to public by politics and terror. Politics, as Sidney Hook has pointed out, determined economics, not the other way round. Marx was refuted by the Marxists.[16]

So Marxism was no nearer the real world than was English political economy. Unlike the classical economists, Marx analysed the evils of *laissez-faire* capitalism as well as its merits, but he did not notice that capitalism was evolving while he was writing, year after year, in the British museum. 'So far as his intellectual development is concerned,' Berlin wrote, 'he might just as well have spent his exile on Madagascar', provided that he had been supplied with books and journals.[17] Despite Marx's relentless study of documents and parliamentary blue books, Marxism is a vast mountain of abstraction. Marx rarely met real workers or real employers; he met chiefly discontented intellectuals. His economic actors are no more real than those of the classical economists. Much of Marx's economics is metaphysical, as a contemporary reviewer pointed out.[18] Indeed, the capitalism that he describes sometimes seems a more ideal or a purer type of capitalism than the capitalism that was in existence at the time.

The materialist conception of history is prophecy and myth, not history or economics. Of course, economics influences politics, but the suggestion that the influence is all one-way is absurd. More probably, 'the ultimate basis of economic activity', M. Jean Baechler has argued, 'must be sought in the realm of politics.'[19] In any case politics, economics, religion and many other factors continually interact with each other. And there was no reason at all why a proletarian revolution and the socialization of the means of production should lead to the end of exploitation and the creation of a classless society. This was clearly recognized by Tolstoy, who, writing in autocratic Russia, predicted that 'even if that which Marx predicted should happen, then the only thing that will happen is that despotism will be passed on. Now the capitalists rule, but then the directors of the working people will rule.'[20] Bukharin, Michels and many others recognized the same truth long before Lenin and Stalin proved that Marx's 'scientific' socialism produced not a classless society but oppression on a gigantic scale.

Marx had given no thought to socialist politics after the revolution, and there was no socialist theory of the state. Consequently, there was no institutional foundation of a socialist state, on paper or anywhere else, for Lenin to build on after the revolution. There was only his own will and power. As he told the Congress of the Community Party in 1922, echoing Louis XIV, 'we are the state.'[21] Thus far from the state's withering away, it became a totalitarian dictatorship. The anarchist, Bakunin, turned out to be a far better prophet than Marx. 'Take the most radical revolutionary', he wrote in 1870, 'and place him on the throne of all the Russias and give him dictatorial power and within a year he will have become worse than the Tsar himself.'[22] Lenin did not wait a year. The terror began in April 1918.

Similarly, the abolition of private ownership in the USSR has not had the socialist effects predicted by Marx. The relations of production have remained the same, except that initially conditions for the workers became a good deal harsher, and they have no chance of forming genuine trade unions. So the relations of production have nothing to do with private ownership. All that has happened is that the state has become the capitalist. Indeed, Lenin said as much. 'Our task', he wrote in *Left-Wing Infantilism and Petit-Bourgeois Mentality*, 'is to study the state capitalism of the Germans, to spare *no effort* in copying it and not shrink from adopting dictatorial methods to hasten the copying of it.'[23] No effort was spared, and there was no question of shrinking from dictatorial methods. Thus the Kulaks and other casualties of the regime were victimized to enable the state to accummulate capital. The capitalism that Marx denounced was much less ruthless than the capitalism of his socialist state.

If Marx had not been so sure of himself, one would be inclined to think that he half-suspected all this, which was why he never spelled out what would happen under socialism or how socialist economics would work. In any case Marx's so-called 'scientific' socialism was at least as utopian as the so-called 'utopian' socialism which he and Engels denounced. Marx refused to outline his utopia, but that did not make his socialism 'scientific'. It was utopian without utopia. Marx not only provided no guidance for socialists, but he provided a system which ensured that socialism, at least of the sort he wanted, could never arrive. He was, therefore, even more useless to the rulers of a socialist state than were the classical economists to the rulers of a liberal state.

In his preface to the first German edition of *Capital* Marx talked of 'the natural laws of capitalist production' and of 'tendencies working with iron necessity towards inevitable results'. He declared that it was his aim 'to lay bare the economic law of motion of modern society'. But his laws were no more laws than were Ricardo's. He was indulging in large-scale prophecy on the assumption that *laissez-faire* would continue unreformed. Had the classical economists had their way, *laissez-faire* would indeed have continued. And had it done so, Marx might well have been proved right. In the event, both were mistaken. Marx was wrong in prophesying the coming of an unreal world. Yet, as we have seen, some of his indictment of the world he was living in was true.

Both Marxism and political economy are stern warnings against the dangers of systems and abstraction in politics and economics. Both have been proved wrong, but experience is no proof against them. Both still have their fanatical devotees. Perhaps they feed on each other. More probably, they are the beneficiaries of what Disraeli called mankind's need for something to worship.

In any case, the synthesis of the two systems was anything but abstract and was itself in no sense a system. The synthesis was provided by political action — something which was opposed and despised by both the classical economists and the Marxists.

4

The Synthesis and the Tory Tradition

Never till now...did the mere manual two-handed worker...
long in vain for...food and warmth....Why, the four-footed
worker has already got all that this two-handed one is
clamouring for! How often must I remind you? There is not
a horse in England, able and willing to work, but has due
food and lodging; and goes about sleek-coated, satisfied in
heart....The human brain, looking at these sleek English
horses, refuses to believe in such impossibility for English
men.

Carlyle[1]

that fortunate inconsequence of our nature which permits
the heart to rectify the errors of the understanding.

Coleridge[2]

Je le dis, et il me semble que je n'ai fait cet ouvrage que pour
le prouver: l'esprit de modération doit être celui du législa-
teur; le bien politique, comme le bien moral, se trouve
toujours entre deux limites.

Montesquieu[3]

The synthesis was political action to protect the economically
weak against the strong, and it had in fact begun well before the
antithesis had been put and indeed even before the thesis had got
fully under way. The first Factory Act was passed as early as
1802. It limited the hours of work of Poor Law apprentices in
factories to twelve hours, but, like the 1819 Act of Peel's father,
which applied to all children in cotton mills, it was largely evaded

because it did not provide for supervision by inspectors. Nevertheless, the 1819 Act struck a blow at *laissez-faire* by affirming the principle that Parliament could interfere in these matters and could override the discretion of parents.[4]

We saw earlier the reaction of the Lake poets and Sir Walter Scott to the evils of industrialism. Such a reaction was not confined to them. The tradition of Tory paternalism had survived even in the House of Lords. Thus the Lords Committee on the Poor Laws in 1817, the year Ricardo's book which called for the abolition of the Poor Laws appeared, was 'decidedly of the opinion that the general system of these laws, interwoven as it is with the habits of the people, ought...to be essentially maintained'.[5]*

But it was in the Tory magazine *Blackwood's* that the Poor Laws were defended with particular vigour and the doctrines of the political economists sharply attacked. The leader of the Tory revivalists who wished to reassert paternalism against competition was Michael Sadler, a Leeds linen merchant, a Tory and an Anglican who entered Parliament in 1829. Sadler opposed Malthus on population and both Ricardo and Malthus on the Poor Laws. So far from agreeing with the economists that they should be abolished, Sadler favoured their extention to Ireland. 'The institution of the Poor Law of England', Sadler told the House of Commons in 1830, 'encourages the demand for, and increases the value of labour, as well as abates distress; in Ireland, in consequence of the want of such a law, labour is discouraged, and distress increased.'[7]† *Blackwood's* was delighted by the performance of its champion in Parliament:

These sages of the Satanic school in politics [it wrote] encountered an adversary...who bid them turn their eyes from the capitalist to the labourer, and who had the spirit and the feeling to ask them...whether that could be a good

---

* Southey held the same view. 'The mischief which the Poor Laws produce', he wrote, 'has arisen wholly from their maladministration or perversion; the system itself is humane, just, necessary, befitting a Christian state and honourable to the English nation'.[6]

† It was characteristic of the political economists not to notice the hole the inferior economy of Ireland made in their case: 'What', asked Southey, 'does this precious philosopher [Malthus] say to Ireland, where there are no Poor Laws?'[8]

system...where national prosperity is made to...proceed upon its course amidst the sweat, and the blood, and the groans of its victims.[9]

Blackwood's also employed some able economists, among whom David Robinson was outstanding. These men opposed the political economists at virtually every point. Robinson attacked Say's Law effectively and saw the folly of cutting wages in a slump. 'The reduction [in wages] diminishes consumption,' he wrote, 'and makes the glut greater, and more general.'[10] Robinson, in what Professor Perkin calls his 'proto-Keynesian economics', thought the Government could and should maintain full employment and maintained that a depression should be dealt with by a reflationary monetary policy, by increased public expenditure on poor relief and public works, and by a protective tariff and the use of taxation. Only through the adoption of such policies and the abandonment of *laissez-faire*, Robinson maintained, could the harmony and the prosperity of the country be restored. All this, Robinson and *Blackwood's* believed should be combined with the beginning of a welfare state.[11] The tide of *laissez-faire*, political economy and *a priori* theory was running too strongly for this advanced common sense to have a chance of withstanding it, but once again we see that there was nothing inevitable about the pseudo-scientific and dogmatic route taken by English economics.

In 1834 the political economists had their way, and the Poor Laws were abolished by the Poor Law Amendment Act. This harshly inhumane law attempted to abolish outdoor relief for the able-bodied pauper, which had been granted to paupers for over two hundred years. 'What is a pauper?' asked Cobbett. 'Only a very poor man.'[12] But henceforward they were to be herded into workhouses, 'pleasantly so-named', said Carlyle, 'because work cannot be done in them'.[13] Conditions inside these establishments were required by the Act to be worse than those available to the poorest able-bodied man outside. Workhouses were accurately called 'bastilles', since living conditions in most of the new ones resembled those in prisons. Thus no inmate, even a child, was allowed to step outside a workhouse, even though there was usually no provision for exercise within it, except to attend church. Before 1842 parents had no right to see their own children even once a day, and married couples were not allowed to live together. Until that year everybody, including children, had to eat all meals in silence. It was only after 1847 that conditions began to improve.

When he got into Parliament some years after its enactment, Disraeli attacked the new Poor Law. But at the time this Whig Bill was not opposed by the Tory Party, though Peel's reasons for supporting it were very different from those of its sponsors. The opposition to the Bill usually numbered only about twenty, consisting of ultra Tories and extreme Radicals.[14] The new Poor Law was political action not to mitigate the hardships of capitalism but to make capitalism more rigorous. It was the legislative embodiment of political economy, but the politicians cannot escape responsibility for passing it. As Byron wrote a dozen years earlier:

For what were all these country patriots born?
To hunt, and vote, and raise the price of corn?[15]

Robert Owen was as strongly opposed to the political economists as were the Tory writers in *Blackwood's*, but from a socialist point of view. The most interesting and impressive thing about Owen is not his naive Rousseauist ideas about the essential goodness of human nature, or his disagreeable views about the upbringing of children, or his ideas about education and sexual freedom, or his utopian project for largely self-contained socialist communities dotted all over the country, but his ability in industry to put his theories into successful practice. What he did actually worked. Starting as a draper's apprentice, he became a prosperous maker of textile machinery in Manchester, before taking over cotton mills at New Lanark. He believed that the capitalists' exploitation of their labourers was not only wrong but also against their own interests, since by keeping wages low they were limiting their own sales. 'The markets of the world', he wrote, 'are created solely by the remuneration allowed for the industry of the working classes, and those markets are more or less extended and profitable, in proportion as those classes are well or ill remunerated for their labour.'[16] This was a long way from Ricardo and Malthus but no great distance from the views a hundred years later of Henry Ford. As well as paying his workers properly, Owen cleaned up the factories, transformed the workers' houses, cut down drunkenness and paid higher dividends. At New Lanark, at least, Owenism was triumphantly successful, and Owen had demonstrated that the filth and squalor and destitution that usually accompanied industrialism could be separated from it.

Owen was less successful when he founded in 1834 the Grand National Consolidated Trades Union. It soon collapsed, though not before it had frightened the Whig Government into confirming the discreditable sentences on the 'Tolpuddle Martyrs'. But on the issue of trade unionism the dogmatism of the political economists for once was helpful. Since, in their view, the level of wages was determined entirely by the laws of supply and demand and by the wages fund, they did not believe that trade unions could have any effect on wages. They therefore favoured the repeal of the Combination Acts. The Combination Laws of 1799 and 1800 were, in fact, relatively mild and ineffective. Combinations of workmen continued much as they had before. Nevertheless, the laws of 1824 and 1825, which were passed under Liverpool's Tory Government but were largely the work of the Radical tailor, Francis Place, notably improved the law by repealing all statutes on the subject from Edward I's reign onwards, and by making combinations legal, while affirming penalties against violence and intimidation. 'Men', said Peel very reasonably, 'who have no property except their manual skill and strength, ought to be allowed to confer together, if they think fit, for the purpose of determining at what rate they will sell their property.'[17] Trade unions were to suffer many vicissitudes in the courts during the nineteenth century, until the Liberal Government of 1906 went to the other extreme and made virtually everything a union might do immune from legal penalty; yet the 1824 and 1825 Acts removed illegality from working men's combinations much earlier in this country than anywhere else in Europe.

This contributed largely to the moderate course that British trade unionism took for the rest of the century. In the 1860s some of its leaders fortuitously became involved with Karl Marx, but none of them, unlike the German trade unionists, was a socialist, let alone a revolutionary.[18] They preferred Garibaldi and Mazzini to Marx, and were more interested in parliamentary reform at home than in revolutionary action abroad.

In any case, Marx himself was ambivalent about trade unions. They were useful instruments for building up the class-consciousness of the workers, but any gains they made tended to strengthen capitalism and to postpone the revolution. Moreover, the sense of community and self-confidence which the unions gave the workers were likely to engender patriotism rather than zeal for the class war. Non-revolutionary trade unions, therefore, were of little use to Marx, and the British unions were anything but revolutionary.

The unions were not overtly political until 1871, when the TUC appointed a political committee.[19] Yet they had in a sense always been political in that their objective was to prevent industrial matters from being decided according to the interests of the employers or solely according to economic criteria. It is, therefore, both historically and logically wrong to argue that trade unions should be only industrial and not political organizations, though their close involvement in party politics can certainly be questioned. Still, a great deal had to be done before trade unionism was firmly established and before industrial conditions for the workforce became tolerable.

Michael Sadler was also the parliamentary champion of the movement to humanize conditions in factories, a movement which cut across party lines. In 1830 the Yorkshire Tory Richard Oastler wrote a series of vastly influential letters to the *Leeds Mercury* on 'Yorkshire Slavery'.

> Thousands of our fellow-creatures and fellow-subjects [he wrote], both male and female, the miserable inhabitants of a Yorkshire town, are this very moment existing in a state of slavery more horrid than the victims of that hellish system 'colonial slavery'.... The system which impoverishes, enslaves and brutalizes the labourer can never be advantageous to any country.... The constitution of this country and the factory system cannot long exist together; and their principles are as opposite as light and darkness.[20]

Sadler drafted a comprehensive Ten Hours Bill to deal with this slavery but lost his seat in the 1832 election and was succeeded as leader of the Ten Hours movement by Lord Ashley. Ashley, who was much influenced by Southey, was, like Sadler, a Tory and an evangelical. In 1833 Ashley's Bill was blocked by the Whig Government, which did, however, pass a much weaker Bill of its own. This Act did not work well, though it brought the important innovation of factory inspectors. And it was during the debates on this Bill that Cobbett made his famous speech supporting an amendment to reduce the hours of work of all young persons in the textile trade from twelve to ten hours:

> Heretofore [he said] ...our ships, our mercantile traffic with foreign nations...together with our body of rich merchants — we have sometimes been told that these form the source of our wealth....But Sir we have this night discovered that the shipping, the land, and the Bank and its credit are all worth nothing compared with the labour of thirty thousand little girls in Lancashire. Aye...if we only deduct two hours a day from their labour, away goes the wealth, away goes the capital, away go the resources, the power, and the glory of England![21]

Even that did not manage to shame the Commons into passing the amendment. Once again the doctrines of the political economists can be used only as a partial excuse for the behaviour of the politicians. Then, as later, MPs were responsible for their vote and for their own selfishness, ignorance or stupidity.

In a very different vein from Cobbett's, the political economist Naussau Senior maintained in a pamphlet four years later that the whole of the factory owner's profit was derived from the 'last hour' of the workers' labour, so a reduction of even one hour in the working day would threaten industry with ruin. This specious argument was later destroyed by Marx, but it was convenient for factory owners.[22] And it was not until 1847 that the Ten Hours Bill was finally passed, by which time Ashley was temporarily out of Parliament and the Bill was in the charge of the Radical manufacturer Fielden. In the vote on the Bill the year before, 81 Liberals voted against and 71 for, 73 Peelites out of 80 voted against, while 117 out of 168 Tory Protectionists voted for it.[23] Yet the Ten Hours Act was eroded by a Whig Bill in 1850 and not fully restored until Disraeli's Government of 1874.

Earlier Ashley had had a greater triumph. The Children's Employment Commission, which had been set up as a result of his efforts, reported on the conditions in the mines in 1842. The revelations of what Peel called the 'mining abominations',[24] which included the employment of 6-year-old children and women down the mines under appalling conditions, produced the Coal Regulation Act, which prohibited work underground by all females and by boys under 10. As usual, the Radical Bright was an opponent of the Bill, but so too was Wellington.

Ashley did not confine himself to factories and mines. 'I feel', he said, 'that my business lies in the gutter, and I have not the least intention to get out of it.'[25] He was active in the Public Health movement in the 1840s and 1850s and, as a Lunacy Commissioner, did much to civilize the laws on insanity. He did more than anyone else for the Ragged Schools movement. These were schools for children who were so dirty or wild that no ordinary school would take them. In 1851, when he became Lord Shaftesbury, he passed the Common Lodging-Houses Act. The conditions in many lodging-houses defied belief. Shaftesbury described how in the main room of one house, which was 15 feet by 10, there lived twenty-seven adults, thirty-one children and several dogs.[26] His Act required all lodging-houses to be registered and to be open to inspection by the police and the local authority. Charles Dickens described it as 'the best measure ever passed in Parliament'.[27]

Even in the 1860s, after Shaftesbury had secured another inquiry into the employment of children, it was discovered that there were children of 6 working in the potteries and other industries for very long hours in dreadful conditions.* But by now Parliament was ready to pass Bills to deal with various industries almost without opposition.[29]

Peel was opposed to Shaftesbury on the Ten Hours Bill, but he

---

* By this time conditions were worse elsewhere. In 1867 Marx thought that other countries would be 'appalled' by what they found if, like England, they 'appointed periodically commissions of enquiry into economic conditions...armed with the same plenary powers to get at the truth; if it was possible to find for this purpose men as competent, as free from partisanship and respect of persons as are the English factory inspectors, her medical reporters on public health, her commissions of enquiry into the exploitation of women and children, into housing and food'.[28] Much of the credit is due to Shaftesbury.

was not a doctrinaire believer in *laissez-faire*.[30] Surprisingly and inexcusably insensitive about the Poor Law and the evils of a largely unregulated factory system, he was yet deeply conscious of the miseries of the poor and of the duty of the Government and the propertied classes to alleviate them. 'Whatever be your financial difficulties and necessities,' he told the House of Commons in his great Budget of 1842, 'you must so adapt and adjust your measures as not to bear on the comforts of the labouring classes of society.' It was therefore, he went on, his duty 'to make an earnest appeal to the possessors of property', and he reintroduced the income tax. It was, he said a few days later, 'for the interest of property that property should bear the burden' of rescuing the finances of the country, while he lowered the cost of living for the benefit of the poor.[31] In the hungry 1840s such a policy was not only right but also necessary if great public disturbances were to be avoided. Similar considerations lay behind Peel's repeal of the Corn Laws. 'The real question at issue', he told Parliament, 'is the improvement of the social and moral condition of the masses of the population.' 'I have a strong belief', he said near the end of his speech before the crucial vote on repeal, 'that the greatest object which we or any other government can contemplate should be to elevate the social condition of that class of people with whom we are brought into no direct relationship by the exercise of the elective franchise.'[32] Peel handled the Chartists leniently and refused to protect employers from what he called 'just and peaceable demands for a rise in wages'.[33] That England suffered nothing more drastic in 1848, when other countries had revolutions, than a failed Chartist rally on Kennington Common, which ended peacefully, was due to Peel more than to any other man.

In the nineteenth century, as Bagehot pointed out in the 1870s, England was governed by the centre. 'A middle Government', he wrote, was 'inevitable'.[34] There were no great differences between the parties. From the late 1820s onwards many leading politicians changed their party, and often the most important differences were within parties not between them. Moreover, parties are necessarily influenced by the intellectual climate of the time; normally they are more the receivers and transmitters of opinion than its creators. From about 1820 onwards Liberalism was the prevailing opinion, and the Tories were naturally affected by it. Similarly, when *laissez-faire* was in partial retreat from about 1850 onwards the Whigs were in turn affected. It would therefore be both wrong and silly to claim that it was the Tories alone who were responsible for overcoming *laissez-faire*.

Nevertheless, there was, despite the liberalism of Peel and his followers, a difference between the parties. As late as 1855, when the textile workers had won a sixty-hour week, Palmerston declared that legislative interference with adult men's freedom to make their own bargains was based upon 'a vicious and wrong principle'. Palmerston was in many ways not a typical Liberal, but he was leader of the party for many years; and it is difficult to imagine a leading Tory at that time allowing doctrine to override both humanity and common sense. Indeed, within a few years many of the men who had been strongly opposed to Shaftesbury's reforms or who had stood aside from the issue (such as the Peelite Graham, the Radical Roebuck, the Whig Brougham, and Gladstone) were prepared to admit that they had been wrong or at least that they had changed their opinions.[35] However, John Bright remained a strong opponent of such legislation until the end of his life.

Laissez-faire was anyway never the doctrine of the Conservative Party, and many Tories strongly opposed the tenets of political economy in the 1820s. Hence the Tories had no doctrinal allegiance to the new economic system, and it was no coincidence that Tories were so prominent in modifying it. They had, after all, an earlier tradition of believing in strong government.

In his attitude to *laissez-faire* and social reform Disraeli was remarkably consistent throughout his political life. He took the trouble to see for himself what was happening in the north, and then described it vividly in *Sybil*. Earlier he had satirized the utilitarians and scathingly attacked the new Poor Law. In a speech at Aylesbury in 1847, he showed how useful a doctrine *laissez-faire* was for many of its devotees:

> Liberal opinions are the opinions of those who would be free from certain restraints and regulations, from a certain dependence and duty which are deemed necessary for the general or popular welfare. Liberal opinions are very

convenient opinions for the rich and powerful. They ensure enjoyment and are opposed to self-sacrifice. The holder of liberal opinions, for example, maintains that the possession of land is to be considered in a commercial light and no other.[36]

Disraeli was here expressing the view which he shared with Coleridge, Carlyle and others that society is more than a framework for economic pursuits and that the state has higher duties than merely keeping that framework in good repair. ' "Laissez-faire", "supply and demand", "cash-payment for the sole nexus", and so forth', thundered Carlyle, 'were not, are not and never will be, a practicable law of union for a society of men.'[37] Tories, like Disraeli, were well aware that the liberal doctrines of self-help and minimal government interference were fine for the winners but did nothing for the losers. And whereas the Liberals tended to blame those who could not help themselves to rise for being inadequate or lacking moral fibre, the Tories accepted that not all could rise and that inability to do so might be as much a matter of luck as of anything else. 'The principle of our society', wrote Disraeli, 'is to aspire and excel.'[38] But those who for whatever reason could not excel or even aspire should not be despised or neglected.

In a famous phrase Richard Oastler had defined Toryism to the Duke of Wellington as 'a place for everything and everything in its place'.[39] In the Tory scheme of things there was a place for everyone whether each was able to help himself or not. Toryism sought to provide a sense of security for all, which could be achieved only if the Tory Party was a truly national party and if the national institutions were preserved.

'To maintain the institutions of the country' was the first of the 'three great objects' of the Tory Party that Disraeli laid down in 1872; the second was 'to uphold the Empire of England' and the third was 'to elevate the condition of the people'. In connection with this third great objective the views Disraeli expressed in his speeches, what he said in his novels in the 1840s, and what he did when he was in power in the 1870s are in striking conformity with each other.

In 1867 he could say that he had supported all of the thirty-two measures which had been passed in three decades on 'the condition of the people' and that the party had opposed none of them. Six years later he said that supporting the Ten Hours Act in 1847 was 'one of the most satisfactory incidents' in his career.[40] In addition, the Government which he formed in 1874 carried through more social reform than any other Government in the nineteenth century.[41] The two labour measures passed in 1875 were far in advance of what Gladstone had proposed, and Disraeli justifiably told the Queen that they were 'the most important of the class... carried in your Majesty's long and eventful reign'.[42]

Reflecting on the Factory Acts and similar legislation, Disraeli had earlier laid bare the issue between the political economists and the doctrinaire Liberals on the one side, and Tories like himself on the other. It was obvious, he said, that nothing important could be done to improve 'the condition of the multitude' without reducing the hours they worked and humanizing their conditions of work. He then reminded his audience that 'many years ago the Tory Party believed...that you might elevate the condition of the people by the reduction of their toil and the mitigation of their labour and at the same time inflict no injury on the wealth of the nation.' The Liberal leaders had replied with all the economists' dogma that the result would be to diminish capital and hence employment, which would lead 'ultimately to the impoverishment of the Kingdom'. But economic dogma had been wrong and the Tories had been right.[43]

Baldwin rightly thought in 1923 that, over the Tory objective of elevating the condition of the people, the Conservatives 'had lagged behind since Disraeli died'.[44] Disraeli's successor, Lord Salisbury, thought it right to be 'forward in the defence of the poor'; 'no system', he added, 'that is not just as between rich and poor can hope to survive.'[45] And he was no believer in *laissez-faire*.[46] But he was not greatly interested in social reform. Luckily, the continued support of Joseph Chamberlain and the Liberal Unionists had to be paid for by the enactment of part of the Radical programme. The Workmen's Compensation Act was the major legislative achievement. But the arrival among the Conservatives of the Whigs and the Liberals made the party 'sodden with whiggery'[47] and, as Sir Angus Maude wrote in 1947, had 'a profound effect on the party, purging it of most of its Tory philosophy and indoctrinating it with that peculiar brand of whiggery and *laissez-faire* Liberalism which still colours the speeches of some of its leaders'.[48]

All the same, when the extreme Liberal, Herbert Spencer, in *Man versus the State* (1892), totted up his blacklist of enactments which had regulated the lives of the people since 1860, he found that the Conservative Party had been responsible for most of them.[49] So, although Toryism had greatly varied in quality over the years, the Tory tradition had not done badly. Just how far it had taken Britain is shown by a near-contemporary case in America. In 1905, in *Lochner v. New York*, the American Supreme Court declared unconstitutional a law limiting night work in bakeries. Justice Peckham said such statutes were 'mere meddlesome interferences with the rights of the individual'. Justice Holmes, dissenting, pointed out that the Court was behaving as though Mr Herbert Spencer's theories were part of the constitution.[50] Not long before, the Court had declared income tax unconstitutional; Britain had had it since Peel. Indeed, Britain had surtax before either France or the United States had income tax.

At varying speeds all free countries had moved to curb the excesses of capitalism while preserving its economic impetus. The Tory tradition is one of balance and community. When *laissez-faire* was in the ascendancy, the Tories defended authority, the state and the weak. Later, when state socialism came to the fore, they defended the individual. But it is of the essence of its tradition of balance that the party should not come down wholly on one side or the other. The Tories are, or should be, free from dogma about the state and the individual. They suffer from no liberal or socialist heresies on these subjects, even though whiggery occasionally surfaces. They know that the individual and the state are mutually dependent and mutually sustaining. And they know, therefore, that the state has the duty to ensure every individual's security, and that every individual has the right to the protection of the state.

Political action was always too late and usually inadequate. The responsibilities that the Government accepted from the beginning of the nineteenth century onwards were not new to the English state. Halévy described the magistrates' right to fix the rate of wages and the protection afforded to the poor which lasted from the Elizabethan age until the nineteenth century as 'state socialism'.[51] But whatever description is given to such measures, the Tory tradition runs deep in British history. Hence there was just enough political action to make capitalism more or less tolerable to the mass of the people, to avoid socialism and to belie the predictions of Marx. The weak were to some extent protected against the strong. Direct economic intervention did take place. For example, a mid-century Act on gasworks limited the permissible dividend and ordered the investment of excess profits in government stocks.[52] And in the last resort there was no question of *laissez-faire* for banks.[53] But Governments tended to deal with social rather than economic evils. They intervened to mitigate the effects of the economic system; they did not seek to interfere with the economic system itself. Apart from anything else, they did not know how to do so. Yet the distinction between social evils and economic evils is largely artificial, and to temper the effects of the economic system affects that system if only at one remove.

In all this the economists played little part. The preservation of a free economy owed virtually nothing to them. They had remained immersed in their own theories and systems, and it is to them we must now return.

5

The Retreat from Political Economy
(or the Neo-Classicals)

Theory is good, but it does not prevent things from existing.

Jean-Martin Charcot[1]

Reality is a thing of infinite diversity, and defies the most ingenious deductions and definitions of abstract thought, nay, abhors the clear and precise classifications in which we so delight. Reality tends to infinite subdivisions of things, and truth is a matter of infinite shadings and differentiations.

Dostoevsky[2]

A little learning misleadeth, and a great deal stupifieth the understanding.

Halifax[3]

Marx's writings had profound effects stretching into the distant future. But one short-term effect they did not have. The 'political' part of political economy was not reasserted. This is surprising. After Marx the whole theory of the capitalist system was under attack. And it was not only a theoretical attack. As a natural result of *laissez-faire*, socialism was gaining strength.[4] On the face of it, therefore, economists should have sought to repulse the Marxian onslaught and to produce a reasoned defence of capitalism.*

There was, it is true, slightly less reason for this to happen in England than in Europe. In this country there were no Marxist

---

* It was not until 1896 that a prominent member of the Austrian school, Böhm-Bawerk, produced his satirical attack on Marxism. *Karl Marx and the close of his system.*

parties or trade union movements, and there was virtually no socialism of any sort. Moreover, the first volume of *Capital* was translated into English only in 1887. Nevertheless, there must have been some economic writers who knew German and were familiar with political events on the Continent. And even though they had never heard of Marx, there should have been some who wished to return economics to the real world.

Yet the opposite happened. The retreat from political economy began, as we have seen, under the classical economists, who were still the dominant influence on English economics until about 1870.[5] Nassau Senior, the first occupant of the Chair of Political Economy at Oxford and in some ways the most 'political' of his contemporaries, laid down that an economist's conclusions did not 'authorize him in adding a single syllable of advice'. Practical questions, he maintained, 'no more form part of the science of Political Economy...than navigation forms part of the science of astronomy'.[6] Economics was a science, and that was that.

The new school which had to some extent been anticipated in its basic theory by Senior and others, continued the flight from political economy. 'Economics,' said Jevons, 'if it is to be a science at all, must be a mathematical science.'[7] Nevertheless, the doctrines of the neo-classical theorists have sometimes been interpreted as an answer to Marx.* The new economics was certainly optimistic about the free market system; it largely evaded the need for social reform, and by placing the consumer instead of the capitalist at the centre of affairs it was less obviously vulnerable to socialist criticism than its predecessor.

All the same, none of the founders of the new school — Jevons, Menger, Walras and Marshall — seems to have been in any way influenced by Marx while devising his system. It is doubtful, indeed, if any of them had even heard of him at that time. Besides, the link between the economics profession and liberalism was less close than it had been before. Walras was a semi-socialist; Wicksell was a bourgeois radical; while Marshall used to say that he sympathized with the ultimate aims of socialism, though his manner of doing so did not please socialists.[9] And if the new doctrine was

---

* Most recently by Lord Balogh in his very acute book *The Irrelevance of Conventional Economics.*[8]

a rebuttal of Marx, it was an oblique one, which was perhaps more effective than a direct answer would have been. The neo-classical economists tended to take the political, economic and social conditions of the time for granted. They sought to explain rather than to defend them, which in the circumstances came to much the same thing. Their explanations satisfied the many who were anxious to be convinced by the optimistic view that everything was as it should be. Hence economic theory remained influential, however little connected it was with the world of affairs.

Jevons in England, Menger in Germany and Walras in Switzerland independently and more or less at the same time promulgated the doctrine of marginal utility, which replaced the labour theory of value. This doctrine held that value sprang from utility, which was taken to be correlative to desire or want, and that value was determined at the margin, since, in Marshall's words, 'the marginal utility of a thing to anyone diminishes with every increase in the amount of it he already has.'[10] 'Happily,' John Stuart Mill had written in his *Principles of Political Economy*, 'there is nothing in the laws of value which remains for the present or any future writer to clear up; the theory of the subject is complete.'[11] Unhappily, Mill was thus quickly proved wrong, and economics became once more absorbed in speculations about value, a largely metaphysical pursuit. The new ideas made possible advances in technique, but under the school of marginal utility economics withdrew even further into itself.

Much as almost the last people to recognize the existence and the problem of joint-stock companies and large-scale production had been the classical economists, so the neo-classical school saw the economic process much as had J. S. Mill or even A. Smith. Economic man still inhabited the globe, and real nations, like real people, were an extinct species. Classes, too, were merely descriptions of economic functions.[12]

Not surprisingly, then, reality broke in only rarely. According to Schumpeter, the marginal utility economists were only imperfectly aware of the formal character of their analysis. They were under the impression that they were teaching much more about what was actually happening than in fact they were.[13] That is a familiar story.

The classical economists had simply assumed that free competition existed. In the circumstances of the time this was reasonable enough, though they might have taken more account of Adam Smith's famous remark that when people of the same trade meet together, the upshot was usually 'a conspiracy against the public or...some contrivance to raise prices'.[14] Only J. S. Mill noted that competition often fell 'short of the maximum'. The marginal utility school also regarded free competition as normal, though its adherents subjected such competition to much analysis and definition. That is to say, they assumed that neither sellers nor buyers could influence prices, which were determined by 'the market'. This, of course, presupposed that in each industry there was a large number of competing firms, none of which was large enough to dominate the market; and this happy state of affairs came to be known as perfect or pure competition.

Clearly, under competition some firms will do better than others and grow at their expense. So unless there is some 'law' which stops them growing before they are in a position to dominate the market, perfect competition will cease. Luckily, there was such a 'law' ready to hand. This was the law of decreasing returns, which was derived from agriculture and the bringing into cultivation of increasingly inferior land. But in manufacturing the opposite is likely to occur. There are likely to be increasing returns as the volume of production grows. In spite of this, in spite of the elements of unreality in the theory and in spite of the growth of oligopoly and the beginning of cartels and trusts (though scarcely yet in England), perfect competition was accepted as the rule and anything else as exceptional. In real life, of course, perfect competition was very much the exception. Anybody who imagined, thought Adam Smith, that employers rarely combined was 'as ignorant of the world as of the subject'. 'Masters', he said, 'are always and everywhere in a sort of tacit, but constant and uniform combination....'[15] But, to the neo-classicals, theory was more important than practice, and pure competition was an integral part of the theory. 'The pattern of income distribution', Professor Deane has pointed out, 'was assumed *given* and the assumption frequently forgotten....'[16] Only if there was full competition was it possible to argue, even in theory, that the system maximized utilities over the whole of society. Without full competition, the system would clearly be distorted, and there would be no maximization of everyone's satisfactions.

As well as perfect competition, the marginal productivity theory of distribution assumed full employment, perfect mobility of labour and perfect knowledge on the part of both sellers and buyers. The problems of technical change and progress were virtually ignored. And, under Jevons's theory of labour, workers were free to decide their hours of work, something which is rare enough today and which was not within the bounds of possibility in the nineteenth century.[17]

Finally, there is one more part of Jevons's economic theory which deserves mention because the mode of argument that produced it has been made familiar by Professor Friedman and his followers. Professor Jevons announced to the world in 1878 that the trade cycle was caused by sun-spots. Sun-spots affected the weather, which affected harvests, which determined the trade cycle. Jevons had discovered that during the previous 150 years the trade cycle had lasted an average of 10.44 years, while the sun-spot cycle had lasted an average of 10.45 years.[18] Clearly, the correlation was so exact that one must cause the other. Presumably the trade cycle did not cause sun-spots; ergo sun-spots caused the trade cycle. Economics was after all, in Jevons's view, a mathematical science.

Once again, then, for the neo-classical school, as for the old classicists, everything was for the best in the best of all possible worlds. Dr Pangloss had changed his clothes, that was all. He was still there.

Alfred Marshall, the greatest and most influential English economist at the end of the nineteenth century and later, was a partial exception to much of this. He had a knowledge of business and understood the economic system; he was a good historian; he wanted his books to be widely read; and, unlike Jevons and the others, he was suspicious of too much mathematics. He wrote in 1901:

> In my view, every economic fact, whether or not it is of such a nature as to be expressed in numbers, stands in relation as cause and effect to many other facts, and since it NEVER happens that all of them can be expressed in numbers, the application of exact mathematical methods to those which

can is nearly always a waste of time, while in the large majority of cases it is positively misleading; and the world would have been further on its way forward if the work had never been done at all.[19]

Marshall was well aware, too, of the country's relative economic decline. Britain had lost her 'industrial leadership', he said in a memorandum in 1903, which was later published as a White Paper. Many of the sons of manufacturers worked shorter hours and exerted themselves less than their fathers had done, and he added the warning (which was not heeded and is still relevant today) that 'Englishmen should take business as seriously as their grandfathers had done and as the Americans and Germans were doing, and should train methodically for it.'[20] Moreover, Marshall was less dogmatic about competition than were others of the utility school. He was always conscious of exceptions. He was opposed to socialism but thought 'the present inequalities of wealth' were excessive.

Notwithstanding all this vision and common sense, Marshall was in tune with the economic theory of the time, which indeed he did much to fashion, and he believed that the fundamental principles of economics had been finally fixed.[21] In a famous passage he likened firms to trees in a forest that grow larger until a certain point at which they wither and die, so that the overall size of the trees remains constant.[22] The simile was brilliant but inaccurate. Firms were no longer almost entirely family ones, and what would have been true of family firms was not true of joint-stock companies. Hence natural growth and decay had little to do with the matter, and Marshall did not succeed in explaining why some firms would not grow large enough to dominate the market.

Marshall was an enlightened Whig: just as there had been progress in the past, so would there be progress in the future, provided that state control did not sap the energies of the nation. He was an optimist who, despite booms and slumps and failures of confidence, believed that the system was self-correcting. According to Joan Robinson, he had 'a foxy way of saving his conscience by mentioning exceptions, but doing so in such a way that his pupils would continue to believe in the rule'. Thus he would point out that Say's Law — supply creates its own demand — occasionally broke down. But 'this was mentioned by the way. It was not meant to disturb the general faith in equilibrium under *laissez-faire*.'[23] A more charitable interpretation would be that Marshall genuinely believed that there was a tendency towards equilibrium under *laissez-faire* but that his intellectual honesty led him to set out the exceptions and the difficulties.

So far as pure theory was concerned, Schumpeter thought Walras was 'the greatest of all economists', and he thought Walras's system of equations was 'the Magna Carta of economic theory'.[24] Walras, who was much more influential in the twentieth century, and especially during the last few years, than in his own, built a skyscraper of abstraction and of algebra and founded general equilibrium theory. In the Walrasian world, which is static and timeless and where pure competition reigns, people come along to markets laden with commodities and marginal utility schedules and announce their prices only tentatively. This system of *tatonnement* enables buyers and sellers to remain uncommitted until they arrive at a price which is the true equilibrium price. Only then does exchange take place. They are helped in these activities by an auctioneer, who is obviously a very busy person.

> The Walrasian Auctioneer [Professor Tobin explains] must collect all the demand and supply schedules....She must solve the simultaneous equations, announce the market clearing prices, and then see that the scheduled transactions are consummated at those prices. For continuous market clearing, the whole process must be repeated every quarter or day or second.[25]

In this world all markets always clear, all resources are used in the best possible way and every wage reflects the exact contribution its recipient has made. Plainly, none of this has anything to do with the real world. In real life markets do not clear, nor does any other part of the Walrasian system occur. But that has not dampened the enthusiasm of Walras's present-day followers.

Wicksell was much wiser. Walras, he noted, imagined that he had found 'the rigorous proof' of his system 'merely because he clothed in a mathematical formula the very arguments which he considered insufficient when they were expressed in ordinary language'.[26] Schumpeter, however, who talked about the 'logical beauty' of the Walrasian structure, thought that anybody who spurned the Walrasian world because of 'its hopeless discrepancy from any process of real life' should ask himself if he considered 'theoretical physics to be useless'.[27]

Just as Marshall was always making exceptions, so a partial exception must always be made of Marshall. But, like their predecessors and like Marx, the neo-classical economists believed themselves to be scientists. They started with theory, and they ended with theory. Cardinal Newman need not have worried. 'Political economy', he had written, 'is a science at the same time dangerous and leading to occasions of sin.'[28] It was no longer dangerous. It had virtually ceased to exist. Only economic science now could lead to 'occasions of sin'.

There is no reason why economics should deal only with the economy of the state and every reason why some economists should wish to concern themselves with pure theory. But Schumpeter's comparison with physics is tendentious. Physicists are not likely to tell unsuspecting politicians, bankers or journalists that unless they alter their behaviour, there will be worrying consequences. Economists, on the other hand, having abstracted their system from the real world, may forget the extent of their abstraction and, when commenting on everyday affairs, give very misleading advice. Besides, theoretical physics led to nuclear weapons; pure economics may have damaging, though less lethal, side-effects. 'The vice of neo-classical economics', ran the verdict of Mr Blaug, was 'the hasty application of static theorems to the real world'.[29]

Economists are fully entitled to disregard 'this actual England' if they so wish. But if they do, those in any way connected with public affairs are unwise to pay much attention to what such economists write or say. If economics ignores the real world and lives in abstractions, it becomes an interesting but peripheral activity, like solving crossword puzzles or pot-holing. Its utility value is marginal.

Socialist economics, too, made little progress. Bernstein's revisionism had much more influence on the tactics of the German Social Democratic Party (which was Marxist) than on socialist ideas. Marx still dominated the scene, and there was scarcely any attempt to fill the vacuum he had created in socialist economics. What attempts there were came from non-socialists. Wieser, Pareto and Barone, who were all antipathetic to socialism, produced 'the pure theory of the socialist economy'.[30] But these efforts were evidently on Walrasian lines, and socialists probably thought they had more than enough on their hands without lumbering themselves with the Walrasian Auctioneer and acres of algebra.

Most of the neo-classical economists were absorbed in their own speculations. Occasionally, however, some of them launched thunderbolts both against socialism and against Governments which, by reforming capitalism, were seeking to prevent the advent of a socialist state.

Ludwig von Mises was one of the last of the great Austrian school of economists which began with Menger* and one of the leading anti-socialist polemicists. Though at first sight Mises was in direct opposition to Marx, he was almost a mirror-image of him. Both men were dogmatic, and neither saw that events were disproving his dogma. Marx believed it was impossible to reform capitalism; Mises believed it was impossible to improve it. Marx thought his socialism was scientific; Mises thought his capitalism was scientific. Both had a taste for prophecy, which often turned out to be inaccurate.

Mises defined intervention as 'a limited order by a social authority forcing the owners of the means of production and entrepreneurs to employ their means in a different manner than they otherwise would'.[31] And for Mises such intervention was always wrong: 'Government cannot make man richer, but it can make him poorer.' Thus not only are tariffs objectionable, but so is factory legislation controlling the employment of women and children. Not only is any form of interference with wages or prices indefensible, but it is even wrong for Governments to

* Happy is the country which has no great economists! France has lacked any since the eighteenth century and has fared very well. Since Friedrich List, Germany too has been spared many of them with even better results. England and the United States are now full of economists, and their economies have not prospered. The great exception is Austria. The Austrian economy has been one of the successes of the post-war world. But that success has in no way been due to the great Austrian school of economists, whose doctrines the Austrian Government has wisely ignored.

prevent railroads from charging discriminatory rates. (Provided that it produces higher profits for the railroad, discrimination is desirable even though ultimately it drives those who are discriminated against out of business and leads to the formation of monopolies.) Government 'regulations for the preservation of competition' are damaging; so are the provision of unemployment pay and 'the denial of the freedom to move from country to country'.[32]

Mises's vision of a completely *laissez-faire* world, without any controls on capital, immigration or anything else and without any protection for the weak, was as mystical as Marx's vision of the state 'withering away' after the socialist revolution. Mises was driven to such absurdity by his dogmatic belief that government 'either abstains from limited interference with the market forces, or it assumes total control over production and distribution. Either capitalism or socialism; there is no middle of the road.'[33] Any attempt by government intervention to achieve an intermediate position would lead to 'a crisis from which either socialism or capitalism alone can emerge'. This was a prediction, which had been proved false even before it was made. The middle of the road, which according to Mises did not exist, is where most free Western countries have usually been, and the result has been greater prosperity for most of the time than ever before.

Mises was disturbed by the degree of interventionism even in the United States, and he was writing at the time of Presidents Harding and Coolidge. President Coolidge proclaimed that 'the business of America is business', and there has probably never been a president less inclined to interference. 'Mr Coolidge's genius for inactivity', wrote Walter Lippman, 'is developed to a very high point....it is a grim, determined, alert inactivity which keeps Mr Coolidge occupied constantly....inactivity is a political philosophy and a party programme with Mr Coolidge.'[34] A less measured observer who had a higher opinion of Coolidge, H. L. Mencken, noted that 'Nero fiddled, but Coolidge only snored.' America suffered least, Mencken believed, when the White House, as with Coolidge, was 'a peaceful dormitory'.[35] Yet Mises managed to be worried by interventionism in America, not by the lack of it.

Mises and Marx were mistaken for similar reasons. In the belief that their approach was scientific and that they had discovered inexorable economic laws, they refused to acknowledge that economics can be affected by politics. And they thought that 'capitalism' and 'socialism' were real and unchanging entities. Baldwin was nearer the mark when he said that socialism and *laissez-faire* are like the North and South Pole — they don't really exist. But, whether or not capitalism exists, it certainly changes.

Thus Marx and Mises were almost equally wrong, though Mises, writing at a much later date than Marx, had far less excuse. Had Marx been writing in the 1920s, he would have considerably modified his views. But his followers did not. Nor did his opponents. Hence the thesis and the antithesis remained as opposed to each other as ever, and both were still no less opposed to the synthesis.

So economics continued separate from politics and from much of the contemporary world. 'Political economy' lasted only a short time, and even then it was something of a misnomer. The connection was always tenuous, and, in view of the route followed by economics, the separation was inevitable.

The British political tradition was strongly empirical both in theory and in practice. Politics, wrote Burke, was, like medicine and physiology, 'not to be taught *a priori*'.[36] The Tories and the Whigs were not affected by the ideological extremism of the right which was prevalent on the Continent after the French Revolution, and there was no revolutionary party on the left. With some occasional backsliding, that empirical tradition has remained strong in all parties for most of the time. Because of the Tory dislike of ideology, dogma and what Burke called 'the hocus-pocus of abstraction',[37] this tradition has been especially strong in the Tory Party. For a Tory, theories have to be grounded in practice. Burke was not opposed to theory as such. When he spoke against theory, he said, 'I mean always a weak, erroneous, fallacious, unfounded or imperfect theory; and one of the ways of discovering that it is false theory is by comparing it with practice.'[38] For Burke, as for other great Conservatives, 'circumstance' is of crucial importance. 'The circumstances', he wrote, 'are what render every civil and political scheme beneficial or noxious to mankind.'[39]

Unfortunately, all this was alien to the political economists.

The great exception to the British empirical tradition was utilitarianism. That was a non-empirical philosophy which relied on *a priori* dogma. But apart from a brief period after 1832, which included such unfortunate episodes as the Poor Law Amendment Act as well as some sensible reforms, and apart from gaining the allegiance of a few Radical MPs, utilitarianism never enjoyed the success in politics that it enjoyed in economics. The politicians spurned it; the economists adopted it.

Thus economics, unlike politics, medicine and physiology, was taught *a priori*. 'Circumstances' were of little account. The political economists preferred to reason with what Burke, in another context, called 'all the nakedness and solitude of metaphysical abstraction'.[40] Nassau Senior, for instance, thought that all political economy could be derived from four postulates.[41] In the pursuit of 'scientific' certainty, empiricism was scorned and deductive logic embraced. Malthus saw the danger early on. 'The principal cause of error' in political economy appeared to him to be 'a precipitate attempt to simplify and generalize'; and he thought that this 'tendency to premature generalization' among some of the principal political economists produced 'an unwillingness to bring their theories to the test of experience'.[42] * But Malthus was almost alone, and the habits he criticized persisted. 'The test of experience' was ignored, and economists dressed up their rationalizations as scientific findings and sought to hide their perplexities behind metaphysics and inexorable laws. The path of *a priori* theorizing, abstraction and scientific pretension was preferred to empiricism.

Burke taught that politics should be based on human nature. There was nobody to do that for economics.† In consequence,

---

* Malthus evidently did not believe that he was vulnerable to the same criticism. He thought 'his steady and unshaken confidence in the theory of population' was due to its having been 'confirmed in the most remarkable manner by the state of society as it exists in every country with which we are acquainted'.[43]

† If one of Burke's last writings, *Thoughts and Details on Scarcity*, is taken in isolation, it is possible to argue that Burke himself believed that politics and economics should follow divergent paths. The pamphlet is replete with impeccably *laissez-faire* dogmatism. As Professor Preece has argued, it comes very close to the rationalistic abstractions which Burke denounces elsewhere as 'barbarous metaphysics'. There is no acknowledgement of the vital importance of 'circumstance' which is fundamental in the rest of Burke's thought. Indeed, *Thoughts and Details* is not only strongly at variance with Burke's

economics was based not on human nature and the ways of the world but on 'economic man' and the allegedly iron laws of economics. 'Economic man' was an abridgement and distortion of man. Utilitarian psychology took part of human nature and treated it as though it were the whole. Man does not think incessantly and exclusively of himself, nor of his own economic advantage. Yet those were the assumptions which the economists made.

In his *Notes from Underground*, Dostoevsky should have killed off 'economic man' once and for all:

Since when, during these thousands of years, has man ever acted solely in accordance with his own interests? What about the millions of facts which go to show that only too often man knowingly...puts that advantage aside in favour of some other plan...? ...You, gentlemen, take your lists of human interests from averages furnished by statistics and economic formulae....Would it not be a good thing if, with one consent, we were to kick all this solemn wisdom to the winds, and to send those logarithms to the devil, and to begin to live our lives again according to our own stupid whims? Who would care to exercise his willpower according to a table of logarithms? ...May it not be that man occasionally loves something besides prosperity?[45]

Unfortunately, economics pays no more attention to literature than it does to life, and economic man lives on. The failure to base economics on human nature as it is and on the world as it is has vitiated much of economic writing from the classical economists onwards.

Utilitarianism would not by itself have been enough to keep economics at variance with the British empirical tradition. Other factors were probably the personalities of the political economists, the urge to be scientific, and the nature of the economic doctrine they taught. Adam Smith was the only economist who, as a

general outlook, but it is also at variance with his observations on economics in, for example, his *Speech on Economical Reform* and his *Letter to a Noble Lord*. It was written, as Professor Preece says, at a time of personal unhappiness and when Burke had a feeling of impending disaster; it is best regarded as an 'aberration'.[44]

thinker, was remotely comparable with Burke in stature, and he was more empirical than his followers. But he lived too soon, and none of his successors was capable of doing what Coleridge advocated: to start with real problems and try to decide how to solve them. The urge to be considered scientists, which still exists among some economists today and is still a source of fog, was too strong. They could not resist the attractions of attempting to formulate laws which were as true as the laws of physics or other sciences.

This urge was almost certainly strengthened by the doctrine which they favoured and by the peculiar place of ethics in that doctrine. Adam Smith, taking up an idea derived from Mandeville's 'Fable of the Bees', separated economics from morality. In the economic sphere, unlike every other sphere of life, man's self-interest and selfishness were to be given full play. Admittedly, at the same time as Adam Smith removed morality from economic life, he seemed to put it back again by invoking the 'invisible hand'. It is, writes M. Louis Dumont, 'as if God told us, "Don't be afraid, my child, of apparently trespassing against my commands. I have so arranged everything that you are justified in neglecting morality in this particular case."'[46]

Nevertheless, the removal of morality from the system put the political economists and their successors, the neo-classical school, under some strain. If the absence of morality led to beneficent results for all, then morality would not be missed. But if the outcome was misery and unfairness, then there would be calls to bring morality back into economics. Thus the economists were under strong pressure to show that the system they had devised did not need morality or that there was no alternative. Iron laws were needed to prevent morality and the politicians from intruding into the economic system.* Hence the political economists claimed that there were inexorable laws which determined economic life and that, if these were not flouted, the system of

---

* Despite the iron laws, Ruskin was a determined intruder. 'So far as I know', he wrote in 1862, 'there is not in history record of anything so disgraceful to the human intellect as the modern idea that the commercial text, "Buy in the cheapest market and sell in the dearest" represents, under any circumstances could represent, an available principle of national economy.' Such an idea was 'perhaps the most insolently futile of all that ever beguiled men through their vices'.[47]

political economy would produce the best possible outcome. Their successors, the neo-classicals, claimed that under certain conditions (which did not, in fact, exist) the free economy would maximize the utilities or the satisfactions of all. Similar attempts have continued down to the present time.

For these reasons the economics taught in the nineteenth century (and since) was more of an ideology than an academic discipline, let alone a science. Tories, therefore, had strong reasons for scepticism. Nineteenth-century liberals and their successors were naturally enthusiastic about the ideology of classical economics and *laissez-faire*. Tories could see the element of truth in it but also the errors and the omissions. They had no cause to be caught in the fog.

Empiricism is as desirable in economics as it is in politics. Indeed, any other approach is bound to fail for the same reason that it fails in politics. As Dostoyevsky and many others have seen, human nature and economic behaviour cannot be confined within the straightjacket of any one theory or ideology, whether it is Marxist or Ricardian. Hence Panglossian theories are as erroneous and as dangerous in economics as they are in politics. The introduction of 'iron' or other laws will keep reality at bay only for a time. The attempt to defend *laissez-faire* and to explain away the glorification of self-love in economics by showing that the market economy produces the best possible outcome for all was bound to fail. It is not unlike the so-called naturalistic fallacy. The free economy cannot be justified by pretending that it is something that it is not. All that can reasonably be said is that, with all its faults, an economy which has self-interest as its driving force works better than one which is under central control and claims to be working in the name of altruism. In other words, the defence of the free economy should be the same as Churchill's defence of democracy: it is the worst known system except all those other forms that have been tried from time to time.

These problems would not have arisen if economics had spurned the Panglossian path. Had economics adopted the British political tradition, economists would have taken human nature and economic behaviour as they found it. They would have seen no cause either to justify selfishness or to try to abolish it. And they would have had no reason to justify the economic system as either perfect or unalterable. They would have set about trying to improve it, and while accepting that self-interest and individual initiative should be dominant, they would have conceded that more generous emotions, such as benevolence, pity and the urge to serve, had a part to play. But the economists' world had no room for such things, and their approach was very different.

Thus much economic theorizing was either irrelevant or erroneous; there was no reason why attempts should not be made to improve the economic system. Marshall, as we have seen, was a partial exception. But he did not swing English economics away from dogma. 'Marshall', wrote Mrs Robinson, 'certainly was a great moralizer, but somehow the moral always came out that whatever is, is *very nearly* best.'[48] The gulf between empirical politics and doctrinaire economics remained wide. It was only Keynes who spanned it. The key fact about Keynes was that he thought of the remedy before he evolved his theory. Practice preceded theory. If this was not characteristically empirical, it certainly was not dogmatic or 'scientific'. Indeed, what Keynes did was in large part empirical. He saw that unemployment was an intolerable evil. He refused to accept that it was an inevitable one or that the problem would solve itself; and he proposed a remedy. Only later did he perfect his theory. Here at last was an economist who repudiated the British economic tradition and behaved as Coleridge had prescribed. Classical dogma and neo-classical dogmas were set aside. Empiricism had come at last to economics.

Admittedly, that was not entirely the approach of Keynes's *General Theory*. In his writings Keynes never completely emancipated himself from his past; there is some metaphysics even in *The General Theory*. But it was his approach in substance, and it had vast influence in this country and in many parts of the world. Unfortunately, Keynesianism soon came under attack from the forces of the old orthodoxy. That intruder, empiricism, had to be expelled, and the old dogma and doctrines returned to their former lecture rooms, from where they could resume their disastrous sway.

6

Keynes and the Inter-War Years

While money can be usefully spent on capital improvements, a large part of it going in payment of labour which might otherwise be unemployed, the argument for spending it is very strong. It would, for example, be ridiculous for the guardians to contribute to the amount of unemployment in Cambridge by refraining from useful building, and then spend money, in order to give relief, to maintain men in idleness or in relatively useless occupations....

J. M. Keynes in 1914[1]

The Community lacks goods, and a million and a quarter people lack work. It is certainly one of the highest functions of national finance and credit to bridge the gulf between the two. This is the only country in the world where this condition exists. The Treasury and the Bank of England policy has been the only policy consistently pursued. It is a terrible responsibility for those who have shaped it, unless they can be sure that there is no connection between the unique British phenomenon of chronic unemployment and the long resolute consistency of a particular financial policy.

Winston Churchill in 1925[2]

The important thing is that society should be organized in such a way as to bring the economic system under conscious direction and control, and that the increased production should be directed towards raising the standard of comfort and security for all the people.

Harold Macmillan in 1938[3]

Quite apart from Keynes, it would be worth pausing for a moment at the inter-war period in Britian, since the resemblances to the present day are so great. Of course, inflation is a menace now, and it was no threat then, except in the immediate post-war years. That is one very important difference. And there is another to which we shall come in a moment. Nevertheless, anybody now reading about the 1920s and 1930s is likely to gain a strong feeling of *déjà vu*. Between 1921 and 1940 unemployment never fell below 10 per cent, and in the early 1930s it was over 20 per cent.[4] Then, as now, the cleavage of opinion as to how to deal with unemployment cut across party lines.[5] Then as now, the bulk of both the major parties appeared to have no answer. Then, as now, the real issue was between interventionist capitalism and *laissez-faire* capitalism,[6] between those who believed that the economy was controlled by the iron laws of *laissez-faire* and those who believed that capitalism had to be altered if it was to survive. Those who saw what needed to be done were, in Mr Brittan's words, 'a strangely assorted group' and included Keynes, Lloyd George, Mosley and Harold Macmillan.[7] But then, as now, the iron laws carried the day.

Then, as now, socialism was irrelevant. The minority Labour Government of 1929—31 was timid, and its Chancellor of the Exchequer, Snowden, was a rigid old-fashioned liberal, whose primary allegiances were to free trade and retrenchment. Even in 1927, 'the microbe of inflation', he told the TUC, 'is always in the atmosphere.... An expansion of the currency issue must respond to a genuine demand arising out of real purchasing power and not to be used to create a demand.'[8] Snowden would have fitted snugly into the Treasury of today. It was only after the fall of the Labour Government that Labour moved sharply to the left. The Labour Party today claims to have the answer to unemployment, but when it was in power it demonstrated that it did not. Although a left-wing Government in other ways, it pursued, at the persuasion of the IMF, 'orthodox' policies, and during its years of office unemployment doubled. Once again, on being driven from office, Labour moved much further to the left. But on both occasions when Labour was in power socialism had nothing of interest to say.

Then, as now, the majority of economists were opposed to the

Government's policies. Then, as now, the response to high unemployment was to take measures which led to still higher unemployment. Then, as now, part of the trouble was an exchange rate which had been pushed too high by government policy. Then, as now, Treasury Ministers maintained that their policies were not the cause of the trouble. The Chancellor of the Exchequer, wrote Keynes, says that 'the return to the Gold Standard is no more responsible for the condition of affairs in the coal industry than is the Gulf Stream. These statements are of the feather-brained order.'[9] Then, as now, there were premature predictions of recovery.[10] Then, as now, the financial system was given a preference, if not a dominance, in the formation of economic policy.[11] The Governor of the Bank of England, wrote Churchill when Chancellor, 'shows himself perfectly happy in the spectacle of Britain possessing the finest credit in the world simultaneously with a million and a quarter unemployed'.[12] Then, as now, the Treasury was clamped in a rigid orthodoxy of a bygone age. Then, as now, international bankers were cautious at home and reckless abroad. Then, as now, when orthodoxy was getting the worse of the argument, there was a tendency to bring in morals.

> Many Conservative bankers [wrote Keynes in 1923] regard it as more consonant with their cloth, and also as economizing thought, to shift public discussion of financial topics off the logical on to an alleged moral plane, which means a realm of thought when vested interest can be triumphant over the common good without further debate....[13]

Today such tactics are not confined to bankers. Then, as now, there was a great shortage of investment at home and a marked increase in British investment abroad, 'In my opinion,' Keynes wrote in 1924,

> there are many reasons for thinking that our present rate of foreign investment is excessive and undesirable....Our traditional, conventional attitude towards foreign investment demands consideration; it is high time to give it a bad name and to call it 'the flight of capital'.[14]

Then, as now, the conventional wisdom, with Keynes dissenting, was that unemployment was caused by wages being too high and that wages should be cut. Then, as now, the Treasury was oblivious of the Keynesian revolution. Then it had not taken place; now it has. But the result is the same. Then, as now, priority was given to the achievement of certain financial targets; what was going on in the real economy was secondary. Today it is M3 and PSBR which hold sway at the Treasury; then it was a balanced budget which was the fetish. Unfortunately, the budget of those days, like the PSBR and the money supply today, was not as straightforward as it looked. 'The exact components of the two sides of the account in any year', wrote U. K. Hicks, a well-qualified observer, 'are to some extent at least a matter of chance and partly even of choice.' And her verdict was that 'the Chancellor's Budget as it stands cannot be an account of primary economic significance, that is to say, that it does not clearly reveal the true economic position of the whole, or indeed any part, of the public finances.'[15] Yet the Treasury devoted its main efforts to balancing these incomplete and often misleading figures and to frustrating anybody who wished to improve the condition of the real economy.

The Treasury's principal weapon against those who saw what needed to be done and produced proposals to lessen unemployment was the so-called 'Treasury view'. According to the Treasury view, existing resources of capital and savings were already fully utilized. Thus if the Government borrowed money for public works, that would reduce the savings which were available to finance private investment. There would, therefore, be no gain in investment. All that would happen would be the displacement of private investment by less profitable public investment. There were three remarkable features about all this. First, both major parties supported the Treasury view. Secondly, the Treasury view was based, as Harrod said, on the idea that there was a lump of savings.[16] It was, therefore, the twentieth-century cousin of the absurd idea of one hundred years earlier that there was a fixed fund for the payment of wages. Thirdly, the Treasury view dismissed from sight the fact of mass unemployment — a notable achievement. Orthodoxy said that the economy was tending towards full employment,[17] so the Treasury simply assumed it was and did not adjust theory to reality. Say's Law was still relied on.[18] Clearly, the Treasury view would have been correct had there been full employment. But in that case there would have been no call for public works or other measures to deal with unemployment, and the Treasury view would not have been formed to frustrate such calls. Thus under full employment the Treasury view was true but irrelevant; under mass unemployment it was relevant but fallacious. In any case, it was 'the orthodox Treasury doctrine, which was steadfastly held', Churchill said in his Budget speech of 1929, 'that whatever might be the political or social advantages, very little additional employment and no permanent additional employment can in fact and as a general rule be created by state borrowing and state expenditure'.[19] Before we are tempted to become too censorious, we should perhaps recall that the Treasury view, or something very like it, is even now entrenched in Whitehall.

Keynes, like the other leading economists who favoured expenditure on public works,[20] attached no credence to the Treasury view. He pointed out that with the money spent on keeping men in unemployment, a million houses could have been built, or a third of all the roads in the country, or the nation's industrial equipment could have been revolutionized.[21] And at the worst of the depression he wrote that 'with what we have spent on the dole in England since the war we could have made our cities the greatest works of man in the world.'[22] As early as 1924 Keynes had come to the conclusion that unemployment needed a drastic remedy and had decided what that remedy should be. *Laissez-faire* should be abandoned, 'not from contempt of that good old doctrine, but because whether we like it or not, the conditions for its success have disappeared'.[23] In its place there should be a large scheme of public investment, chiefly in housing, roads and electricity. There should also be credit control to flatten the credit cycle and some check on the export of capital. Thus, as Harrod comments, the main framework of Keynesianism was already there in 1924.[24] The remedies had been thought of. The theory came later.

In the meantime, the industrial position was worsened by Churchill's decision, reached after Treasury persuasion had overcome his own misgivings, to return to the Gold Standard at the pre-war parity.[25] This action was soon violently unpopular, but at the time Keynes was almost its only opponent.

The Labour Party did not even vote against it in Parliament.

In his *Economic Consequences of Mr Churchill* Keynes pointed out that as a result of the return to gold the pound was 10 per cent over-valued and the Government's policy was, therefore, one of 'reducing everyone's wages by 2s. in the pound'. This was what the coal owners duly proposed. Coal, wrote Keynes, was 'a victim of our monetary policy', and he added, 'on grounds of social justice no case can be made for reducing the wages of the miners. They are the victims of the economic juggernaut.'[26] The clash between the juggernaut and the miners produced the General Strike, which was followed by increased unemployment. The return to gold had indeed, as Churchill feared, favoured 'finance' at the expense of industry.[27]

At the same time, the Government successfully opposed the attempt of the protectionists to safeguard British industries, so the protectionist route to lowering unemployment was effectively barred. In the 1920s protection was, from the Conservative point of view, the natural remedy for unemployment, but after the 1923 election Baldwin was understandably cautious on the issue; and he had then sold the protectionist pass by making the free trader, Churchill, his Chancellor of the Exchequer. With Neville Chamberlain at the Ministry of Health, pursuing in conjunction with Churchill an active and successful social policy, there was a return to the Disraelian tradition of social reform, while Baldwin himself sought to conciliate the Labour Party and to soften class antagonisms. Economically, however, the Government was sunk in inertia, pursuing old policies which had failed and following old theories which were false.

In these circumstances Lloyd George and the Liberals, the only party not locked into outworn attitudes to the economy, produced in March 1929, in good time for the election, *We can Conquer Unemployment*. This embodied a Keynesian programme of public works and was backed up by a pamphlet, *Can Lloyd George Do It?*, written by Keynes and H. D. Henderson. The Lloyd George pamphlet asserted:

At the moment individual enterprise alone cannot restore the situation within a time for which we can wait. The state must, therefore, lend its aid and, by a deliberate policy of national development, help to set going at full speed the great machine of industry.[28]

Unusually, and mildly unconstitutionally, the Conservative Government set the Treasury and not the Treasury Ministers the task of trying to answer Lloyd George. It produced the same old mish-mash, with the 'Treasury view' prominently displayed. Keynes summarized the Conservative attitude as 'you must not do anything, because this will only mean you can't do something else', and 'we will not promise more than we can perform. We, therefore, promise nothing.' These, he said, were 'the slogans of depression and decay — the timidities and obstructions and stupidities of a sinking administrative vitality'. The Government's watchwords were 'negation, restriction, inactivity'.[29]

The Government was defeated not by Lloyd George, who had imaginative policies to deal with unemployment, but by the Labour Party, which had no imaginative policies to deal with unemployment or with anything else. Ramsay MacDonald formed his second minority Government to face the world slump of 1929—31, and unemployment remorselessly rose. In the Labour Government only Mosley had anything to propose, and he soon left the party to form his own. Nor, fortunately, at the crisis of capitalism, had the Labour Government any serious socialist measures to hand. The Labour Party at that time 'owed more to Methodism than Marx'. But for the purpose of dealing with unemployment or introducing socialism the methodist tradition was no more helpful than the Marxist. If capitalism was bankrupt, so was socialism; and so was traditional economics.

After the break-up of the Labour Government and the formation of a national coalition, the Government naturally went on deflating. Keynes, who favoured instead lower interest rates, a tariff and a large programme of public investment,[30] thought the coalition Government's first budget was 'replete with folly and injustice' and stated rightly that its effect on unemployment would be 'disastrous'. In a sentence, which again calls present-day conditions to mind, he added that the Government had noticed that there was one point, the employers' insurance contribution, where their activities raised the cost of production. 'So in order to prove for certain they are quite mad,' he wrote, 'the government have decided to increase it.'[31] *

Unemployment duly rose to nearly 3 million. Nevertheless, Chamberlain pursued a policy of cheap money, imperial preference and protection, combined with much government intervention in industry and agriculture; and Britain recovered from the slump more quickly than other countries. The departure from the Gold Standard and the imposition of a general tariff had swept away many of the old orthodoxies. *Laissez-faire* had been abandoned. That dismayed Dr Hayek[32] and delighted Harold Macmillan. 'It seemed to me', wrote Macmillan in *The Middle Way*, 'that the idea of an unplanned self-adjusting economic system had been finally and irrevocably destroyed.'[33]

That is the second great difference from today. The Government of the 1930s believed in a strong state, and its economic policy was highly interventionist. The Government of today is opposed to intervention and leans towards *laissez-faire*, whatever happens in practice. Chamberlain had no doubt that he was making 'changes of a really revolutionary character'.[34] He used the tariff as a lever for forcing industry to reorganize itself. Steel was a notable example. With Government support, there were reorganizations and amalgamations, and output and prices were controlled. Special assistance was given to industries such as shipbuilding and cotton. And the Government entered into various 'mercantilist' trade agreements under which, in return for help for British exports, quotas were given for agricultural imports. At the same time British agriculture was assisted by direct subsidy, and marketing boards were set up. What Professor Beer calls 'this structure of "quasi-corporatism"'[35] was certainly very different from anything that had happened before, and the British economy was more successful than it had been for a long time. All the same, the fetish of a balanced budget remained, even though to cut expenditure in a slump necessarily increased unemployment. 'By cuts, by economy and by severe taxation', Neville Chamberlain, the Chancellor of the Exchequer, said proudly in 1935, 'the Budget was balanced.'[36] The 'Treasury

* The present Government have not increased the National Insurance Surcharge, introduced by Mr Healey, but waited until the 1982 budget before slightly reducing it instead of abolishing it.

view' also survived. In the same year Chamberlain told Parliament that a large expenditure of public money and public works would not help employment 'because the whole experience of the past shows that, for the purpose of providing employment, this policy of public works is always disappointing....'[37] Just what Chamberlain meant by 'the whole experience of the past' is not clear, but his final sentence has a fine contemporary ring.

Cheap money and protection had been advocated by Keynes, but Keynesianism was not adopted. Both officially through his membership of the Economic Advisory Council and in the newspapers Keynes had been advocating a public works policy since 1932, but though by 1937 his ideas had become respectable in Whitehall, little was done.[38] The depressed areas remained depressed; some of them became more so. Governmental promises to help were not kept, and Chamberlain himself thought the 1936 Reconstruction Bill 'pretty thin'.[39] In consequence, five years after Chamberlain's speech, at the time of Dunkirk, Britain still had over 10 per cent unemployment; more than a million people were unemployed.

Keynes's *The General Theory of Employment, Interest and Money* was published in 1936 but had little practical effect before the war. As Professor Skidelsky has pointed out, Hitler's New Deal was the only one that succeeded in dealing with unemployment. Roosevelt's did not: in none of the pre-war years did his fiscal policy stimulate the economy as much as Hoover had done in 1931. And nothing much happened in the Swedish New Deal.[40] But during and after the war Keynes's influence was immense. *The General Theory* demolished — for the time being — the ideas that the economy is totally self-regulating and that full employment is its natural state. There would not be full employment, said Keynes, if demand were not high enough. Savings might exceed investment, in which case demand would be too low. Say's Law was false. Supply did not create its own demand.

If there was unemployment, the way to cure it was not, as previous theory had held, to lower wages and to cut everything in sight. Deflation did not help countries out of depression; it made the depression worse, and increased unemployment. The way to reduce unemployment was for the Government to increase demand by fiscal measures and by public investment. Investment had a 'multiplier' or snowball effect on output and unemployment, just as cuts in investment had in the opposite direction. We need not go into the complexities of *The General Theory*. Such matters as 'liquidity preference' and 'the propensity to consume' and (Lord Kahn's) multiplier need not detain us. The essential points of Keynesianism are, first, that full employment does not come automatically. Hence the Government must ensure that effective demand is adequate. In other words, there is no natural harmony of interests. The 'invisible hand' does not exist, and the Government has to intervene to remedy the defects of the economic system. Secondly, we live in an uncertain world. Consequently, economic dogmas which purport confidently to predict what will happen are what Burke called 'solemn trifling', suitable for diagrams and lectures and learned journals, but out of place in the real world, where we do not know what the future holds and where neither the present nor the future is ever in equilibrium. Finally, Keynes brought together the theory of value and monetary theory. Previously they had generally lived in separate compartments, to the disadvantage of both. (Now they have returned to separate compartments.)

Keynes thus demythologized economics — for a time. After him economics was no longer a matter of algebra and imaginary clearing markets; it was a matter of dealing with real problems. Before Keynes economics had been concerned chiefly with explaining why politicians could not and should not do things. Economics was a self-regulating and politician-regulating system. And from the socialist point of view, capitalism was bound to collapse. There was, therefore, no point in tinkering with it. Keynes swept all that away. Political economy was restored for a time. The economy was no longer an occult mystery on which Governments should not lay profane hands. And since Governments could prevent high unemployment, capitalism was no longer bound to collapse. By banishing *laissez-faire*, capitalism could be saved. And by banishing high unemployment, socialism would be prevented. Keynes thus provided a true *via media* between *laissez-faire* and socialism. Managed capitalism was the solution. Economics had been put to the service of politics.

That of course caused problems. All the same, economics at the service of politicians has been far more successful than it was when it was at the service of central bankers, the forces of orthodoxy and the *status quo*. Even Dr Hayek conceded there had been 'a unique twenty-five year period of great prosperity', though he thought that Keynesianism had inevitably produced its Nemesis.[41]

In his *History of the World* Dr Roberts has described how Pythagorean influence on Greek thought led to a

> view of the universe, which because it was constructed on mathematical and deductive principles, rather than from observation, fixed astronomy on the wrong lines for nearly two thousand years. From it came the vision of a universe built up of successively enclosing spheres on which moved, sun, moon and planets in a fixed and circular pattern round the earth. The Greeks noticed that this did not seem to be the way the heavens moved in practice.

But appearances, Dr Roberts concludes, were saved 'by introducing more and more refinements into the basic scheme while refusing to scrutinize the principles from which it was deducted'.[42] As we have seen, much the same thing happened to economics until Keynes changed fundamentally the basic scheme. He made the economic system move round man, as it were, instead of man moving round the economic system. It was a striking intellectual achievement. Unfortunately, as we shall see, Pythagoras soon came creeping back and attempted with some success to reimpose the old, out-worn system.

The blame for this lies partly with Keynes himself, partly with some of his followers, but primarily with those economists who refused to accept that the old orthodoxy, having been destroyed by Keynes, was like Humpty Dumpty and that all their ingenuity and all their abstractions could not put it together again. Keynes wrote in the Preface to *The General Theory* that he himself had 'held with conviction for many years' the theories which he was attacking and that the writing of the book had for him been 'a long struggle of escape...a struggle of escape from habitual modes of thought and expression'. The difficulty, he added, was 'not in the new ideas, but in escaping from the old ones, which ramify, for those brought up as most of us have been, into every corner of our minds'.[43] As far as his ideas were concerned, Keynes was largely successful in escaping. True, he did not discard the law of diminishing returns or the theory of marginal productivity. But he really did produce a new way of looking at economics and at the economic system of the country. 'Life', as Dostoevsky once wrote, 'had stepped into the place of theory.'[44] Keynes was concerned with what was actually happening and what should be done about it.

Yet Keynes's method of argument was far less revolutionary than his results. His years of being a monetary economist at Cambridge had left their mark. Thus although his objective was to get away from the old equilibrium economics and to move into the actual historical world, he used for *The General Theory* a static equilibrium model. His method, as opposed to his ideas, was not so very different from that of the classical economists. Indeed, instead of burying Ricardian economics, he has been accused of praising it.[45] And there was one sentence in *The General Theory* which almost invited the old guard to re-form: 'But if our central controls succeed in establishing an aggregate volume of output corresponding to full employment...,' wrote Keynes in his concluding notes, 'the classical theory comes into its own again from this point onwards.'[46] Keynes meant, of course, that the classical theory could return only as a superstructure, on top of a non-classical or Keynesian foundation of demand sufficient to secure full employment.[47]

In any event, while Keynesian ideas were generally accepted after the war, the ideas which he had refuted also lingered on. That they had been exposed as mistaken was not sufficient to persuade the economics profession to give up the habits of thought of more than a lifetime. In the textbooks, Joan Robinson complained, 'all the old slogans are repeated unchanged.'[48] Keynes was grafted on to the old system, and neo-classical economics went on its way as though nothing much had happened. Keynesianism was even grafted on to, of all things, the Walrasian general equilibrium tradition. In any other subject such sleight of hand would surely have been impossible. But economic theory is a world of its own, and economic theorists were determined to protect it from reality. The best way to do so was to bring reality within the system and thus make it unreal. The result of this unnatural union was aptly christened by Professor Hahn the 'neo-classical bastard'.[49] Maybe this was only to be expected. After all, it was not until 1823 that the Papacy finally accepted that Galileo had been right two hundred years before and that the earth does revolve round the sun and not vice versa. Still, the comparison is not exact. To be in fundamental error about the solar system does not affect many people's lives: to try to rehabilitate obsolete economic dogma affects millions of lives and millions of jobs.

Keynes also suffered from some of his followers, who turned his theory into an orthodoxy almost as rigid as the neo-classical one. They did not properly appreciate that all theories are imperfect and that new difficulties need new remedies. Thus Keynes had rightly demolished Say's Law, but some of his followers came near to creating the reverse of Say's Law: demand creates its own supply. Not enough attention was paid to seeing that the demand created by Keynesian policies would lead to the right kind of production. More important, *The General Theory* had been produced to deal with a depression. Its ideas were instrumental in preventing serious depressions for twenty-five years. Yet full employment, combined with free collective bargaining, brought the problem of inflation to the fore. Keynes anticipated the problem as early as the last years of the war. 'I do not doubt', he wrote in 1944, 'that a serious problem will arise when we have a combination of collective bargaining and full employment.' He added the profound remark that it was 'a political rather than an economic problem'.[50] Some Keynesians also realized what was bound to happen. But others of his followers – and nearly all politicians – were slower off the mark and did not see that Keynesianism was not enough. Probably, too, the Keynesians were remiss in not making greater efforts to secure wider and fuller public understanding of what Keynes had tried to do. In particular, they did not manage to instil the realization that rules suitable for running an individual's economic affairs are unlikely to be equally suitable for running the national economy.

Nevertheless, it was the addiction to myths of many economists, their antipathy to the empirical approach to their subject, their attachment to abstract 'scientific' theory and their resolute determination to ignore present-day events and conditions which were the prime causes of the probably temporary eclipse of the Keynesian approach to economics.

Harrod's great biography of Keynes was published near the beginning of the Keynesian era in 1951. He had no inkling that there could ever be a return to the bad old ways of the 1920s and

the 1930s or that the same ancient fallacies would before long
be back on parade, pretending that they had not been routed a
generation before. He wrote for instance that 'the idea that supply
creates its own demand disappeared; so also did the idea that
unemployment is primarily due to unwillingness to work for
sufficiently low wage rewards.'[51]

And he included in his book a satirical paragraph on the sort
of pre-Keynesian economic thinking which he thought Keynes
had destroyed for ever:

If you can increase investment or government expenditure,
that can only be at the expense of something else. If there is
unemployment, you must consider a reduction of wages;
otherwise you will merely make confusion worse confoun-
ded. As an ancillary measure you should encourage all-round
economy by precept and example, as that will always help to
tune up the economic system.[52]

Roy Harrod was wrong, of course. His satire reads like an advance
parody of a currently fashionable economic outlook.

7

The Post-War Years and How Monetarism Captured the Conservatives

Surely experience might have taught
Thy firmest promises are naught....

Byron: 'To Woman'[1]

...nothing is so firmly believed, as that which a man knoweth least.

Montaigne[2]

If the Pope wishes to change his religion, that is his affair; I see no reason to change mine.

Lord Acton[3]

Keynesianism was enshrined as government policy in the wartime coalition's 1944 White Paper on Employment Policy.[4] There it was laid down that 'the Government accept as one of their primary aims and responsibilities a high and stable level of employment after the war'. As a result of a palace revolution in the wartime Treasury, an eminent Treasury official has said, 'Keynesian economics' reigned there from the war years until the counter-revolution took place in the 1970s.[5] Certainly, full employment was an important objective of economic policy and was achieved for just over a quarter of a century. For most of that period, indeed, unemployment was considerably lower than the authors of the White Paper had envisaged. But whether full employment was the result of Keynesian policies, and whether Keynesian policies were in fact followed, are matters of greater uncertainty.

The post-war world boom, which lasted longer than any other, owed much to the international financial arrangements made at

Bretton Woods, where Keynes was the British negotiator. Although he dominated the conference,[6] he got by no means all that he wanted. And on top of that the agreements did not function as Keynes hoped they would. For instance, as he told the House of Lords before Bretton Woods, Keynes was determined that the external value of sterling 'should be altered if necessary so as to conform to whatever *de facto* internal value results from domestic policies'.[7] In the event exchange-rate adjustments were much more difficult and much less frequent than Keynes had expected. Nevertheless, the agreements provided financial stability for nearly thirty years, and it is since their breakdown that the international economy has sharply deteriorated.

Worldwide, the Keynesian era was successful. By every criterion, the world economy performed outstandingly well. And so, by our standards, did we. Britain's economic performance between 1945 and 1974 was better than it had been either in the inter-war years or before 1914 and much better than it has been since. Full employment was combined with only a mild rate of inflation and with more growth than for almost a century. Yet when our performance is compared with that of other countries, a very different picture emerges.

Apart from Switzerland and Sweden and the Irish Republic, Britain was the only country in Western Europe not to suffer Nazi occupation, a bloody civil war or a long-running colonial war in Africa. Yet our economic performance was worse than that of any other country in Western Europe save Portugal. Having been the richest country in Western Europe in 1950, we were by 1979 almost the poorest. Only Spain, Portugal, Greece and Italy were behind us, and even some of the Eastern European countries were drawing uncomfortably close. Britain's gross national product per head is only just over half that of her immediate neighbours.[8] Some of these competitors no doubt had advantages that we did not possess, but it is unreasonable to believe that all of them did. So the divergent case is Britain's relative failure, not other countries' successes. And it cannot be explained away by saying that we did worse in most other recent periods of our history.

The causes of Britain's relative economic decline are many and various: too many changes in government policy; a primitive trade union structure; the failure to give as much power and status as did, for example, the French and Germans to middle management; the failure to commit sufficient resources to marketing; the attempt to spread the marketing effort too widely instead of concentrating it on particular areas; too little investment; too much nationalization; excessively high taxation; bad industrial relations; restrictive practices; hostility to change; and so on. Britain was at a disadvantage, too, compared with her competitors, in having to export a higher proportion of her national product than any other country. This necessarily subjected her industrialists to additional uncertainties. But the proximate causes of our failure to grow in step with other countries were our appalling low productivity and the endemic tendency of the annual round of wage claims to exceed the miserably small increase in that productivity by a larger margin than did those of our competitors. Added to these grim recurring features were excessive commitments and expenditure abroad. The consequence was regular crises brought on by fears of inflation and a sterling crisis, which in turn led to the growth of the economy being frequently and sharply stopped.

The question at issue, therefore, is whether this was caused by the application of Keynesian economic policies. Was the British failure the result of erroneous economic theory slavishly followed, or was it the result of weaknesses in the British economy, of mistakes by Governments and of sundry other causes? Keynes's *The General Theory*, Mr Eltis wrote in 1977, made 'a significant contribution to human welfare' for a quarter of a century. 'The Governments which like Britain's applied the tools that Keynes invented achieved full employment and, in addition, declining inflation rates for most of the 1950s.' But the 1960s and 1970s were different, and Mr Eltis believes that the countries most susceptible to the influence of Keynesian policy making 'suffered most'.[9] Yet before making a judgement on Keynesian economics, we have to decide whether Keynesianism was, in fact, followed here and abroad. There is no certain criterion for applying or withholding the label, but one rough definition might be the willingness of Government to manage demand so as to achieve full employment.

Keynesianism has broadly come under two contradictory lines of attack by monetarists. The first was best expressed by Sir Keith Joseph in his Preston speech shortly before the second 1974 election. 'It is the method that successive Governments have used to reduce unemployment — namely, expanding aggregate demand by deficit financing — which has created inflation, and without really helping the unemployed either.'[10] The second line of attack has been pressed by Mr Samuel Brittan and others. So long as the world system prevailed, he maintains, 'the over-riding aim of economic policy in most countries — despite their Keynesian rhetoric — was to maintain the parity of their currency against the dollar.' And since Mr Brittan believes that Keynesianism did not come to the USA 'until well into the 1960s', other countries had to follow policies similar to those of the United States to avoid devaluing against the dollar.[11] * At the very least both these arguments cannot be right. One says that Keynesian policies were disastrous; the other says they were not even tried — at least until the late 1960s and 1970s. In seeking the answer it will be convenient, for the time being, to stick to the British experience.

In a well-known article written in 1968,[12] Professor Matthews posed the question whether the high post-war level of demand had been due to the Government or to other forces which had made Government action unnecessary. 'The hypothesis is that the change was due to fiscal policy is', he wrote,

> open to a simple basic objection. That is that throughout the post war period the government so far from injecting demand into the system, has persistently had a large current account surplus. Government saving has averaged about 3 per cent of the national income...Fiscal policy as such therefore appears on the face of it to have been deflationary in the post war period, quite strongly deflationary in fact, rather than the reverse. This is not to deny that in various post war years fiscal policy has been adjusted with the object of increasing demand above its existing level. But in the years when this was done it was a matter of reducing the size of the surplus rather than turning it into a deficit.[13]

In other words, we did not have budget deficits to boost demand; we had budget surpluses to restrain it.[14] That seems to wash out Keith Joseph and possibly Keynes as well. But in his valuable book

---

* Having had a strong Keynesian period and then a strong monetarist period, Mr Brittan now seems anxious to act as a referee. His refereeing is above the standard seen in the 1982 World Cup.

Can We Get Back to Full Employment? Mr Maurice Scott argues, in answer to Matthews, that different government policies would have produced unemployment, which indeed Matthews conceded, and that it was the knowledge that, if private investment had not increased, fiscal demand would have been kept up which was important. So it was after all, he thinks, 'the commitment to full employment which really mattered'.[15]

Keynes can therefore be given credit for full employment. Should he be debited with Britain's failure to grow as fast as her main competitors?

In a recent fine polemic against the management of the British economy since the war, Professor Pollard maintains that Britain's 'abysmal' record was due to our refusal or inability to invest sufficiently in productive equipment. He asks why the country does not enjoy an income per head roughly double what it is now, and answers that Britain does not 'produce double the current output because she lacks the productive capacity to do so'. Much of the blame for this he ascribes to the stop-go cycle which was caused by recurrent balance of payment crises. Stop-go meant the sacrifice of economic growth for the sake of preserving the balance of payments. These crises took place in 1947, 1949, 1951, 1955, 1957, 1964—7, 1968 and 1973—6. During the stop-go cycle, demand was expanded until there was a run on the pound, or the danger of one, whereupon demand was deflated until unemployment was high enough to make the foreign holders of sterling happy and calm. And then the cycle started again. Thus during the Keynesian era of full employment Governments were continuously creating unemployment for the sake of the balance of payments. This does not look like the 'hubristic Keynesianism' which Professor Beer has talked about.[16] But it does not look like sensible Keynesianism either.

The post-war British Governments were thus unable consistently to pursue Keynesian policies of so managing demand as to maintain full employment, because they failed to combine those policies with other kinds of intervention which would have secured increased productive investment. That investment would have enabled the Keynesian stimulus to be consistently applied without overheating the economy or running into balance-of-payments difficulties. Without it, Keynesianism had continually to be put into reverse. In other words, Keynesianism by itself was not enough.

It is possible, like Mr Scott,[17] to be relaxed about stop-go and to reflect that it was at least better than the perpetual stop that we have had since. Yet Professor Pollard believes that stop-go lies near the root of our troubles. It was a way of solving successive short-term problems at the expense of the long-term failure to sustain economic growth. As a result, businessmen lost the confidence to invest, and the workforce, because its standard of living grew so slowly, became 'radicalized'. Because the necessary investment in productive capacity had never been made, a boom could never be sustained. And each cut-back (in which industrial investment was always the hardest-hit) put us further behind our competitors. He finds it astonishing that nobody ever bothered to ensure that there had been sufficient investment to provide productive capacity to support a boom before that boom was unleashed. Pollard makes a convincing case.[18]

The extraordinary thing is that the Government never learned. It was evidently as unaware of what it was doing as a sleepwalker. It went on going round the same route, or rather the same cycle, which always led to the same results. Experience was apparently irrelevant.

It seems therefore as though Mr Brittan is at least partly right. Keynesian instruments were used to manipulate demand, but they were used to achieve a non-Keynesian result, increased unemployment, even though by previous and future standards unemployment remained low. We did not have 'hubristic Keynesianism'; we had Treasury Keynesianism, and in that hybrid the Treasury part dominated the Keynesian part. The wartime 'revolution' in the Treasury was only superficial. It was not so much a palace revolution, more a change of uniform. Before the war the Treasury's obsession was a balanced budget, after the war the balance of payments. 'The criticism', wrote Mr Brittan during his Keynesian period in 1964, 'is that Britain was playing the wrong economic game during the last dozen years or so.'[20]

---

* Sir Roy Harrod would have agreed with him. 'It is surely very irrational indeed', he wrote in 1967 'to tolerate "stop" measures, lasting two years or more, causing a loss of output of perhaps 3 per cent of national income in the first year and 6 per cent in the second year , merely to correct a deficit amounting to 0.85 per cent of national income'.[19]

The British economy suffered not from too much government interference but from too little and of the wrong kind.

Most other countries had been less affected by *laissez-faire* than Britain. Many of them in the nineteenth century had tended to see British political economy as an argument for free trade and therefore for British ascendancy. They believed that their Governments had to act if Britain was to be overtaken. In the 1930s Britain was much more interventionist than formerly, but most other countries were more so.

Hence, for most of them, Keynesianism was much less of a break with the past than it was for Britain and was much less necessary. There was no *laissez-faire* to displace. Their degree of intervention was already often greater than that envisaged by Keynes. What was new was the conscious pursuit of full employment. 'The deliberate attempt to influence the level of effective demand', Professor Deane has written, 'was a feature of all advanced capitalist economies in the post-Second World War era.'[21] And for Keynes theory had been less important than practice.

France had a long history of *dirigisme* and sustained a high level of demand by indicative planning and other means. Keynesianism did not reach Germany until the late 1950s, and surprisingly its point of entry there was the Bundesbank.[22] Although Germany represented her policies as being fully in accordance with market orthodoxies; the Government did not hesitate to intervene in order to hasten growth in the economy. Moreover, its intervention was often highly discriminatory.[23] Even the great Erhard himself, despite his rhetoric, was not averse to speeding up the processes of the market. He was, wrote Andrew Schonfield, 'a jogger and nudger'.[24]

The intellectual influence of Keynes was strong in America from an early stage. Professor Hirschman has talked of the Keynesian revolution becoming 'the new economics and almost a new orthodoxy' in the 1940s and 1950s.[25] And 'the wide acceptance of Keynesian views', Milton Friedman said in 1967, 'meant that for some two decades monetary policy was believed by all but a few reactionary souls to have been rendered obsolete by new economic knowledge.... These views produced a widespread adoption of cheap money policies after the war.'[26] In 1946 the 'Keynesian' Employment Act was passed. But apart from that Act the influence of Keynes remained mainly intellectual for some time. Both President Eisenhower and his Secretary of the Treasury, George Humphreys, were anxious to balance the budget, come what may. Yet Eisenhower's first Chairman of the Council of Economic Advisers, Arthur Burns, made muted Keynesian noises in his economic report of 1955, and the Eisenhower Administration ran up a deficit of nearly $10 billion in overcoming the recession of 1958. At that time it was by far the biggest deficit America had ever seen in peacetime.[27]

In the 1960s American policy became openly 'Keynesian', though the methods President Johnson and Congress employed to finance the Vietnam war were very different from those advocated by Keynes in his 1940 booklet *How to Pay for the War.*

President Nixon promised in his election campaign of 1968 'to balance the Federal budget' and, when elected, took strong deflationary action. This hit output and jobs but had little effect on prices. The Republicans did badly in the mid-term elections, and in 1971 Nixon reversed his policies. Government expenditure was increased; the money supply rose; tax increases were abandoned; and the Government intervened to reduce wage and price increases. Well might Nixon say in an aside: 'I am now a Keynesian.'[28] Thus, near the end of the Keynesian era, Keynesianism received its most improbable convert.

By and large, therefore, if specifically Keynesian policies were not followed abroad, the alternative was not *laissez-faire* but increased, if often hidden, intervention. Hence it seems unlikely that Keynesian policies were the cause of Britain's economic failure, except in the sense that, unlike in other countries, they were not accompanied by other government measures. Undoubtedly, Keynesians — whether politicians, economists or civil servants — made many mistakes, some of which have already been mentioned. There was too much chopping and changing of government policies. Keynesianism tended to become a mechanical orthodoxy, like neo-classical economics into which indeed it was partially absorbed, rather than a new approach to economics which should be varied by experience. The 'Phillips curve', for example, which claimed a stable relationship between the rate of unemployment and the rate of wage increases, was treated as a law instead of a passing phenomenon. Insufficient attention was paid to structural problems. Immense pains were lavished on the management of demand; supply was left largely to look after itself – which it did not. The problem of wage inflation proved intractable. Trade-union reform was tackled too late. Churchill had promised in 1951 to leave the issue 'to the working of common sense and public opinion'.[29] But when, ten years later, those forces had proved insufficient, the Government should have acted.

Thus the main problems of the British economy had at that time little to do with theory. They had much more to do with attitudes, politics, institutions, management, trade unions and excessive foreign commitments. Yet Britain's poor economic performance, the world oil crisis, rising inflation together with rising unemployment, the defeat of Mr Heath's Conservative Government and the disarray of Keynesian economics produced what may be called a revolutionary situation in political and economic theory.

There had for some time been academic monetarists in this country, and the Institute of Economic Affairs had for some years produced some high-class specialist publications. At the end of the 1960s Mr Peter Jay introduced the British public to the new monetarism in the pages of *The Times*. But, politically, the beginning of monetarism can be dated from Sir Keith Joseph's Preston speech of 5 September 1974, which has been mentioned above. Preston was the first of a series of brave and eloquent speeches in which Keith Joseph set out to change the views of the Conservative Party, and of much outside opinion, on economics, the post-war consensus and a lot else besides. His success was a notable achievement, however unfortunate the consequences.

Yet, despite Keith Joseph's missionary fervour, the acceptance of monetarism by much of the Conservative leadership is one of the most surprising episodes in Conservative history.* Conservative politicians, after all, are supposed to be cautious and practical, suspicious almost to a fault of new ideas, and acutely aware of the importance of social cohesion and its dependence upon a degree of moderation and political consensus. They are almost the last

---

* Not everybody succumbed. The most notable exceptions were Mr Edward Heath and Mr Reginald Maudling. See also Appendix.

people one would expect to want to explore the wilder shores of politics or economics.

There were, as has been seen, economic reasons why Conservative leaders should have thought that a change of course was desirable. There were also political reasons and reasons based upon economic theory. In the 1950s the successful moderation and centrism of successive Conservative Governments had a powerful effect on the Labour Party. Moderation was infectious, and the centrism of the Tories made Labour centrist too. In the 1970s the Labour Party returned (or, rather, reversed) the compliment. Labour resiled from the consensus that had prevailed since the immediate post-war period and lurched to the left. Extremism, like moderation, proved infectious, and the Conservatives lurched to the right. Just as Labour sought consolation and refuge in nineteenth-century socialism, so the Conservatives found inspiration and relief in nineteenth-century capitalism.

Yet Labour extremism would not have been able to affect Conservative policy if Labour had still been in opposition. It was the two Conservative defeats in 1974, and the consequent change in leadership, which precipitated the Conservative swing to the right. And the fact that the Conservative downfall had been at the hands of the trade unions did much to determine the party's policy. The belated and over-elaborate attempt to curb the trade unions by means of the Industrial Relations Act had ended in the defeat of the Heath Government. The Industrial Relations Act was not the cause of that defeat, but the trade unions were. How a future Conservative Government could conjure up a reasonable economic performance despite the presence of over-mighty trade unions, and at the same time avoid overthrow by those unions, was thus the chief problem facing the new Conservative leadership. Monetarism seemed the obvious solution to that problem.* It appeared to take the politics out

---

* This point is well made in Mr Peter Tapsell's entertaining lecture, *Monetarism in Practice*. Mr Tapsell goes on to say: 'It has become convenient for the present leadership of both the Conservative and Labour Parties in Britain to find excuses for the harshness of their own economic policies by blaming the Chancellorship of Mr Anthony Barber, in Mr Heath's Government, for inadequately controlling the Money Supply – a prime example of two burnt pots calling the kettle black....Mr Anthony Barber's money supply policy was too lax, as I said at the time, but the deleterious effects of this have been grossly exaggerated since (the M1 and M3 figures were very different) to provide a smoke-screen for the failures of others, and, in particular the failure to restrain excessive wage awards far in excess of anything justified by increases in production or productivity.'[30]

of economics and perhaps out of politics as well. Monetarism taught that inflation was caused not by inflationary wage claims but by an excessive money stock. Hence with monetarism there would be no more occasion for those lengthy meetings at No. 10 Downing Street when, on the eve of a major strike or perhaps after it had begun, Ministers plied trade-union chiefs with sandwiches and tea and, as the shadows lengthened, with whisky in an attempt to buy them off. Indeed, if the money supply were properly controlled, monetarism taught, there would be no need for the TUC ever to come to No. 10 at all. An abstraction or an economic statistic, the money supply, would at a stroke, solve the problem of inflation and keep the trade-union leaders out of Whitehall. It would exorcise the spectre of union power. Perhaps, too, it would help to exorcise the spectre of the Conservative leader who had been overthrown, Mr Edward Heath.

Monetarism is, or can be, politically neutral. Indeed, it was first practised in an adulterated form by the Labour Chancellor, Mr Healey. But it exerted far greater fascination and enjoyed much more success in the Conservative Party than in the Labour Party. This was partly because Labour did not need monetarism to solve the union problem. The Labour Government could not have kept the TUC at a distance even if it had wanted to: the constitution of the Labour Party entrenches the power of the unions. Besides, Labour had its own nostrum for dealing with the unions: the social contract. Where monetarism was to keep the Government and trade unions apart, the social contract bound them together. In the event, the two solutions were about equally expensive.

Monetarism's most eminent propagandist, Professor Milton Friedman, is not, however, politically neutral. He is an enthusiast for a free market economy and a fanatical opponent of state intervention. This partially explains the adoption of his views by many Conservatives, even though prior to 1979 the Governments most receptive to his doctrines were the right-wing military dictatorships of Argentina and Chile. A number of Conservatives had never liked the mixed economy, which they regarded as a long step towards a socialist state. The contention of Friedman that government intervention was invariably self-defeating was, therefore, in tune with their prejudices. Sir Keith Joseph even seems to have decided that a belief in monetarism was a necessary condition not only for the control of inflation but for being a Conservative. At any rate, he announced that it was only in April 1974 that he had been converted to Conservatism.[31] What he had been before was not revealed.

As Mr Rogie Opie pointed out in a letter to *The Times*, monetarism did not make much headway in the economics profession. Equally, however, as Mr Opie conceded, the profession did not make much headway against it. Instead the profession largely ignored the new phenomenon, which is indeed the treatment it often reserves for new developments. But this one was not an event or a series of events in the real world, which, if recognized, might have had an upsetting effect on current economic teaching. It was itself an economic theory, and the relative insouciance of the economics profession, which Mr Opie called 'the treason of the academics', was surprising. Apart from a heavy attack by Professor Kaldor in 1970, most academic economists pursued their recondite studies undisturbed. In the resulting near-vacuum the monetarists prospered like Jehovah's Witnesses when the Churches slumber. And important conversions were made in Fleet Street, in the City and in the Conservative Party.

Some of the reasons why elements in the Conservative Party were receptive to monetarism have been given. Similar, though very much less drastic, shifts of opinion were also occurring in other countries. Yet the largely uncritical adoption of its tenets by so many Conservatives, especially those most concerned with the formation of the party's economic policies, still remains a puzzle.

The dominant traits in the Conservative intellectual tradition, to be found in Halifax, Hume, Burke, Coleridge, Disraeli and Salisbury, are scepticism, a sense of the limitations of human reason, a rejection of abstraction or abstract doctrines, a distrust of systems and a belief instead in the importance of experience and of 'circumstance'. These things are closely related, and for Conservatives to embrace monetarism was contrary to all of them. A sense of the limitations of human reason, for example, should surely have raised Conservative eyebrows when the monetarist notion of rational expectations was expounded. A suspicion of abstract doctrines should similarly have led to misgivings about the monetarist tenet that there is no place for government to interfere to influence unemployment or output. The Tory distrust of systems should have induced suspicion of the large claims made by the monetarists for their theory. Experience, after all, had shown that every economic system had its faults; and no economic doctrine hitherto had turned out to be wholly true. As Salisbury once wrote, 'the promise of the most hopeful theories is so often deceptive....'[32] Experience had also shown that economic ideas or doctrines had radically different results depending on the circumstances that prevailed. Yet disbelief was suspended; credulity took its place; and monetarism was enthroned in the Conservative Party.

This was all the more remarkable in that the monetarist counter-revolution in the mid- and later 1970s, while far from meeting its Thermidor, was no longer carrying all before it. Some leading monetarists were shading the doctrine and introducing a number of caveats. Unfortunately, the politicians, the City and many of the journalists remained stuck to the theory and oblivious to the modifications. There is nothing unusual about followers being more dogmatic than leaders, but it is rare for practitioners to be more wedded to a theory than the theorists themselves.

The acceptance of the monetarist revolution by much of the Conservative Party was accompanied, as revolutions usually are, by a rewriting of history on a large scale. The shaky economic edifice of monetarism needed to be shored up by some political and historical masonry. The sans-culottes of the monetarist revolution also wished to strengthen the party's new leadership by denouncing the alleged follies of the Ancien Régime. Ideally, perhaps, this could best have been achieved by a bell, book and candle condemnation of the Heath Government alone. The snag was that some of the leading monetarists had served without demur in that Government. The trail of heresy had, therefore, to be extended back to the thirteen Conservative years of 1951 to 1964. The new ideological fervour would, in any case, probably have demanded the commination of all post-war Conservative Governments. Indeed, even poor Disraeli, because he has been rightly identified as a moderate, recently came in for a good deal of right-wing contempt. If this sort of thing continues, Conservatives will soon have to choose their heroes from a short list of Montague Norman, Lord Eldon, Judge Jeffreys and President Hoover.

The right-wing or monetarist indictment of the Conservative Party and Conservative Governments in the post-war era up to 1975 can be summarized as follows: all previous post-war Governments went for soft options and easy answers; in retrospect it could be seen that the post-war policies of stimulating demand and high taxation had begun to eat away at the sinews of the economy; inflation is a self-inflicted wound; successive Governments caused it by trying to do too much too quickly by way of deficit financing; grossly excessive government expenditure is the main cause of inflation, in other words, inflation is politically induced and caused by Governments; if Governments get the money supply wrong, nothing else will come right; post-war Conservatives followed the false trails of social democracy, embracing the delusion of the efficacy of government action in the economic sphere and failing to pay sufficiently respectful attention either to the quantity theory of money or to the spontaneous, in-built correctives in the economy; the unemployment statistics were misleading, since they greatly exaggerated the number of the unemployed; Conservatives had talked about plans and strategies, and they had talked to trade unions and other corporate bodies — this activity was unnecessary as well as damaging; Conservative Governments and the Conservative Party since the war made the fatal mistake of seeking the middle ground; in consequence, the party pendulum was replaced by a socialist ratchet, and the middle ground moved continually to the left; the Conservative obsession with the middle ground became a rake's progress and swept us down towards the abyss; indeed, it even drove the Labour Party to the left; similarly, Keynesianism, so far from being an alternative to red-blooded socialism, merely paved the way for socialist advance, if indeed it was not socialist itself. Such were the monetarist charges against the pre-monetarist Conservative Party.

The rewriting of history was not, however, confined to the Keynesian years. Thus it was claimed that the return to gold at the pre-war parity in 1925 was 'interventionism...in conflict with orthodox economic theory and a far cry from *laissez-faire*'.[33] In fact, all the orthodox were in favour of it, and Keynes was one of its few opponents. Belief in the Gold Standard was the orthodox economics of the day, and there was precious little economic intervention between 1925 and 1931. One could as plausibly argue that the present Government, because its policies have raised the exchange rate, is 'interventionist'. Even more curiously, it was argued that the national Government of 1931 'simply relinquished many of the interventionist measures, maintained a 2 per cent interest rate and let the economy look after itself, with occasional bouts of *dirigisme*, none of any great magnitude'.[34]

This is the reverse of the truth. The national Government was much more interventionist than the Conservative Government of the 1920s, and its policy was not remotely one of 'letting the economy look after itself'. As Mr David Clarke put it, the period was 'one of notable government intervention in industry'.[35] The monetarist attempt to repudiate the 1920s and to take over the 1930s is understandable if illegitimate: the interventionist policies of the 1930s were much more successful than the largely *laissez-faire* policies of the 1920s.

There was a grain of truth in some of the monetarist contentions as well as a good deal of hysteria. Britain's post-war record has just been looked at and found wanting. Nevertheless, the thirteen Conservative years from 1951–64 saw a transformation of the country, and the British performance was not markedly worse than the American up to the early 1960s. The standard of living rose more than it had in the previous half century. Those who were hardest-hit by economic and social forces beyond their control were protected. Full employment was combined with growth and relative price stability (the average rise in prices from 1952 to 1964 was 3 per cent a year).

If we look at the monetarist charges in more detail, the general picture, allegedly, is one of ever-rising inflation and ever-increasing deficits. But the rate of inflation did not rise during the 1950s. It fell. The resignation of Lord Thorneycroft, Mr Enoch Powell and Mr Nigel Birch from the Treasury in January 1958 has come to be thought of as the crucial event in the slide towards increasing inflation. In fact, inflation in 1958–9 was negligible at 0.6 per cent, and in 1959–60 it was 1.1 per cent. In the 1960s, as the Government's Chief Economic Adviser has recently said, the inflation rate drifted upwards, 'but no more than in other countries'. Indeed, the average annual rate for the UK in the 1960s was 4 per cent. But, Professor Burns went on, 'following the oil price shock in 1973—4 UK inflation far exceeded the average rate in other industrial countries.'

Probably most people regard deficit financing in certain circumstances with some equanimity. Only some monetarists regard it with horror. But in any case, as we have seen, it did not happen. Central government ran a financial surplus in every year from 1950 to 1973; 1974 was the first in which there was a deficit, and there has continued to be a deficit throughout the monetarist era, which began under Mr Healey in 1976. The Public Sector Borrowing Requirement (PSBR), which is the total borrowings of the public sector, tells the same story. The aggregate total of the PSBR from 1952 to 1970 inclusive is only slightly more than it was in either of the single years of 1979 or 1980. Even allowing for the great fall in the value of money, that is surely quite striking. The allegation of financial profligacy during the Keynesian years is therefore false. In general, both fiscal and monetary policy were fairly strict.

The politics of the period can be interpreted in many different ways. But the monetarists' political history does not seem to be based any more firmly than their economic history. The allegation that Britain moved sharply to the left between 1951 and 1974 invites the question: when did this sharp move occur? Under that well-known leftie, Sir Winston Churchill? After all, he was once a Liberal. Or under Sir Anthony Eden, who did, after all, resign from the Chamberlain Government in 1938? Or under Mr Harold Macmillan, who before the war was right on both home policy and foreign affairs and therefore a prime suspect? In fact, all these Prime Ministers were prominent in the Conservative Party before and during the war as well as after it, and there was no break in continuity. The most zealous sniffer-out of heresy would have difficulty in detecting much socialism in Sir Alec Douglas-Home, and the party moved slightly to the right under Mr Heath until 1972. In that year there was a change, but there was no sign of dissent within the Government. Monetarists may criticize some of Mr Heath's policies, but they can scarcely consider his term of office left-wing. So the sharp move to the left, if it occurred, must have been the responsibility of that notoriously inflexible socialist ideologue, Sir Harold Wilson. The Labour Government of 1964—70 was singularly unsuccessful.

'Nobody', wrote Anthony Crossland, a prominent member of it, 'disputes the central failure of economic policy.'[36] But, whatever else that Government was, it was not extremist or very left-wing. In other words, the alleged sharp move to the left between 1951 and 1974 is imaginary.

It follows that the similar allegation that the Tory search for the middle ground turned the party pendulum into a ratchet for socialism is also imaginary. The only nationalization measure carried out by the first Wilson Government was steel. Regrettable, no doubt, but steel originally had been nationalized by the Attlee Government, and one jolt does not make a ratchet.

Nor did Tory moderation drive the socialists to the left. From 1951 to 1970 Tory centrism helped to keep Labour well away from the far left. This can easily be shown by comparing Sir Harold Wilson's Labour Government of 1964–70 with Mr Michael Foot's present Labour Party. In politics, moderation tends to breed moderation, just as extremism tends to encourage extremism.

Finally, the allegation that Keynesians merely paved the way for socialist advance implies that there were better alternative policies that the Churchill Government and its successors could have adopted. One wonders what these might have been. Perhaps a stiff bout of early monetarism? But, unfairly or not, the Conservatives were still blamed for the unemployment of the inter-war years, and for the party to have been associated again after only a short interval with high unemployment would have put it out of power for a generation. And then there really would have been a lurch to the left! Indeed, probably the only feasible alternative to the policies which were implemented was a whole-hearted Keynesian policy, which is presumably not what the monetarists had in mind.

By adopting hybrid Keynesianism, the Conservatives maintained themselves in power for thirteen years and helped to retain moderation in the Labour Party for twenty. Conservatives should surely applaud such achievements, not go out of their way to denigrate them. Admittedly, the Heath Government lasted only three and a half years. But it was defeated because, to use a favourite monetarist phrase, the country chose the soft option and refused to support the Government's counter-inflation policy.

For people to seek to rewrite history in accordance with their current economic dogmas is a barren and trivial activity, especially when they did not hold those dogmas at the relevant time and may well not hold them for much longer. Not surprisingly, nearly everything that the monetarists say about their Conservative predecessors is not history but ideology. History has been rewritten and what actually happened ignored. But that makes all the more remarkable the achievements of the monetarists in converting to their views, and to their 'facts', so much of the Conservative Party, the City and Fleet Street. The party — or the bulk of it — committed what is for Tories the unforgivable sin: it abandoned scepticism and embraced what almost amounted to a system.

It is hard to find anything comparable with this strange interlude. But the history of Arianism, the heresy which denied the true Divinity of Christ, has some similarities. Though Arianism was condemned by the Council of Nicaea in 325, it remained strong and was favoured by Constantine's sister, Constantia, and by his successor in the East, Constantius. And, after a number of other councils and much banishment and counter-banishment of prelates, Arianism was accepted by both Eastern and Western bishops in 359. As St Jerome later sadly commented, 'the whole world groaned in astonishment at finding itself Arian.'[37] In much the same way, though more cheerfully, Keith Joseph claimed a few years ago, 'We are all monetarists now.' Yet the adoption and apparent triumph of Arianism were the beginning of its downfall. The West returned to orthodox Catholicism shortly afterwards, and the East followed later. Arianism was popular until it won; its adoption spelled its end. As with Arianism and Catholicism, so, let us hope, with monetarism and Conservatism.

8

The Socialist Alternative

The death of socialism is the unrealized political fact of this century.

Daniel Bell[1]

Socialism is not a science, a sociology in miniature — it is a cry of pain, sometimes of anger, uttered by men who feel most keenly our collective *malaise.*

Emile Durkheim[2]

'Albion is sick!' said every Valley, every mournful Hill
And every River: 'our brother Albion is sick to death.
He hath leagued himself with robbers; he hath studied the arts
of unbelief. Envy hovers over him; his friends are his
abhorrence.'

William Blake: 'Jerusalem' [3]

Marx refused to explain how society and the economy would function in the socialist future. The Labour Party refuses to remember the socialist past. An unwary reader of *Labour's Programme 1982* might think that the Conservatives had been in power for the last thirty years. Even a careful one without previous knowledge would have no inkling that since 1964 Labour had been in power for most of the time. Thus in the key section 'Work for All' the document says that 'the right to work is of central importance to socialism', and it refers to the Employment White Paper of 1944; but there is no mention of what happened under the Labour Government which left office in 1979. Again, 'the central aim of our economic strategy', we are told, 'will be to reduce unemployment to below a million within five years of taking office.' Any doubts that such an aim will be achieved are stilled by a reference to the achievements of the Labour Government of 1945—50. The experience of the Labour Government of 1974—9, which might be thought to be more relevant — in that Government, after all, the present leader of the party, Mr Foot, was Secretary of State for Employment — is ignored. But then under that Government unemployment, so far from coming down to a million, rose to well above a million and, in fact, doubled.

Similarly, the *Programme* 'totally rejects the use of higher unemployment as a weapon against inflation' and proclaims that 'Labour will have nothing to do with monetarism.' The reader is evidently not intended to remember that the last Labour Government did use higher unemployment as a weapon against inflation and did have quite a lot to do with monetarism. One last example: 'over the last twenty years,' the Labour *Programme* tells us, 'our immigration laws and practice have become increasingly racially discriminatory....' and therefore the highest priority will be given to the repeal of the 1971 Immigration Act.[4] But out of those last twenty 'increasingly racially discriminatory' years Labour has been in office for more than half of them; and if the 1971 Act was so bad, why was it not repealed by Mr Wilson or Mr Callaghan?

Like the Conservative monetarists, then, the Labour left, which has become increasingly dominant, is seeking to repudiate its own party's past. The monetarists have rewritten history; the socialists have erased it. This is not, however, the only aspect of socialist amnesia and schizophrenia. The left has abstracted itself from experience everywhere. What has happened in socialist countries abroad is also ignored. If people behaved in a similar way in their private lives, they would be certifiable. And *Labour's Programme 1982* is, in that sense, a mad document. Yet that programme was endorsed at the 1982 party conference by 6,420,000 votes to 220,000.

Just why Labour should have abandoned its moderate, empiricist tradition is not fully clear. Some movement to the left was to be expected. Recent Labour Governments have been failures, and the cynicism of the Wilson era left its mark. There has also been a fundamentalist revival, which Professor Hook has called 'the second coming of Karl Marx'.[5] This phenomenon is surprising in that Marxism did not have a revival in the 1930s, when the economic conditions were ripe for it and when many intellectuals had a deep admiration for Stalin's Russia. Yet now that the full horror of Stalinist rule has been revealed, Marxism is more popular than it was before. Admittedly, the latter-day Marxists seek to avoid the Stalinist problem by embracing Trotsky. They also rely more on the young than on the older Marx. Yet the Communist Terror began under Lenin, not Stalin, and Trotsky was fully implicated. And it is perverse to pay more attention to Marx's early writings, which were not intended for publication, than to the published products of his mature thought. Even allowing for governmental failure and Marxist resurgence, the extent of Labour's drift to extremism is still surprising. The same has not happened with other European socialist parties. In the main the opposite has occurred. Even the Italian Communist Party has displayed much more moderation than the Labour Party and is now well to the right of it. But if the reason for the great shift in Labour's attitude and policies is obscure, the mechanics of the shift are not.

The victory of the Conservative right was due to ideology; the victory of the Labour left was due to organization. One might have expected the reverse. But the organizational *coups* of the Labour left soon led to ideological victory. In 1973, owing to the negligence or inadvertence of Sir Harold Wilson and the Labour leadership, the 'proscribed list' which declared various far-left organizations ineligible for affiliation to the Labour Party, and members of those organizations ineligible for membership of the party, was abolished. From then on various organizations of the 'outside left', as they called themselves, began to prosper. Some of them, such as the Campaign for Labour Party Democracy led by Vladimir Derer, would have been eligible under the old rules; others, such as the Militant Tendency and other Trotskyist factions, would not. Several years of diligent committee work, procedural expertise, delicate manoeuvring and incessant propaganda followed. This coincided with the decay of the Labour Party as a mass organization, many of its constituency parties becoming mere shells ready for takeover. In consequence, when Labour was defeated in 1979, 'small groups of activists' were able to 'dictate events' within the Labour Party.[6] These activists belonged to the 'outside left', which may be roughly defined as being to the left of Mr Benn. Mr Benn is perhaps more their figurehead than their leader.

The party moved further and further to the left both in its constitution and in its policy. At the 1982 party conference the union leaders took fright at the possible electoral consequences and used their block votes to give the party's National Executive Committee (NEC) a right-wing majority, which in true fraternal style proceeded to kick out of their committee posts all the left-wingers in sight. But the left-wing policy gains over the preceding few years were not clawed back. Labour's repudiation of its past was left undisturbed.

Yet Labour's contempt for what it claimed was its non-socialist past did not lead to careful planning of the socialist future. Just as Marx had ignored socialist economics, so did the new left-wing Labour Party. It just assumed that it would be able to do everything it wanted. All that was needed was 'accountability', the key word of the 'outside left', and much talk of 'socialism' and 'democracy'. That would be enough to bring about utopia. Thus, in defiance of all previous experience, a socialist Government would apparently be able to increase all social security benefits as well as lowering the male pension age to 60, increase local government expenditure, substantially increase all public investment and greatly expand the economy; and it would be able to do this while rejecting 'policies of wage restraint', providing more scope for industrial action (i.e. strikes), rejecting any kind of 'planning which is bureaucratic or authoritative', and nationalizing or threatening to nationalize 'the bulk of private ownership'.[7] Labour at the same time also proposes to leave the European Community, abolish our nuclear weapons and banish American ones, politicize the Civil Service, abolish the remaining grammar schools and all private education, politicize the police by taking senior appointments out of the hands of Chief Constables, abolish the House of Lords, make the press and media more favourable to the Labour Party, as well as such trifling matters as democratizing the arts, unionizing the armed forces, allowing small businesses to be taken over by their workers and seeing that our military forces are 'recognizably equipped and deployed for recognizably defensive purposes'.[8] *

* This last is perhaps the most absurd phrase in a document in which competition for that title is keen. Virtually all weapons can be used either for defence or for attack. Artillery for example may be used as a prelude to an attack or in an attempt to stop one. The same is true of aeroplanes, tanks and ships. How then could our forces be 'recognizably equipped and deployed for recognizably defensive purposes'? Perhaps they could be equipped with shields not swords and deployed in castles where they could pour not boiling oil but propaganda leaflets on their attackers.

Sir Leo Pliatsky, Second Permanent Secretary at the Treasury, called the first year of the 1974 Wilson Government 'a period of collective madness'.[9] It will be seen that the period of collective madness which is planned for us next time will be lengthy and intense. Indeed, Labour intends to cut us off from our neighbours by offending them in a variety of ways and by imposing a siege economy. Those neighbours will presumably respond by putting Britain in quarantine until the fever subsides.

Western defence has included nuclear weapons for thirty years, and Labour has supported that policy. Indeed, the last Labour Government spent about £1,000 million on modernizing Britain's nuclear deterrent.[10] Now, however, Labour proposes to disrupt NATO by removing all nuclear weapons from these shores. The British people voted overwhelmingly to stay in Europe in a referendum in 1975. The Wilson and Callaghan Governments knew they could not withdraw. As the Labour Chief Secretary, Joel Barnett, put it, 'it was quite impossible to consider leaving the EEC'.[11] Now apparently that no longer applies, and although 43 per cent of our exports now go to the Community and hundreds of thousands of jobs would be lost if we withdrew from it, Labour plans to take the country out without a referendum. They said a referendum was necessary if our entry into the Community was to be made legitimate; they claim a referendum is not necessary to legitimize our withdrawal.

Nobody disputes that there is an economic problem. And the proposal of a siege economy cannot be dismissed out of hand. The deindustrialization of the country has been proceeding, and the idea of pulling up the drawbridge until British industry has been modernized and is fully able to compete with other countries is not inherently implausible. Such a scheme, it can be claimed, is based on the experience of Britain's post-war industrial failure under a regime of free trade. Unfortunately, the other economic proposals show that Labour's policies stem not from experience but from socialist theory, which is divorced from all past practice. While there are many possible explanations of Britain's poor industrial performance, a shortage of nationalized industries is not one of them. A defence can be made for many of those industries, but it is not possible to maintain that they have been more efficient than the private sector. In addition, nearly all our competitors have a smaller public sector than we have, and they have performed better. Labour's response is to propose a massive programme of public ownership.

Again, much of trade-union obstructionism may be ascribed to bad management or incompetent Governments. Yet Britain has probably the most powerful and the most legally privileged unions in the world. The suggestion that the British economy has suffered from the weakness of our unions and from an insufficient number of strikes is simply not tenable. Nevertheless, *Labour's Programme 1982* proposes to increase the power of the unions and to facilitate 'industrial action'. Moreover, a siege economy would in any event increase union monopoly power: there would be no foreign competition to put firms out of business if wage claims were excessive. In a siege economy a strict incomes policy would be vital, yet *Labour's Programme 1982* is fully committed to so-called free collective bargaining.

The conclusion must be, therefore, that Labour's economic proposals are based not on a rational analysis of the problem but on Marxist dogma, which is a defiance of experience. They are designed to make the country socialist, not to modernize industry or to make the economy more efficient.

Marx made much of the undoubted contradictions of capitalism. But they are as nothing compared with the contradictions in Labour's current socialism and in the Labour Party itself. The Labour left sets much store by 'democracy', and Mr Tony Benn has produced a book on the subject.* Yet the left's attitude to democracy is the greatest of its contradictions. Its basic article of faith is that there must be democracy in the party. The party conference is the parliament of the party, and conference decisions and 'democratic law' are not to be flouted (unlike the law of the land, which may be flouted if it is not to socialist taste); party leaders must be accountable to the party, and MPs must be accountable to their constituency management committees.

---

* In a hilarious chapter Mr Benn maintains that Britain is a colony, and a peculiarly unfortunate one. Most colonies, after all, suffer from only one colonial oppressor. Not so, Britain. We are subject to many colonial powers: the Crown, the House of Lords, the multinational companies, the International Monetary Fund, the European Community, American nuclear weapons, and the Pentagon. Luckily Mr Benn and the British Labour movement are available to lead us in the 'liberation struggle to end our colonial status....'[12]

Hence the mandatory re-selection of MPs, forced through by the outside left.

The first difficulty is that the party conference is less like a parliament than the Supreme Soviet, except that it is less well behaved. It is profoundly undemocratic. The big unions control the proceedings, and they control the election of the majority of the NEC. In 1977 the union share of conference votes was 89 per cent; the two biggest unions held 25 per cent of the total conference vote, and the six largest just over half of it.[13] To talk about democracy in such circumstances is an abuse of language. Yet the situation is even worse than it looks. For one thing, the unions can 'affiliate' as many members as they like; it is just a question of paying for them. Secondly, a great many of the members on whose behalf they are allegedly voting are opponents of the Labour Party. In 1979 over a third of trade unionists voted Conservative, and only a half voted Labour;[14] there are, in addition, numerous communists in the unions. And, thirdly, there is no reason to suppose that the votes cast are representative of the wishes even of Labour members of the unions.

The biggest union of all, the Transport and General Workers, recently demonstrated that it is the wishes of the leaders and activists which count, not the wishes of the rank and file. In the election for the deputy leadership of the party the union consulted its regional organization. A majority of the regions voted for Mr Healey. Undeterred, the union's executive committee recommended a vote for Mr Benn. Whereupon at the conference the union's delegation voted for Mr Silkin, and then, on the second ballot, for Mr Benn. (To be fair, the National Union of Public Employees, by contrast, consulted its members individually, who supported Mr Healey, and the union cast its vote accordingly.)

In their passion for intra-party democracy and their almost religious belief in the sanctity of conference decisions, Mr Benn and the left thus ignore that the Labour Party conference is a large rotten borough controlled by a few large unions, and that the votes cast at the conference by the unions — which are almost 90 per cent of the whole — have little to do with the wishes of union members. In the name of reducing oligarchy in the Labour Party, they are merely substituting the oligarchy of the TUC. Moreover, the leaders of the Parliamentary Party have all been elected democratically by the voters, and the leader of the Parliamentary Labour Party has been democratically elected by Members of Parliament. All of them are subject to removal by their respective electorates. Trade-union leaders, on the other hand, obtain their jobs by a variety of methods, and unless there is a postal vote, as there is with the Amalgamated Engineering Union, the turnout is often miserable. Many of them are virtually irremoveable. They are not, therefore, accountable to their members. The General Secretary of the Transport Union, for instance, once elected, retains his job until he reaches retiring age.

Yet, remarkably, these passionate democrats on the far left devote their efforts to what they claim to be the democratization of the Labour Party; and nothing is done to democratize the unions. Mr Benn and the left thus favour oligarchy in the unions and 'democracy' in the Labour Party. This is directly contrary to both what is desirable and what is democratic.* The advance of the extreme left was two-pronged: as it captured the Labour Party, it also captured the leadership of some of the major unions. There has been one fortunate consequence of this takeover. It has emphasized the gulf between extremist union leaderships and their wiser rank and file. No doubt this explains the left's reluctance to see the unions democratized.

Many trade unionists have little option as to which union they can join. There may be only one possible union. Even if there is a choice, there may be little to choose between them. Members of trade unions cannot shop around. There should, therefore, be a special obligation on the union leaders to represent their membership. In any case, there is certainly no good reason why they should not do so. While they should provide leadership and should be influenced by the national interest, they should also be guided by the wishes of their membership and not by outside influences or by ideological prejudices which are not shared by their members. The trade unions have in the past often kept the Labour Party sensible; they may do so again. In any case, democratic unions will have an important role to play in any non-socialist Britain.

---

* In his book Mr Benn thinks 'it would be quite natural if within the unions there was growing pressure' for democracy. But whereas he favours measures to produce instant 'democracy' elsewhere, he leaves the unions to themselves.[15]

With a political party the democratic argument is different. The party leadership has to take account not only of the wishes of the members of the party but also of the far greater number of people who vote for it without belonging to it. And if the leader of the party is Prime Minister as well, both he or she and other Ministers must also take account of those who did not vote for them, of the national interest, of international realities and of many other things. To say that in all circumstances the wishes of the party faithful expressed in conference decisions should be paramount and everything else should be disregarded is, therefore, mere ideological bluster. It is not rational, and it is not democratic. And that would be so even if the composition and procedures of the Labour Party conference were defensible, which they are not.

These are not, however, the only contradictions in the left's attitude to democracy. It is not only the party leadership which has to be made accountable. 'Large concentrations of economic power should be accountable to the community as a whole'; 'the principle of accountability' should be 'extended to every level of planning'; multi-nationals will be brought in; there should be 'greater accountability' for agriculture; broadcasting is to be made 'more democratically accountable'; the aim is 'a truly accountable police force'; and even the security services are to 'become accountable to democratic institutions'.[16] Virtually everything, then, is to become 'accountable', with two exceptions. The first is the trade unions. They are to be given full rein. Far from being made accountable, their privileges and powers are to be increased and the closed shop strengthened.[17] The second exception is government. *Labour's Programme 1982* says, 'for us, socialism and liberty are indivisible.'[18] But like Marx the socialists have no theory of liberty, and it seems inconceivable that liberty could survive the carrying out of Labour's programme.

Tories do not have the liberal aversion to using the power of the state. As that great Conservative, the late Lord Butler, said in 1956, 'Conservatives have always been ready to use the power of the state. This has been our tradition since Bolingbroke.'[19] The state power is there to be used to curb other centres of power, and it has been used throughout British history. But to think there is no constitutional or political problem about enormously increasing the powers and the scope of government is on

the same level of unreality as the belief of the *laissez-faire* school
that all problems will be solved by the abstention of government
and by the 'invisible hand'. Clearly, a large extension of public
ownership will limit the freedom of some workers to find other
jobs. 'In a country where the sole employer is the state,' said
Trotsky who knew what he was talking about, 'opposition means
death by slow starvation.'[20] The left constantly employs the
words 'democracy' and 'socialism' as if trying to purify itself and
to defend its policies from the charge of authoritarianism, much
as the French Jacobins used the word 'revolution' to justify all
their actions. And just as there was no constitutional restraint on
the Jacobins, there would be no constitutional restraint on a
Bennite Government. The House of Lords would be abolished.
(Not that the Lords are much of a restraint except in one important respect: they are able to prevent a House of Commons from
prolonging itself beyond its allotted span of five years.) The House
of Commons would not be a restraint. Its Bennite majority would
be urging the Government to carry out the policy of the party
conference. And that Government would not be responsive to
public opinion or the needs of the hour. Its duty would be to
carry out the party manifesto and not to deviate from it. Parliament would thus be subjugated to an outside interest.

With no checks on the Government, and with the Government
composed of people with a fierce determination to achieve ideological goals and to brook no opposition, egged on by people with
an even greater attachment to those goals and with even more contempt for those with differing views, there is no doubt at all what
would happen. Parliamentary democracy would be replaced by
mandated government; the constitution would wither away. 'C'est
un expérience éternelle', wrote Montesquieu, 'que tout homme qui
a du pouvoir est porté à en abuser; il va jusqu'à ce qu'il trouve de
limites.'[21]

That brings us to the biggest contradiction in the left's attitude
to democracy. The policies which Mr Benn and his friends wish to
impose upon the country are profoundly antipathetic to the British
people. The Labour Party has been in electoral decline for many
years. Whereas in 1950 Labour won over 40 per cent of the votes
of the electorate of Britain, in 1979 it won less than 30 per cent.[22]
Except for 1966, the decline has been continuous since 1951.

Unpopular as the Labour Party is, however, it is much more popular than its policies. 'For at least the last fifteen years', Professor Crewe has written, 'people have voted Labour despite its policies....'. In 1979 manual workers, who should be Labour's natural sympathizers, found Conservative proposals slightly more to their liking than Labour proposals.[23] And it is the two crucial elements in the Bennite policy which are the most unpopular of all. Labour won just over a third of the vote at the last election: 36.9 per cent, to be exact. And of that small proportion only 32 per cent were in favour of more nationalization, and only 36 per cent did not believe that trade unions have 'too much power'.[24] Labour's Programme 1982 proposes a vast extension of nationalization and proposes to give the trade unions yet more power. Those policies are supported by roughly one third of one third of the electorate, that is to say, just 10 per cent. Yet those are the policies, together with much of a similar ilk, which the Bennites propose to fasten on the British people. And they say they are democrats! Mr Benn may be a populist, but his populism is profoundly unpopular.

Socialist contempt for the wishes of the electorate in general and of Labour supporters in particular is not confined to matters which could be considered fundamental to socialist strategy. In 1979 85 per cent of the voters were in favour of council house tenants being given the right to buy their houses.[25] Yet *Labour's Programme 1982* proposes to remove that right. Such is socialist democracy!

The contradictions and absurdities of the socialist treatment of democracy raise serious doubts as to whether the left can in any sense, save the Eastern European, be considered democratic.* It seeks to fetter the democratically elected parliamentary leadership with undemocratic party conference resolutions; it supports undemocratic union leaderships; it favours policies which are opposed by an overwhelming majority of the British people; and

---

* In his attempt to show that his policies do not have an Eastern European flavour, Mr Benn writes in his book that 'the institutions at the disposal of the East European establishment have far more in common with the corporatism now consolidating itself in Britain and other capitalist countries than with any proposals made here'.[26] Provided the leaders of both East and West find Mr Benn convincing, this seems to offer a good prospect of ending the cold war.

it opposes popular policies which are favoured by the same overwhelming majority.

These doubts about the left's democratic credentials are confirmed by the way in which the socialists hope to achieve power. Granted the unpopularity of their policies and themselves, the only chance the socialists have of gaining office is by a wave of revulsion against the Government of the day. (Elections tend to be plebiscites on the record of the outgoing Government rather than anything else.)[27] If that happened, Labour would be likely to achieve office on a very small popular vote — probably, owing to the SDP—Liberal Alliance, on an even smaller percentage (39 per cent) than it did in October 1974 — and on a vote which would not be an endorsement of its extremist policies. Yet on the strength of a negative vote by a minority of the electorate, the socialists would embark on the profoundly undemocratic course of enacting legislation which was opposed by the great majority of the country.

That is the only way the left could achieve power. No wonder Mr Benn in 1981 expressed strong opposition to electoral reform.[28] Such a democratic safeguard would keep him out of office indefinitely, since he has not the remotest chance of ever gaining the support of more than 50 per cent of the voters. Yet, according to Mr Benn, 'Decisions, in a democratic society, must ultimately be made by the people as a whole.'[29]

There is, however, a more sinister interpretation of what the left has been doing. At a time when conditions would normally have been expected to favour the party, Labour has been strikingly unpopular, and much of that unpopularity has been due to the campaigns of the far left in general and of Mr Benn in particular. They can hardly have been unaware of the likely effect of their activities on Labour's electoral fortunes. Possibly the Social Democrats would have left the party anyway, but the left's absurd insistence upon changing the mode of election of the party leader made their departure certain. In consequence, the Labour Party lost some of its leaders who had most appeal for the uncommitted voters, and the dislike felt by much of the party for the far left was clearly revealed — a high price to pay for a creaking piece of electoral machinery. So has the left been trying to bring about Labour's electoral defeat?

This suspicion is strengthened by *Labour's Programme 1982*. It is hard to believe that anybody seriously thinks that such an unpopular and disastrous programme should be carried out. 'A socialist party without an incomes policy', John Mackintosh wrote, 'is a contradiction in terms.'[30] Yet the socialist left goes out of its way not to have an incomes policy. There is to be socialism for everybody except the trade unions. The policies seem to make sense only if they are not supposed to be put into action – if they are designed entirely for opposition. On this interpretation militant trade unionism will be used to smash the system by wrecking Conservative policies and the mixed economy; and when it has done so, it will itself be an early casualty of the socialist revolution.

Another possible interpretation is that the contradictions of British socialism are the consequences of the unique relationship between the trade unions and the Labour Party. Because of this relationship and because of the trade-union control of the party conference, the left has decided to ignore the fatal contradiction between a fully socialist state and completely unfettered trade unions and to support the unions because that is where power lies. It will then see what happens and pick up the pieces afterwards.

Whichever interpretation is correct – and none of them confers credit on the left – poor Mr Foot is saddled with an impossible programme (much of which, however, he characteristically supports) and a party which is distrusted because of the Bennite antics. Sir Harold Wilson recently said that 'today we hardly present the image of the natural party of opposition', and he went on to refer to 'Labour's pantomime performance in these recent years: a party of prehistoric policies, giving the image of prematurely old men and of old women of both sexes....'[31] That was unkind, especially as the present state of the Labour Party and the present strength of the left owe much to Sir Harold's benign neglect when he was leader. But it was also true. Labour looks incredible as a governing party. It looked scarcely less incredible in 1973, however, yet it won in 1974. Evidently, incredibility – by which I mean the absurdity and extremism of the policies adopted by a party – is not necessarily a bar to winning an election.

Moreover, by the time of the election Mr Foot may have been able to drop or trim some of the party's more outlandish policies, though he will have less freedom than his predecessors because the whole party has shifted to the left. It still seems likely, therefore, that Labour will be rejected, as it deserves. And had the Government pursued different economic policies, a Labour victory would have been inconceivable. As it is, unemployment is high, the electorate is volatile, and the present electoral system, with three sizeable national parties, is a lottery. So a Labour win cannot be ruled out. If disaster did strike and Mr Foot won by default, the country and the Conservative Party would pay a heavy price for the Conservative neglect of constitutional reform.

9

The Monetarist Diagnosis

Monetary theory is like a Japanese garden. It has aesthetic unity born of variety; an apparent simplicity that conceals a sophisticated reality; a surface view that dissolves in ever deeper perspectives. Both can be fully appreciated only if examined from many different angles, only if studied leisurely but in depth. Both have elements that can be enjoyed independently of the whole, yet attain their full realization only as part of the whole.

Milton Friedman in 1969 [1]

...there would be the certainty of disaster if a Conservative pro-market sector Government came to power and just sat back, balanced the budget, and let unemployment mount waiting for the market to solve its problems. That is not how France, West Germany, and Japan recovered from the war, and it is not how Sir Winston Churchill and Mr R. A. Butler reacted to the opportunities and responsibilities of 1951.

Robert Bacon and Walter Ellis in 1976 [2]

Our present troubles...are not of a monetary character, and are not to be cured by monetary means.

Sir John Hicks in 1975 [3]

With monetarism we are in a world in which politicians and their advisers, as well as journalists, bankers and industrialists, disagree sharply with each other. And this fundamental disagreement has its counterpart in a deeply divided and confused economics profession. Nevertheless, there are issues here which are central to the country's politics, and it is difficult for politicians to evade them. While, therefore, it is probably impossible to put forward a proposition which will not be disputed by reputable people, it is worth trying to describe the present state of the discussion and to attempt a brief summary of the main tenets and assumptions of monetarism. Obviously, not all monetarists believe exactly the same things at all times. The summary here is based chiefly on the views of Professor Milton Friedman.

Monetarism possesses a rare 'historical continuity and theoretical completeness'.[4] The economy, its adherents believe, is fundamentally stable. Therefore, it should be left alone as much as possible, so that its inbuilt equilibrating mechanisms can do their work. The quantity theory of money is of fundamental importance. Economic instability is caused chiefly by instability in the money supply.[5] By itself, fiscal policy is not important for inflation.[6] Asset preferences are stable and predictable.[7] There is a consistent though not precise relation between the rate of growth of the quantity of money and the rate of growth of nominal income.[8]

There is a causal link between the money supply and inflation.[9] The time lag is likely to be about two years, but the relation is far from perfect, so the money supply cannot be varied in an attempt to bring stability.[10] But the government is able to determine the quantity of money.[11] It is difficult to explain, the way in which the quantity of money affects income, Professor Friedman concedes, but it undoubtedly does.[12] Inflation is always and everywhere a monetary phenomenon;[13] all inflations are demand inflations. There is no such thing as a cost-push inflation. Both Friedman and Hayek are agreed on that.[14] Restraint in the rate of monetary growth is both a necessary and a sufficient condition for controlling inflation.[15] It follows that trade unions cannot be a source of continuous inflation.[16] Money alone determines such 'money' things as money GNP, the price level or the exchange rate, but it cannot affect (except temporarily) 'real' things, such as output or employment, without causing inflation.[17] This is because employees no longer suffer from money 'illusion'. They have come to expect inflation, and so any trade-off between increased output and increased employment as a result of the Government expanding the economy and of inflation is at best only temporary. Therefore it is idle for Government to attempt to increase output or reduce employment. There is a natural rate of unemployment, to which unemployment will automatically tend in the long run, whatever the government does; unfortunately, though, nobody knows what the natural rate is.[18]

Accordingly, the Government should concern itself with its own finances — the balance between income and expenditure in the public sector and the PSBR — with removing distortions in the market, with improving incentives and with improving and promoting the system of private enterprise. It should not concern itself with aggregate demand for goods and services in the economy as a whole. Indeed, the Keynesian concept of effective demand is irrelevant and should be discarded.

The various manifestations of monetarism, of which the Rational Expectations school, sometimes called the New Classical school is the latest and most extreme, are all agreed that it is impossible for the Government, through its fiscal and monetary policy, to change real demand other than temporarily. The attempt to do so only changes the rate of inflation. Hence price stability should be the Government's prime and, possibly, only objective.[19] In one of his cautious moods Friedman stressed the danger of assigning to monetary policy a larger role than it could perform. 'A steady rate of monetary growth at a moderate level', he wrote, 'will not produce perfect stability; it will not produce heaven on earth; but it can make an important contribution to a stable economic society.'[20]

Monetarism, therefore, claims to provide not only a diagnosis for the disease but also a prescription for its cure. Indeed, it claims to do more. At least as propounded by its most energetic evangelist, Professor Friedman, it provides a complete economic system and a political ideology as well. These three things do not necessarily stand or fall together. Monetarism, 'like a Japanese garden', has 'elements that can be enjoyed independently of the whole'. The diagnosis could be right and the cure ineffective or damaging, and the cure might work even though the diagnosis was faulty. Another possibility is that both the diagnosis and cure are wrong, yet the ideology is helpful; or they could both be right and the ideology inadequate or mistaken. Or all three could in their different ways be erroneous and damaging.

In any case, although there is inevitably some arbitrariness in deciding under which heading some propositions are discussed, it will be convenient to discuss diagnosis, cure and ideology in turn.

And since Professor Friedman himself has said that the quantity theory of money is 'a classical term', which he much prefers to 'the unlovely word monetarism',[21] the quantity theory is plainly central to the doctrine and provides an obvious place to start. The theory has a distinguished ancestry going back to Hume and Cantillon, though Schumpeter contended that what he called the 'strict quantity theorem' was, among the major classical writers, held only by Ricardo, James Mill and McCulloch. Marx rejected it as an 'insipid hypothesis', and J. S. Mill thought it was no longer true when there was a developed system of credit.[22] Still, the theory in one form or another was influential and popular in the nineteenth century, and nobody provided a theory to counter it. It was put in its modern form by Irving Fisher in *The Purchasing Power of Money*, which was first published in 1911. Fisher stated the equation $MV = PT$. M is the quantity of money, V its velocity of circulation, P the price level and T the physical volume of transactions. Despite his important role in its history, Fisher was by no means a rigid quantity theorist, and if he were living now, he would probably be regarded in monetarist circles as something of a backslider. The quantity theory, he believed, held only when the economy was in a state of equilibrium (that is to say, at times of full employment) and not in 'transition periods'. Secondly, he admitted that T could influence both V and M. And, thirdly, he went out of his way to emphasize that M, V, and T were only the 'proximate causes of P'.[23] (Incidentally, in the Great Depression Fisher, like Keynes, thought the cure was reflation not deflation.)[24]

$MV = PT$ is an identity or tautology and can only be made into something more if V is assumed to be constant, or nearly constant, and if T is also assumed to be constant, which it could be at full employment. The leading Cambridge economists, Marshall, Pigou, Robertson and the Keynes of *A Tract on Monetary Reform* in 1923, were not far removed from Fisher's ideas. Even then, however, Keynes believed that the quantity theory in its crude form was true only in the long run, and it was in this connection that he made his famous remark that 'in the long run we are all dead'.[25] In his *Treatise on Money* in 1930 Keynes still remained pretty close to the quantity theory, but in his *General Theory* in 1936 he shot it down, regarding changes in prices as being largely determined by changes in wages. In 1940 he wrote to an offending editor: 'if you are not too old, as to which I have no information, I strongly recommend an operation. By modern methods an inflamed quantity theory can always be removed with much less danger than formerly.'[26] A more temperate verdict on the quantity theory came earlier from Keynes's friend and adversary, Professor Pigou, who wrote:

> The Quantity Theory is often defended and opposed as though it were a definite set of propositions that must either be true or false. But in fact the formulae employed in the exposition of that theory are merely devices for enabling us to bring together in an orderly way the principal causes by which the value of money is determined.[27]

In other words, if you do not take the quantity theory in excess but as part of a balanced diet, you will not need the operation.

The quantity theory of money was revived after the war by Milton Friedman and the Chicago School. But there are striking differences from the earlier version, which was primarily concerned to show how changes in the price level were determined. The new Friedmanite version is concerned to show how money national income is determined, and in particular how a change in the rate of growth in the money supply brings about first a change in money national income and later a change in the rate of inflation. We have thus come to the central monetarist proposition: this is based on the claim that since 'experience has shown that people are pretty stubborn' about how much of their incomes they want to keep in money,[28] the demand for money is stable. It follows, if the theory is to have any value, that the velocity of circulation is also either stable or changes only gradually over the years. Otherwise changes in the supply of money could be offset by changes in its velocity and would not have a direct effect on the level of prices or the rate of inflation. 'Empirically,' Friedman has said, 'the movements of velocity tend to reinforce those of money instead of to offset them.'[29] It is also fundamental to the monetarist position that an increase in the stock of money will, except in the short run, have no effect on output or T.

The key point of controversy in all this, of course, is whether changes in the money supply are mainly the cause or mainly the effect of changes in economic activity, or, as Irving Fisher put it, whether the cycle is largely a 'dance of the dollar' or whether the dollar is largely a dance of the cycle.[30] Professor Friedman has cited several kinds of evidence for his contention that it is largely money which calls the tune. The most important is what he calls 'qualitative historical circumstances', which he believes to be 'perhaps the most directly relevant kind of evidence'.[31] This comes from the monetary history of the United States, and Friedman took what happened in the Great Contraction as an important example. He told the American Economic Association in 1967:

> The revival of belief in the potency of monetary policy was fostered also by a re-evaluation of the role of money from 1929 to 1933. Keynes and most other economists of the time believed that the Great Contraction in the United States occurred despite aggressive expansionary policies by the monetary authorities.... Recent studies have demonstrated that the facts are precisely the reverse: the US monetary authorities followed highly deflationary policies. The quantity of money in the United States fell by one-third in the course of the contraction. And it fell because the Federal Reserve system forced or permitted a sharp reduction in the monetary base, because it failed to exercise the responsibilities assigned to it in the Federal Reserve Act to provide liquidity to the banking system. The Great Contraction is tragic testimony to the power of monetary policy – not, as Keynes and so many of his contemporaries believed, evidence of its impotence.[32]

If all this was true, it obviously made a strong case for Milton Friedman. But Professor Kaldor pointed out[33] that on Friedman's own figures in his book *A Monetary History of the United States 1867–1960*, written with Anna Schwartz, the monetary base was actually rising during the period when the money supply fell. The monetary base (or the total of high-powered money) is the part of the money supply which is under the direct control of the monetary authorities and is the reserve base of the banks. The monetary authority can therefore increase the monetary base, but it cannot force the banks to lend. Kaldor's explanation is thus the opposite of Friedman's. The central bank did provide the banks with more reserves on which they could base more loans, but the banks did not want to lend because there were no credit-worthy people to lend to. In other words, the episode remains an example of the impotence of monetary policy, not of its power.

In his answer to Kaldor's article Friedman conspicuously failed to deal with this important point. But the revised monetarist case now seems to concede that what Friedman said about the monetary base was wrong and to argue that the key factor was the financial crisis caused by bank failures particularly in 1932. The banks, it is admitted, did hoard reserves, but this was because of the fear of failure rather than a scarcity of credit-worthy clients. If more and more reserves had been available, there would, it is contended, have come a point at which the banks would have started to lend again.[34]

Plainly, Kaldor had the better of the argument. No doubt the banks were frightened of failure, but the fact remains that although the Federal Reserve enlarged the monetary base, the banks could not find suitable people to take up loans. That was Kaldor's point, which is in accordance with what was generally thought at the time; and the monetarist rejoinder, which amounts to saying that the banks would have lent more if they had had more reserves, is weak as well as lacking direct evidence to support it.

Maybe Friedman appreciated its weakness. That is perhaps why, in his evidence to the Treasury Committee,[35] he said that he now regarded American experience between the wars, which used to be one of his strongest arguments in favour of monetarism, as 'idiosyncratic'. There were, no doubt, other reasons for Friedman's change of front, but it seems not unlikely that his forced retreat on the question of the monetary base during the Great Contraction was one of them.

One of the difficulties about Friedman's historical evidence is that for nearly all of the period that has been studied, monetary authorities were not aware of the doctrines of Professor Friedman. They therefore concentrated on what they thought were the proper duties of central bankers — preserving the stability of the financial system, controlling the rate of interest, acting as lenders of last resort — rather than on controlling the quantity of money (assuming that they could have done so had they wished). Indeed, Friedman's collaborator, Mrs Schwartz, has said that this control was exercised at best 'fitfully'.[36]

The American humorist, Will Rogers, used to say that President Roosevelt would take a difficult subject like banking and explain it so clearly that everybody could understand it — even the bankers. Friedman likewise seems to believe that bankers do not understand banking, and he has found them sadly wanting in monetarist rigour. He told the House of Commons Treasury Committee in 1980:

> Central bankers throughout the world have rendered lip service to the control of monetary aggregates by announcing monetary growth targets. However, few have altered their policies to match their professions of faith. Most have continued to try to ride several horses at once by simultaneously trying to control monetary aggregates, interest rates, and foreign exchange rates — in the process introducing variability into all three. And few have altered their operating procedures to make them consistent with the professed goal of controlling monetary growth.

The Bank of England was singled out for particular condemnation, being accused of ignorance of monetarist literature, of an inability to distinguish between money and credit, of 'myopia engendered by long-established practices', of failure to adjust its 'outlook to changed circumstances', and of surrender through standing ready passively to provide reserves to the banking system at the option of the banks.[37]

If the Bank of England — run by highly intelligent men who had had the benefit over the years of much Friedmanite advice as to how central bankers should conduct their business, and operating under the control of a strongly monetarist Government — still felt compelled to behave in the ways criticized by Friedman, it is reasonably safe to assume that bankers in the past, who did not enjoy such advantages, followed traditional banking practices and supplied money to meet the economy's demands. So it is not easy for Friedman's historical researches to provide the evidence he seeks.

Another type of evidence comes from the cyclical timing of monetary changes. Friedman has conceded that although 'these regular and sizeable leads of the money series are themselves suggestive of an influence running from money to business, they are by no means decisive', because, among other reasons, the apparent lead may be a 'lag' from previous business activity.[38] And when Professor Tobin, in an article written in 1970,[39] showed that all Friedman's evidence on timing was no more consistent with the timing implications of a Friedmanite model than it was with that of an ultra-Keynesian one (which Tobin did not believe either), Friedman's angry reply seemed to downgrade still further this type of evidence;[40] his attitude has been described as 'biased agnosticism'.[41] Biased or not, agnosticism seems appropriate, so we need not dwell on cyclical timing.

Friedman's remaining important evidence is evidence from foreign countries. To take Britain first, the money supply data before 1914 are not accurate; all the same it seems clear that during the last quarter of the nineteenth century and in the years up to 1914 there was a large increase in the money supply, yet the price level did not rise; it fell.* The inter-war years provide no support for monetarism. Professor Alan Walters, a fervent monetarist, writing in 1969, found that while for the whole period 1878 to 1938 money was 'the most efficient independent variable', the inter-war years were by coincidence 'strongly Keynesian'.[43]

More recently, the then editor of The Times, Sir William Rees-Mogg, wrote a notable article in 1976 entitled 'How a 9.4 per cent Excess Money Supply gave Britain 9.4 per cent Inflation'.[44] Sir William began with the striking words, 'The strongest case for monetarism has always been that it works', and he went on to say that 'the theory of monetarism can be tested scientifically. It can be used to make predictions and the fulfilment of the predictions can be observed.' 'Dr Friedman', Rees-Mogg explained, 'established that there was a time lag, normally of about two

---

* Professor Friedman's explanation is that 'the decline in the stock of money per unit of output occurred not only in Britain as a result of (1) exhaustion of then-known gold mines; (2) the shift of many countries from a silver to a gold standard; (3) the rapid increase in output'.[42] But in Britain the average growth rate from 1873 to 1914 was in fact only 1.5 per cent.

years, between changes in the money supply and consequential changes in prices', and Rees-Mogg showed that, taking the years 1965—73, the excess money supply, which is the annual rate of growth of the money supply minus the annual rate of growth of the domestic product, fitted the inflation rate exactly for 1967—75. 'Excess money supply', argued Sir William, 'is like water flowing from a tap to a hosepipe which is about two years in length. Once you have turned the tap on, nothing will stop the water coming out at the other end of the hosepipe in the form of price increases.' This uncompromising statement of the doctrine received the endorsement of the master himself, who wrote to Rees-Mogg, 'you certainly have not misstated the theory.'[45]

Now, certainly the average excess money supply for the nine years was exactly the same as the average rate of inflation. But, as Rees-Mogg conceded, in individual years the theory performed much less happily. More important, Professor Wynne Godley demonstrated that the close relationship between the two series 'depended entirely on the inclusion of the observations for 1974 and 1975 when price changes were predominantly determined by the rise in world commodity prices, including oil, and the subsequent wage increases' generated by the rise in import prices and the scheme of threshold awards.[46] Moreover, much of the rise in M3 (but not M1) in the years 1972 and 1973 was caused by the Bank of England's having introduced a new system of credit control. The causation was, therefore, the Bank of England and the 1973 Arab—Israel war rather than the money supply.*

In a correspondence in *The Times* in the following year the most significant feature was Milton Friedman's admission that

---

* In his useful book *Monetarism: An Essay in Definition*, Mr Tim Congdon managed to sketch the financial and economic developments from 1972 to 1975 without even mentioning the Arab—Israel war and the quadrupling of the price of oil. As a result of this considerable feat, he was able to claim that 'the monetarist predictions of early 1973 had, by late 1975, been completely vindicated'![47] He did not, however, claim that Professor Friedman's prediction in May 1974 that OPEC oil prices would soon return to normal since the Arabs would not for long be able to keep the price of oil at $10 a barrel had been completely vindicated. Like the Arab—Israel war, that was forgotten. Clearly, as was seen in chapter 8, monetarism and history do not go well together.

'many factors affect the precise rate of inflation that will follow a given rate of monetary growth, most notably, the potential for real growth, the state of expectations, the exchange rate regime, and the course of prices in the rest of the world.'[48] Evidently Sir William Rees-Mogg's hosepipe had not only sprung a leak; it was joined to more than one tap.

As a postscript Professor Godley wrote to *The Times* in 1980 reminding the Editor of his claim that the theory of monetarism could be tested scientifically and showing that in the five years following his famous article retail prices from 1975–80 had risen about 25 per cent more than the growth of the excess money supply in the years 1973–8.[49] According to the scientific test chosen by Sir William Rees-Mogg, therefore, monetarism during that period had evidently not worked. Indeed, the Governor of the Bank in a lecture in 1978 drew attention to the sharp fluctuations in the velocity of M3 during the 1970s.[50]

In his 1970 encounter with Kaldor, Professor Friedman wondered how Kaldor would explain 'the existence of essentially the same relation between money and income for the UK after the Second World War as before the First World War, for the UK as for the USA, Yugoslavia, Greece, Israel, India, Japan, Korea, Chile and Brazil'. If the relation between money and income was a supply response, as Professor Kaldor maintained, how was it, demanded Friedman, that 'major differences among countries and periods in monetary institutions and other factors affecting the supply of money [did] not produce widely different relations between money and income'?[51]

Kaldor replied to this seemingly formidable challenge that international comparisons showed nothing of the sort and, indeed, that they cast grave doubt on the Friedmanite claim that there was a 'stable demand function for money'.[52] Earlier in his evidence to the Radcliffe Committee in 1958[53] Professor Kaldor had pointed out that 'the ratio of the money supply...to the gross national product', which is the same thing as what Friedman called 'the relation between money and income' and which he claimed was 'essentially the same' in different countries at different times, in fact varied from 54 per cent in Switzerland, 36 per cent in France, 30 per cent in the US, 27.5 per cent in the UK to 18 per cent in Germany and 13 per cent in Mexico.

Kaldor added that since 1951 the ratio had fallen in some 'inflationary' countries such as the US, the UK and Mexico and had risen in some 'non-inflationary' countries such as Germany and Belgium, and that there was 'no systematic connection between these movements and the rate of increase in the money value of the GNP'.[54]

More recently Lord Kaldor has shown from IMF statistics that the ratio of money (M3) to income in 1978 was in Switzerland 125 per cent, in Italy 96 per cent and in Japan 87 per cent, while in Britain it was only 34 per cent and in Chile and Brazil about 15 per cent. In Germany the ratio was 10 to 15 per cent after the monetary reform, 36 per cent in 1958, 52 per cent in 1968 and nearly 57 per cent in 1978.

In other words [Kaldor continued], it is in the country with the lowest inflation rate that the money supply has shown a persistent rate of growth in excess of the rise in money income — something which on Friedman's principles is bound to lead to inflation, with a two-year lag. In Germany, however, it failed to do so with a twenty-year lag.[55]

There does not, therefore, seem to be much left of Friedman's claim that the relation between money and income in different countries and in different periods is 'essentially the same'.

So much for Friedman's various kinds of evidence. Before looking at other elements of the theory and also at some of the difficulties in it, one point should be got out of the way. Friedman often writes as though unbelievers think that changes in the quantity of money do not matter.[56] That is true of a few, but only of a few. The great majority believe that of course money is important. It would be very surprising if something which played such a large and conspicuous part in economic life were not important. In the Keynesian years insufficient attention was often paid to monetary policy — though monetary policy in Britain in those days was not in general more lax than in, for example, West Germany. But now most people would agree that due attention should be paid to money and monetary policy. Where non-monetarists part company from the monetarists is that they do not believe that monetary policy has the unique importance ascribed to it by Friedman, to the virtual exclusion of other policy instruments.

Monetarists believe that the chain of causation always runs from money supply to national income to prices. Non-monetarists, or neo-Keynesians, or unbelievers think that the chain often runs from income to demand for money to stock of money. Accordingly, monetarists believe that inflations are always caused by an excess of demand; non-monetarists believe there is more than one kind of inflation and more than one cause of inflation. The monetarist contention is that 'the ultimate source of inflation is always [an] increase in demand.'[57] It follows that trade unions 'do not and cannot cause inflation'.[58] Wages are determined by supply and demand. Obviously this is a very important matter for the monetarists: their cure for inflation is the cutting of demand, which is unlikely to be appropriate if the disease is not excessive demand.

This monetarist view is supported by the fact that the presence of strong unions has not always led to high inflation, and the absence of strong unions has not prevented high inflation. From 1959 to 1974, for example, Turkey and Spain had a higher inflation rate than any of the OECD countries, though their unions were either very weak or under the control of the government. Clearly, then, unions do not always cause inflation; but that is a very different thing from saying that they never do.

Non-monetarists concede that an increase in the quantity of money is a necessary accompaniment to inflation (unless the velocity of circulation increases) if unemployment is to be avoided; and many monetarists, most notably Professor Hayek,[59] concede that trade unions, by increasing the general level of wages faster than production, can more or less force Governments to increase the supply of money in order to prevent heavy unemployment. To some extent, therefore, the argument is semantic, but only to some extent. To deny that the trade unions have any responsibility in these circumstances and to argue that the behaviour of the Government is 'the sole cause of the inflation' seems, in Lord Robbins's tactful words, 'a little fanciful'.[60]

It is more than a little fanciful to lump together 'demand' inflation, 'cost-push' inflation and inflation caused by happenings abroad such as the quadrupling of the price of oil. 'It is cost inflation, coming in from outside', wrote Sir John Hicks, 'which upsets the monetarist's case....' He complained that monetarism tried to put 'all the kinds of inflation into the same box'.

> Monetarists [he went on] cannot deny that there is at least one distinction, the familiar distinction between demand inflation and cost inflation — 'demand pull and cost-push'. For this is a distinction which, on the most casual survey of inflationary experience, simply leaps to the eye.[61]

Sir John should not have used the words 'cannot deny', because that is precisely what Professors Hayek, Friedman and other monetarists do deny. All inflation, they believe, is caused by excessive demand.[62]

This attempt to reduce the complicated phenomenon of inflation, which is not solely economic, to a single cause is yet another example of the wilful exclusion of reality to which economic theory is prone. It is supported neither by the facts nor by common sense. While there has occasionally been excessive demand (in 1955 and 1966, for example), Britain's inflation since the war has been mainly a cost inflation. The 'wage-wage spiral',[63] in which various unions or parts of unions compete with each other in winning large wage settlements, has long been a feature of the British scene. The institutional reasons for this, such as powerful trade unions, the fact that a high percentage of the workforce belongs to trade unions, the decentralization of union power, the weakness of employers' associations, etc., seem much more convincing as causes of inflation than a lax monetary policy or an excess of demand, which is alleged to be present despite high unemployment.

In his illuminating book *The Causes of the Present Inflation* Andrew Tylecote calls inflation 'a spiral process, in which wages affect prices, prices affect wages, and the wages of one group affect those of another'.[64] In a wage negotiation each side will be influenced by a number of factors. The management will be influenced, among other things, by whether the cost of conceding the claim will be greater than the cost of a strike; by the number of workers who will either immediately or later be affected by the claim; by whether or not its giving in will lead to its competitors doing the same, so that its relative position will be unaltered;

by whether it will be able to raise its prices to pay for the claim; by its profitability; and by the state of the economy. The union side will be influenced, among other things, by what other unions are getting and what other companies have conceded; by what the costs of a strike will be and the chances of its success; by the need to maintain or restore differentials; by the strength of the company with which it is bargaining; by the level of inflation over the previous year and its expected level in the coming year; by the standard of living of its members; by the amount of unemployment in the industry; by the state of the economy generally; and by the degree of militancy in the union.[65]

Plainly, in most cases the state of the market and the level of demand influence the outcome of the bargaining. But to suggest that all the considerations mentioned above are insignificant and that ultimately the level of demand is all that matters seems highly implausible. Towards the end of the 1960s, for example, unions in nearly all countries became much more militant. Just as in 1848 revolutions spread across Europe − a historian who thought like a monetarist would presumably say that there was only one kind of revolution and that there was only one cause of revolution − so 120 years later union militancy spread from one country to another. This was probably caused by the arrival of a new generation of union leaders and rank and file who did not remember the inter-war depression, took prosperity for granted and did not understand the need for restraint.[66] This new generation of union leaders and the influence of the 'May events' in France seem more plausible causes of union militancy than market forces, unleashed by the war in Vietnam. Monetarism thus offers a 'Keynesian' technique of demand management to deal with a problem which is not caused by demand.

Before turning to the monetarist doctrine of the natural rate of unemployment, let us see how far the monetarist view of inflation is borne out by what happened in an earlier inflation, that of the sixteenth and seventeenth centuries. 'Inflation', according to Friedman, 'is always and everywhere a monetary phenomenon.'[67] It is an increase in the quantity of money that is always the cause of inflation.

The inflation in the sixteenth and seventeenth centuries used to be ascribed to the debasement of the currency and to the flow into England of gold and silver coming from the New World via Spain. Such an explanation is, of course, in full accord with Friedmanite ideas. Yet in England debasement was severe only for a few years after 1544, and Elizabeth's recoinage of 1561 ended it. No doubt this was the cause of some inflation, but inflation had begun long before the debasement and continued for a century after it had ended.

The inflation had begun, too, well before much gold and silver had got to Spain, let alone anywhere else. If and when it was brought to England, it was presumably disseminated by mercantile spending. It might be expected, therefore, to have produced a strong demand for relative luxuries. But in fact, in England and in other European countries as well, agricultural prices rose far more sharply than the prices of relative luxuries. A more probable cause of the inflation, it is now thought, was the combination of a rising population and limited agricultural resources. Indeed, in England in particular food prices and the population rose and fell together.

If this is so, then a rise in the quantity of money was not the cause of inflation. It is more likely that rising output and rising prices led to additional demands for money, as a result of which the supply of money expanded. Thus a distinctly Keynesian explanation of the inflation is probably the right one.[68]

Central to the monetarist position is the conception of the 'natural rate of unemployment'. According to this doctrine, if unemployment is above this 'natural' level, the rate of increase of wages and prices will slow down; if unemployment is below it, the rate of increase will accelerate; and if unemployment is at the natural level, the rate of increase will be constant. This level is called natural by analogy with Wicksell's natural rate of interest.[69] Professor Friedman, who thought of the idea, described it in these words:

The 'natural rate of unemployment'...is the level that would be ground out by the Walrasian system of general equilibrium equations, provided there is embedded in them the actual structural characteristics of the labour and commodity markets, including market imperfections, stochastic variability in demands and supplies, the cost of mobility, and so on.[70]

Perhaps the most notable part of this description is the last three words, 'and so on'. Certainly they are the most comprehensible. Not only is there nothing particularly 'natural' about this natural level, but nobody knows what it is. Nor can they know. The concept is largely metaphysical. And to claim that it is the rate 'that would be ground out by the Walrasian system of general equilibrium equations' does nothing to make it more real. Whatever relevance the Walrasian system had in the world of allegedly perfect competition, it has none today in the world of union power and oligopolistic industry.

If the monetarists merely said that if unemployment is very low, there will be bottlenecks and overheating and inflation, and if unemployment is very high, this will tend to reduce inflation, at least in the short term, they would be stating the obvious and there could be no objection. But if that is merely what they mean, presumably they would say it. By importing a metaphysical conception, they are trying to show that the level of unemployment depends solely upon the real cost of labour and cannot be affected by government action to increase effective demand without producing inflation. What Professor Tobin has called monetarism Mark II has gone further. For this school 'the natural rate, at least in the sense relevant for policy makers, is whatever situation prevails.'[71] Thus the Mark II monetarists remove the metaphysical content of the doctrine but at the cost of removing, too, any residual credibility it might have possessed.

So far, it will have been noticed, one thing is lacking in monetarism. A purely 'money' diagnosis has been put forward as a cause of inflation, and a purely 'money' cure has been prescribed for it. As was seen earlier, Friedman told the House of Commons Treasury Committee that control of the quantity of money was a necessary and sufficient condition for curing inflation. Now, even if these propositions are fully granted, the cure, on the theory so far, is unlikely to be effective without a considerable increase in unemployment and a large loss of output, which are not usually thought to be the proper objectives of economic policy. In other words, under cover of a lot of high-sounding theory, the monetarists seem to be prescribing merely a sharp dose of old-fashioned deflation. To fill this gap in the theory, Professor Sargent and Messrs Muth, Lucas, Barro and others produced in

America the Rational Expectations Hypothesis. Professor Minford of Liverpool, who has been so unlucky in his predictions of the course of the economy since the monetarist experiment began, is perhaps the foremost proponent of the Rational Expectations Hypothesis in this country.

The Rational Expectations Hypothesis brings the Walrasian system up to date in the sense of making it dynamic instead of static and so theoretically suitable for helping to fashion policy. We are thus back in the dream world in which all markets are clearing at the same time all the time. Indeed, the Rational Expectations Hypothesis makes the natural theory of unemployment almost seem down to earth and empirical — it is metaphysics run wild. Most economic theories, rightly or wrongly, assume a degree of rationality in economic agents. This one assumes a good deal more. Professor Minford and Mr Peel defend their assumptions on the grounds that they 'constitute a powerful theory able to generate a multitude of predictions about economic behaviour'. To the charge that their assumptions are 'unrealistic' and violate known facts about human behaviour, they reply '*any* theory must be unrealistic.'[72] That may or may not be so, but it does not seem a good reason for making a theory as unrealistic as possible, or rather for not making efforts to make it as realistic as you can. But the methodology of the monetarists will be considered later.

The basis of the Rational Expectations approach, as described by Minford and Peel, is 'the assumption that people use information efficiently in the pursuit of their interests'.

To make this operational, we suppose first that 'their interests' are 'normal' (i.e. they like more rather than less of commodities and leisure, they avoid pain, etc.) and, secondly, that given perfect knowledge they would know how best to pursue them. Let us call these respectively 'normality' and 'technical competence'. We suppose, thirdly, that their efficiency in the use of information is absolute, that they know the *true* probabilities attached to possible outcomes, given all the publicly available information; this is 'rational expectations'.[73] *

---

* The authors' own efficiency in the use of information is not absolute. They imply that the Medium-Term Financial Strategy was announced at the outset of the Government's term, whereas in fact it was not unveiled until the 1980 budget (see chapter 10).

This sounds bizarre enough, but the Rational Expectations Hypothesis is not just our old friend 'perfect competition' in modern
dress. As Professor Hahn has pointed out,[74] the theory entails
the belief that all firms can sell as much as they like at going
prices; that they are not restricted by demand; and that at the
going money wage everyone who wants to work can do so.

That most of the unemployed want to work does not disturb
these theorists. They could establish that fact quite easily by
going and talking to the unemployed. But once again the theory
is more important than reality, and the facts must not be allowed
to spoil 'a powerful theory able to generate a multitude of predictions about economic behaviour'. This, then, is how the theory
runs. Since the Government has reduced the rate of monetary
growth, people know that unless they reduce their wage claims
they are liable to lose their jobs. If in these circumstances, they
do not reduce their wage claims, it follows that they are not
prepared to be employed at a realistic wage which would save
their jobs. Therefore, they have decided that they would be
better off on the dole. They are better off in the sense that they
have decided that increased leisure is better for them than employment at a lower wage than they wished to receive. Therefore all
unemployment is voluntary. Anybody who wishes to keep his
job has only to lower his wages in line with the Government's
economic policy or move somewhere else to find work.

In this way the gap in monetarism is filled, and deflation can
take place harmlessly. Only those who want to be hurt will be
hurt; and they are not really hurt since they are enjoying increased
leisure.

The Rational Expectations theorists, therefore, go much further
than the classical economists or their neo-classical successors in
building a fantasy world. Even if they are not prepared to talk
to the real unemployed, a merely cursory acquaintance with a
stock exchange or any real market might have been expected to
rid them of their illusions. As Keynes said in the 1930s:

> the theory we devise in the study of how we behave in the
> market place should not itself submit to market-place idols.
> I accuse the classical economic theory of being itself one of
> these pretty, polite techniques which tries to deal with the

present by abstracting from the fact that we know very little about the future.[75]

Whether the unemployed, however, would think the Rational Expectations Hypothesis 'a pretty, polite technique' seems doubtful. To suggest that their employment is voluntary is not only false; it is insulting. But unless the Rational Expectations Hypothesis is broadly correct, then the effect of monetarist measures will be far greater on output and unemployment than on prices. Going back to our old friend the quantity theory, the reduction of M will affect T more than P.

The last monetarist tenet to be considered in this chapter is that the economy is fundamentally stable and therefore should be left alone as much as possible so that its in-built self-adjusting mechanisms can do their work undisturbed. It can be disposed of quickly. The many fluctuations that there have been in the capitalist system or the market economy show that it is not stable and that the alleged self-adjusting mechanisms do not make it stable. In other words, the self-adjustment does not take place.

The development of new drugs since the war has saved many lives and done a great deal of good. Occasionally development has ended in tragedy, as with thalidomide. But normally the stringent rules and procedures which govern the introduction of a new drug provide adequate safeguards for the public. Unfortunately, there are no such rules or procedures to control the introduction of new economic panaceas or doctrines. Our examination has shown that had monetarism been a drug, the Committee on the Safety of Medicines would not have allowed anybody to take it, since the claims of its makers had not been proved. Many more tests would have been ordered before it would have been adjudged safe for the market. Until such tests had been concluded, its damaging side-effects would have been considered too certain and its alleged benefits too questionable for it to have gained a certificate of safety.

Professor Friedman and his followers maintain, however, that it does not matter whether their assumptions are right or wrong provided that the results are good. And, as we saw earlier, monetarism as a cure can be considered separately from monetarism as a diagnosis. So we shall now examine the cure.

10

The Monetarist Cure

There is perhaps no empirical regularity among economic phenomena that is based on so much evidence for so wide a range of circumstances as the connection between substantial changes in the stock of money and in the level of prices.

Milton Friedman[1]

In this otherwise wintry season it is a pleasure to come to London and find the crocuses and Professor Milton Friedman in full bloom. But I wonder if Professor Friedman can be entirely content? It is a dangerous thing for an economist to have his ideas put into practice. They may not work. If unemployment continues high in Britain and if inflation continues and if exports continue to lag, there will be no doubt as to who was wrong. In past times my friend has undertaken, as in the case of Israel and Chile, to detach himself when his disciples made things worse: the Israelis were insufficient in the faith, the Chileans reprehensibly oppressive, however good their economic intentions. But such has been the British embrace that this will not be possible. Professor Friedman will surely agree, he is now fully and fairly on trial.

John Kenneth Galbraith[2]

I argue that there are limits to the good which Governments can do to help the economy but no limits to the harm....

Sir Keith Joseph[3]

In considering the value of monetarism as a cure, we can rely more on practice and less on theory.* The economic and financial

* This chapter is solely an examination of the efficacy of monetarism as a cure for the nation's economic ills. It, therefore, does not attempt an assessment of the Government's general achievements nor of its industrial and social policies.

policies of the present Government have been in the hands of convinced believers in monetarist ideas. Of course, not all its policies have been monetarist, and one or two of them have been criticized by Milton Friedman. But even a Government led by Milton Friedman would not be wholly monetarist and would no doubt be criticized as insufficiently orthodox by the Professor himself. In 1980 such a level-headed observer as Sir Henry Phelps Brown thought that the Chancellor of the Exchequer had in a broadcast interview 'treated monetarism not as one theory among others but as an incontrovertible principle like the law of gravitation'.[4] Another Treasury Minister went further. In the House of Lords he likened monetarism to the proposition that 'if twice one is two, then twice two is four.'[5] And Professor Tobin, in his evidence to the Select Committee in the same year, described what was being done as a 'very interesting laboratory experiment for economics...a risky experiment in macroeconomic policy and monetary policy'.[6] For any monetarist, therefore, to try to pretend that his doctrine has not been put into practice would be futile and evasive. He could, however, maintain that the present Government's policies were not a completely unheralded revolution. Other countries had used a monetarist approach.[7] Besides, monetary targets were first introduced in Britain when Mr Healey was Chancellor in 1976, and in the same year Mr Callaghan made his (or his son-in-law's) famous remark that we could no longer spend our way out of recession. At the insistence of the IMF, moreover, the Labour Government had made substantial cuts in public expenditure and had eschewed devaluation. Finally, when the Governor of the Bank of England said that the Bank had not 'adopted a wholehearted monetarist philosophy', but that 'what we do is likely to give a monetarist a good deal of the prescription he would recommend',[8] he was speaking in 1978 about policy under a Labour Government. Yet much of what Mr Richardson had to say showed a heretical disregard for some of the canons of monetarism. For instance, he thought that the blame for inflation rested 'not on any simple cause, but rather on a multitude of political and economic pressures'. He shrank from suggesting that there is always 'a direct, simple chain of causation running from the money supply to the price level'. And he even wondered if in certain circumstances 'the causality could not run as much from prices to money as from

money to prices'.[9] On the whole, therefore, it is probably safe
to accept the judgement both of an opponent of monetarism,
Professor Ford, that monetarism has recently been pursued in the
UK and the US in a uniquely 'fundamentalist' way,[10] and of two
supporters of monetarism, Professor Minford and Mr Peel, that
'this Government's economic strategy is, at least in conception, a
complete departure from the past.'[11]

The departure was from a starting place that nobody would have
chosen. Britain's economic record had in the previous ten years
been worse than that of her competitors. Output had increased
less here than elsewhere. The growth of productivity had been
much lower than in any of the OECD countries except the United
States, and inflation had been higher than anywhere else except
Italy. That record would have been sorry enough, even if we had
not had the advantage of oil from the North Sea. In addition, the
British system of pay negotiations, which fluctuates between the
rigidities of incomes policies and the anarchy of so-called free
collective bargaining, has strong claims to being the worst in the
world. So the incoming Conservative Government did not take
possession of a prosperous and well-run estate. It inherited a
gravely weakened industry, poisoned industrial relations, an
inflation rate which was over 10 per cent and rising, a demoralized
public sector and a string of post-dated cheques. Some of the
trade-union leaders were ashamed, as well they might be, of the
winter of discontent which had followed the Labour Government's
attempt to impose a 5 per cent pay norm, but there was no
possibility of close or fruitful co-operation between the new
Conservative Government and the TUC, at least for some time.

Undeterred by any of this, the Government's economic Ministers
lost no time in demonstrating their impeccably monetarist convic-
tions. In the Chancellor's first Budget interest rates were raised;
the monetary target was tightened from the previous Government's
range of 8 to 12 per cent to one of 7 to 11 per cent; income tax
was cut to improve incentives, as the Conservatives had promised
at the election; and, to pay for this, VAT was raised from 8 to 15
per cent. At first sight this last measure was surprising, since it
was bound to increase the level of wage settlements, and the
Government's chief priority was the control of inflation. But
in the monetarist scheme of things trade unions cannot cause

inflation, and restraint in the rate of growth of the stock of money is both a necessary and a sufficient condition for controlling inflation. Hence wages would be kept in check by the Government's control of the money supply, and the increase in VAT could not cause inflation any more than trade unions could.

Indeed as late as July 1980, when a wage explosion had undeniably taken place, one of the ablest and most sceptical of the economic Ministers told the House of Commons that, 'broadly speaking', he did not think the wage increases in the previous twelve months had been a contributing factor to the rise in inflation and that 'the present rate' (20 per cent) was 'mainly determined by the expansion in the money supply' two years before. [12] The contradiction between the Government's having as its main objective the reduction of inflation and then proceeding to increase it by raising indirect taxes and hence wage settlements was a contradiction only to non-monetarists. And it was only the first of many.

The Government set out its economic objectives and attitude in a letter from the Treasury to the House of Commons Treasury and Civil Service Committee in June 1980. The letter was a model of monetarist orthodoxy. [13] The reduction of inflation and the creation of conditions in which 'sustainable economic growth can be achieved' were the main objectives. 'Pride of place' was no longer given to 'short-term stabilization of output, employment and the external current account'. Reduction of inflation had necessarily to be the first concern of policy. Governments themselves, the Treasury letter went on, could not ensure high employment and 'a commitment to high employment at a time when pay bargainers were pushing nominal incomes far ahead of improvements in productivity could not be met'. This was the first time since the war that a Government had explicitly abandoned the commitment to full employment. The previous Labour Government had in practice abandoned it but without saying so.

Under the heading of 'Intermediate Targets', there then came two key sentences.

The Government has deliberately not set its targets in terms of the ultimate objectives of price stability and high output and employment, because...these are not within its direct control. It has instead set a target for the growth of money supply, which is more directly under its influence, and has stated that it will frame its policies for taxation and public expenditure to secure a deceleration of money supply without excessive reliance on interest rates.

Earlier, in its second Budget at the end of March, the Government had unveiled what was called its Medium-Term Financial Strategy (MTFS). This stated that to reduce inflation the Government would 'progressively reduce the growth of the money stock.' Thus the percentage range of growth of Sterling M3 was to be 7–11 in 1980–1, 6–10 in 1981–2, 5–9 in 1982–3 and 4–8 in 1983–4. To this end the PSBR as a percentage of Gross Domestic Product was also to be progressively reduced by the cutting of public expenditure. The decision to base policy on the intermediate targets of the PSBR and the stock of money instead of on the real objectives of growth and full employment and price stability was fateful for the success of the policy of the Government and the future of the British economy. And this decision, which was of course fully in accordance with monetarist doctrines, was taken at least partly because these intermediate targets were believed to be more directly under the control of the Government. Indeed, the Financial Secretary to the Treasury, in a lecture in August 1980, confidently reasserted what he called a 'basic proposition', that the Government was 'able to determine the quantity of money'.[14]

But what is it that the Government is, allegedly, able to control? Monetarists, as we saw in chapter 9, are very sure of the effects of money; they are less sure what money is. They have a theory which states that changes in the quantity of certain financial assets have a direct causal link with money GNP and thence with the rate of inflation, but they are unable to say which those financial assets are. In the nineteenth century, of course, there was also no agreement as to what constituted money, but since in those days there was no call to base economic policy on the achievement of monetary aggregates, the absence of agreement was not important. If your behaviour is not dependent on the weather, the lack of a reliable barometer is largely immaterial. If, on the other hand, your behaviour is determined by a barometer, it is a handicap to have an instrument which is defective. Yet after a quarter of a century of monetarism, there is no agreement on what is and what is not money, or rather on which collection of monetary assets constitute the monetary aggregate that should be controlled. The number of definitions of money has grown, but the inability to state which is the right one has grown with them. Indeed, under 'Goodhart's Law' it is now widely accepted that any collection of monetary assets which is chosen as the right indicator of how the Government's monetary policy is faring becomes in quite a short time the wrong one. After stating that from 1963 to 1978 M1 had shown a closer relationship with incomes and interest rates than M3, the Governor of the Bank of England thought that the relationship would not necessarily remain so stable under differing conditions, 'particularly if the authorities were to seek to control it more closely'![15] Thus neither the Government nor anybody else knows which collection of financial assets has the effect on nominal income, and thence on prices, which the monetarists assert is so important; and as soon as the Government tries to control a certain monetary aggregate, it is liable to become an unreliable indicator. This seems to raise doubts about the reliability of the doctrine. After all, if you don't know what to control, how can you be so certain that you ought to control it?

In any case, in his 1982 Budget the Chancellor implicitly admitted defeat and announced that the Government would pay attention to three monetary aggregates. However, in the event of wide differences between them, the question of which one, so to speak, the Government's money would be on was left unclear. One of the chief reasons for announcing money supply targets was to influence the behaviour of trade-union negotiators. How those negotiators were to know which indicator was the one that mattered when the Government itself did not know was not explained. Even a negotiator who attained Professor Minford's ideal of absolute efficiency in the use of information, and whose expectations were, therefore, fully rational, might be forgiven some confusion about what he should expect, let alone about how he should act. Indeed, the 'Minfordian' must also have been at something of a loss when the corset was removed in 1980 and there was a jump in M3. At that time there were important people in Whitehall who were rumoured to think that even the Bank of England had no idea how fast the money supply was growing.

Still, the Government's difficulty in defining money was trifling compared with its difficulty in controlling it. 'It is', said the Minister of State at the Treasury in the 1980 Budget debate, 'because the money supply is the critical factor in determining the level of inflation that it is crucial both to set monetary targets and ensure that the money supply is kept within the specified range.'[16] Yet for the first two years of the MTFS the Treasury came nowhere near hitting its financial targets. In 1980–1, when the target was midway between 7 and 10 per cent, the outcome was 18.8 per cent, and in 1981–2 when the target was midway between 6 and 10 per cent, the outcome was 13.5 per cent. Finally, after two years of failing to hit the target, the Chancellor in the 1982 Budget decided to move the target, so that he might at last be able to hit it.* For 1982–3, instead of the 5–9 per cent laid down by the MTFS, the target became 8–12 per cent, which was probably within the Government's marksmanship if well outside its original policy. In view of this sobering experience, monetarism may be termed the uncontrollable in pursuit of the indefinable. Similar vicissitudes attended the attempt to reduce the PSBR, to which we shall return in a moment.

The best feature of the Government's monetary policy was its failure. While the Treasury was concentrating its attention on intermediate targets, startling things were happening to the real economy, and they would have been even more startling if the Government had succeeded in hitting its monetary and PSBR targets. As it was, the country suffered the worst depression since systematic measurement began — which rules out of consideration, for instance, the years after the Black Death. Between the election in 1979 and the first half of 1981 total output fell by 6 per cent, industrial production (excluding oil) by 15 per cent and manufacturing output by 17 per cent. Bankruptcies and closures — not all, by any means, those of inefficient businesses — took place at an

---

* This was like the marksman who found it easier to shoot his arrows first and then paint the bulls eyes where they had landed.

unprecedented rate,* and unemployment nearly doubled. All this was done in the cause of slaying the dragon of inflation. But the dragon remained unslain. For long, indeed, he was more bloated than he had been before the Government came to power; and it was only after the Government had been in office for nearly three years that the dragon became appreciably more shrunken than in June 1979. Meanwhile, St George had suffered more damage than the dragon. Since the first half of 1981 there has been no recovery, and unemployment has risen to well over 3 million.† How did this disaster happen?

The new Government's announced tough monetary policy, together with North Sea oil, raised the exchange rate. At the same time there was a wage explosion, unhindered (indeed, arguably, stimulated by) government policy. The combination of the high exchange rate and the greatly increased labour costs led to a dramatic fall in British competitiveness. The Treasury and Civil Service Committee's Report on the 1982 Budget said that 'competitiveness improved by 10 per cent between the first and third quarters of 1981 reversing some of the 50 per cent deterioration in the previous two years.'[20] Yet exports held up remarkably well. Exporters were able however, to maintain their share of the market only by slashing profit margins. This loss of profitability, combined with high interest rates and the restrictive fiscal policy of the Government, led to large-scale destocking, greatly reduced output and soaring unemployment.

---

* The President of the Birmingham Chamber of Commerce, scarcely a left-wing source, told the Chancellor of the Exchequer in April 1982 that too many good companies had been wiped out 'not necessarily because their products or their marketing strategy were bad, but rather they failed as a major extent as a result of government policies'.[17]

† This was the sort of outcome of monetarist policies that non-monetarists have always expected. Monetarists naturally thought the outcome would be very different. Professor Minford, for instance, believed in July 1979 that the recession would not be serious. 'Any temporary loss of output', he wrote, 'is likely to be of modest significance.'[18] On 30 June 1980 the Professor was asked about unemployment. He forecast there would be an increase of 300,000 in the eighteen months till the end of 1981.[19] In fact, this was wrong by a factor of four. The increase was nearly 1.2 million. In his article in July 1979 Minford derided the idea that the switch to indirect taxes in the 1979 budget which increased the Retail Price Index by 3.5 per cent would have any effect on wages. When asked about this by the Treasury Committee a year later, after the wages explosion had taken place, he still clung to his view. This is a good illustration of how economic dogma remains undisturbed even when disproved by events.

So the short answer to our question about how all this happened is the Treasury's faith in monetarism. 'Deflation', wrote Keynes in 1925, 'does not reduce wages "automatically". It reduces them by causing unemployment. The proper object of dear money is to check an incipient boom. Woe to those whose faith leads them to use it to aggravate a depression.'[21] The Treasury's obsession with its textbook monetarist targets, its abandonment of any policy of stabilization and its neglect of the proper objectives of economic policy — growth, full employment and price stability — contributed largely to the slump. The automatic pilot of monetarism put the economy into a steep dive, and reliance on monetarist dogma prevented the Treasury from taking steps to regain height. The automatic pilot was left undisturbed, though it was clear to anybody who looked out of the window that something was badly wrong.

The PSBR was an even more unsuitable target for policy than Sterling M3, though in this the Government was once again following the example of its Labour predecessors. Sir Geoffrey Howe himself described it in his first Budget as 'a fickle and elusive statistic', and so it proved. But there is not just the difficulty of estimating the PSBR with any precision. There is also the difficulty, analagous to that of deciding which monetary aggregate should be the guiding light, of knowing what should be in the PSBR and why. 'I thought I had done a fair amount of juggling with figures as an accountant,' wrote Joel Barnett, Labour's Chief Secretary 1974—9,

> but when it came to the sort of sophisticated 'massaging and fudging' I learned as Chief Secretary, I realized I had been a babe in arms by comparison. It was a case of changing this and that 'assumption', and abracadabra — the Public Sector Borrowing Requirement is about the figure you first thought of!

And, he added, 'the particular methods adopted to cut the PSBR might have little or no effect on real resources.'[22]

Nearly everybody who has had anything whatever to do with this matter in Whitehall would agree with Mr Barnett. Yet the reduction of the PSBR was still chosen as the objective of the

Government's fiscal policy. There seems to have been two major reasons for this damaging decision. The first was given in the MTFS. It was conceded that the relationship between the PSBR and M3 was erratic from year to year, but the Treasury had 'no doubt that public sector borrowing has made a major contribution to the excessive growth of the money supply in recent years'.[23]

On the face of it some association between the two things seems likely, but let us look at the evidence. In the three years 1977–80 the unfunded PSBR was very low, while the increase in Sterling M3 was relatively large. In the previous three years, on the other hand, the unfunded PSBR was much larger, while the increase in the money supply was less than half of what it was in the years 1977–80. Taking the PSBR as a whole, when it was large, as in the years from 1974–7, the growth of the money supply was relatively small; while in the years in which the PSBR was relatively low, such as 1977–8, the growth of the money supply was relatively large.[24] The same thing has happened during the last two years. In 1980–1 the unfunded PSBR was small, yet Sterling M3 grew substantially. And in 1981–2 when the PSBR was much smaller and the unfunded PSBR was substantially negative, the rise in the money supply was again high.[25] The Government's reasons, given in the MTFS, for making large reductions in the PSBR a key policy objective must on clear empirical evidence, therefore, be dismissed. Not surprisingly, as OECD figures demonstrate, the experience of other countries leads to the same conclusion.[26]

The second reason was similar in that it was superficially plausible but fallacious. The Government believed that the nation's borrowing should be treated, whatever the cost, as it would be in an ordinary household. But, not surprisingly, the analogy with the prudent (or imprudent) housewife is wholly inappropriate. If a housewife cuts her household expenses, she does not thereby cut her income. Not so a national Government. Unlike a housewife, a Government has responsibilities not only for its own finances but also for the national economy. And when a Government spends less, it indirectly causes its own income to fall. A Government which cuts its spending on goods or services reduces national income and increases unemployment. As a consequence, it has to spend more on unemployment benefit and is bound to receive lower income from taxes. The loss of government revenue and higher expenditure caused by the recession may largely cancel out the effects of the previous cuts in spending, so that the gap between expenditure and income, the PSBR, remains wide. That was indeed the self-defeating game the Treasury played for two years or so. It was always seeking to balance the books at an even lower level of economic activity.* Hence the nine or ten attempts of various sorts to cut government expenditure since the last election — the Treasury chasing its own tail. In 1982 the Treasury finally managed to catch its tail. Instead of being substantially higher than forecast, as in the past, the PBSR turned out to be £2 billion lower than forecast. Unfortunately, as with Sterling M3, the partially redeeming feature of the Government's efforts to reduce the PSBR was that they had failed, and the reduced PSBR did not presage or produce recovery.

The reason, of course, as was implicit in what has just been said about the false analogy with the housewife's budget, is that the PSBR has a role to play in stabilizing the economy. In a recession public expenditure will naturally rise because of the increase in unemployment pay, and the public revenue will naturally fall. In these circumstances a reduction in the PSBR merely intensifies the recession, and that is what happened. Moreover, the crude PSBR is not a proper measure of the fiscal stance. The proper measure is the so-called 'constant unemployment deficit'. This measures what public expenditure and tax receipts would be if unemployment remained at a constant level. By failing to use this measurement, the Treasury probably misled itself and went on deflating an economy which had already been deflated far too much. In other words, the Government has gone on cutting demand when demand was already far too low. In consequence, not only have we had a disastrous slump, but there has been virtually no recovery.

Monetarists, of course, deny that there has been a shortage of

---

* 'If we carry "economy" of every kind to its logical conclusion', Keynes wrote of a deflating government in 1931, 'we shall find that we have balanced the Budget at nought on both sides, with all of us flat on our backs starving to death from a refusal, for reasons of economy, to buy one another's services'.[27] Luckily the Treasury did not carry 'economy' that far, but it carried it far enough to put much of industry flat on its back.

demand. Indeed, they seem to deny the validity of the very idea of aggregate demand. Whatever became of the laws of supply and demand, one wonders? Monetarists claim that since money national income rose by about 15 per cent in the Government's first year of office and has risen by about 10 per cent a year since then, there cannot have been insufficient demand. The answer is that the rise in prices was substantially faster than the rise in money national income. Hence, in real terms, income and output fell. If wages and prices had risen less, money demand would have been lower without any presumption that real demand would have been significantly higher.

The pursuit of textbook monetarist goals, Sterling M3 and the *ignis fatuus* of the PSBR, instead of the real goals of economic policy, for long even hindered the attainment of the Government's main economic objective, the defeat of inflation. Thus in order to secure a reduction in the PSBR, which was supposed to bring down inflation, the Government had to increase taxation, which put inflation up. The same thing happened with the nationalized industries. In order to lower the PSBR, they had to increase their prices and charges. In August 1981 the retail price index (RPI) was 11.5 per cent higher than a year earlier. Those components of the index which were closely influenced by government fiscal policy (about one-third of the total) rose over that period by no less than 18.5 per cent. The price of goods and services produced by nationalized industries rose by over 20 per cent, rents by 39 per cent, rates by 21 per cent. The other two-thirds of the RPI comprising retail sales of food, durables, clothing and so on, rose only 7.5 per cent.

In other words, the gain that had been achieved through the relative stability of food prices, through lower wage inflation and through the moderate trend of import prices was for long more than offset by increases directly caused by the Government's own fiscal policy. In short, the Government's pursuit of textbook monetarist targets not only helped to cause a slump, it initially put up prices as well. In doing so it still further reduced demand.

Yet in the course of 1982 the Government's fight against inflation met with dramatic success. The struggle to keep wage settlements low was gaining its reward. A no less important cause of lower inflation was the sharp fall in commodity prices, which were lower in real terms than at any time since the Korean War. The cost of fuel and material bought by manufacturing industry rose by 20 per cent in 1980, by 14 per cent in 1981 and by 3 or 4 per cent in 1982. This was highly beneficial for inflation in Britain. But it has caused havoc in the Third World, and by cutting down the purchasing power of the poorer countries it has lessened the demand for the exports of Britain and other countries and deepened the depression.

All the same it is the rise in unemployment to a record level which has been the most spectacular result of monetarism. The headline total of 3,295,000 unemployed in October 1982 considerably understated the actual level of unemployment. There were then 645,500 people covered by special employment and training measures, though their direct effect on the unemployment register was probably only about 375,000.[28] There was also a large group of people who were unemployed but not registered. Recent evidence suggests that in 1981 this group numbered about 400,000.[29]

The Government began its term of office firmly and ideologically opposed to any form of incomes policy. The problem of excessive wage claims, it was believed, could safely be left to the control of the money supply and to the influence this would have on wage bargainers. However, here as elsewhere, monetarist doctrine turned out to be misleading, as the 1979—80 wages spree unmistakeably demonstrated. The Government was soon compelled, therefore, to evolve an incomes policy of a sort, while carefully avoiding the impiety of using the phrase. This took the form of incessant exhortation by Ministers to workers not to price themselves or other people out of their jobs, the announcement of cash-limited figures for wage increases in the public service, which were selectively enforced according to the strength of the union, and continued deflation. It was undoubtedly this last element, large-scale unemployment, which was the most influential in securing lower and more realistic wage settlements.

That this should be so, and that the expectations of the monetarists about 'real expectations' should be disappointed, was inevitable. For several years many unions had demanded and received excessive wage increases. These had been inflationary and had damaged the competitiveness of British industry without making their recipients better off. Nevertheless, the Government's appeals to workers to make themselves more competitive by reducing wage claims rang hollow in many a trade-union ear when they could argue that it was some of the Government's own policies which had done so much to make industry less competitive and when British wages were already low by international standards. There was, furthermore, no suggestion that there was going to be parity of sacrifice. The Government was shouting at the unions but not talking to them. It announced that it was going to stick to its monetary targets and not accommodate excessive wage increases, come what may. The trouble is, as Professor Tobin told the Treasury Committee, 'that kind of a threat is a threat to everybody in general and nobody in particular.' People, Tobin went on, were not 'playing a game just with the central bank'.

Those people, they are playing a game with other workers.... and they are going to be concerned whether anybody else is going to respond to that threat.... Their main concern is about how they stand in wages and prices relative to other people whom they regard as important reference groups for themselves. They will figure, not knowing what the rest of the private economy is going to do, that the safest thing may be to let those other guys do the disinflating if anybody is going to do it at all.[30]

Professor Tobin might have added that other people who are playing a game are the Rational Expectations monetarists, with their convenient conceit that workers use information with absolute efficiency and know the true probability of every outcome. Tobin was talking about what happens in the real world. Economically, the only connection that Professor Minford and his school have with the real world is the damage that is done if policy makers act on their advice. As Keynes wrote more than fifty years ago, 'the working classes cannot be expected to understand, better than Cabinet Ministers, what is happening.'[31]

Some workers have undoubtedly priced themselves out of a job. But most have lost their jobs through no fault of their own, and for a huge and growing number of people there is not a job to go to at any wage. The fundamental cause is the shortage of demand, and there is little reason to suppose that lower inflation and lower wages will increase either demand or employment.

Various monetarist defences have been put forward for what happened: the recession is worldwide; the high exchange rate was the result of North Sea oil and nothing could be done to bring it down; the slump is the result not of the policies followed since 1979 but of mistaken policies followed during the last thirty years; the rise in unemployment is the fault of the workers themselves and their unions — they have priced themselves out of jobs; other countries have followed substantially the same policies as Britain with substantially the same results. And, finally, there is really nothing to defend: what has happened is good and was inevitable; overmanning has been eliminated; productivity has greatly increased; there is a more realistic attitude to pay bargaining; and there are many fewer strikes. Altogether British industry (or what is left of it) is now in better shape than ever before.

Of course, unemployment and the recession are not confined to this country. The recession *is* world-wide. But the rest of the world is a large net importer of oil. Britain is a net exporter of oil. We should, therefore, have had a relatively mild recession instead of the first and just about the worst in the world.* There was nothing in the world recession which decreed that Britain should move faster and deeper into recession than other countries. Yet that is what happened.†

Probably only a small part of the rise in the pound can be attributed to North Sea oil.[34] Most of that rise was due to the tight monetary policies of the Government.[35] The Government

---

* For an economy that is self-sufficient in oil, as Buiter and Miller have pointed out, 'there is no need for real incomes to fall as the price of oil rises. For the economy as a whole the decline in real wages required to maintain competitiveness and full employment will be matched by an increase in real oil rents. Unless these rents are distributed to wage-earners in a way that maintains their standards of living, the necessary real wage cut is likely to be resisted.'[32]

† A parliamentary answer on 25 October 1982 stated that 'between the first half of 1979 and the second quarter of this year manufacturing output in the United Kingdom fell by 16 per cent. Betwen the same two periods, the level of manufacturing output in France did not change. In West Germany and the United States of America production fell by 2 per cent and 10 per cent respectively, and in Japan production increased by 13 per cent.'[33]

did abolish exchange controls, but whether or not that was desirable, the likely effect on the exchange rate was almost certainly not the chief reason for that decision. Nor in the event did the ending of exchange controls have much effect on the pound. In any case, with lower interest rates and a less restrictive fiscal policy leading to higher imports and a deficit in the balance of payments sterling would not have appreciated, or if it had, the rise would have been small. Norway has comparable energy resources, but her currency did not appreciate.

Certainly the unions have played their part over the years in swelling the number of unemployed. But to blame unemployment solely on the workers is unjustified and is a negation of government. Government has a responsibility in this as in other matters. To blame the slump on the last thirty years does not explain why unemployment should have begun to rise to unprecedented heights only in 1979–80. It is also at variance with another monetarist defence, which is that other countries are now pursuing similar policies with similar results. Unless it is thought that they also pursued mistaken policies for thirty years, it cannot be our allegedly erroneous past policies which are to blame. And, as has already been indicated, other countries are heavy importers of oil, so their recession should be more severe than ours, not less.

Nevertheless, as Mr William Keegan has pointed out, the Government is entitled to claim that other countries have adopted its policy.[36] Where Britain has led, other countries have followed. But such knowledge can have given only momentary comfort to the leading ranks of the gadarene swine. And the prolonging of the world recession caused by almost every Government's pursuit of beggar-my-neighbour deflation policies has made economic recovery more difficult. Britain would have been in a better position if other countries had not followed her example. In any case, as Mr Brittan has sharply noted, 'for the political leaders of every country to point at the bad performance of other countries as the main reason why they are performing so badly themselves is surely a logical fallacy.'[37]

The view that there is nothing to defend contradicts all the other defences. If there is nothing to defend, why bother to blame what has happened on somebody or something else? According to this theory, no blame should be attached to anybody. Certainly, amidst the gloom there have been some rays of hope. Productivity has increased. Between the first half of 1979 and the first quarter of 1982 output per head in manufacturing industry increased by 5.2 per cent.[38] That is not a staggering increase, and there is limited advantage in producing fewer goods more efficiently, but it is encouraging so far as it goes. Some firms have done very well. Wage settlements have become smaller, and strikes have become fewer. And inflation declined sharply during 1982 and will fall further. The Government will be the first one for a very long time to go into an election with a lower rate of inflation than when it came to office. Between 1974 and 1979 prices rose by 110 per cent. Even if the Government runs its full five years, the rise in prices during its term of office will be only about half that which occurred under its predecessors. But those achievements scarcely make up for the large drop in output — growth lost for ever — the loss of factories and the tragic doubling of unemployment. There are, of course, those who think that suffering is good for the soul and that something quite so painful must have worthwhile effects. In *Man and Superman* Shaw laughed at the 'pious English habit of regarding the world as a moral gymnasium built expressly to strengthen your character in'. But that is not the purpose of the economy. Similarly, many people believe that if a medicine tastes sufficiently disgusting, it must cure their illness. But, regrettably, the nastiness of a medicine is not a reliable indication of its effectiveness. On the other hand, it is true that, if you go on banging your head against the wall you get a headache, and that if you stop doing so, your headache is likely to get better quite soon.

The monetarist defences of the last three years are not important in themselves. Their importance lies in their having helped to delay or prevent recovery. The battered British economy, contemplating the Treasury, might well feel with Dean Swift:

It'd rather choose that I should die,
Than its prediction prove a lie.[39]

Perhaps the most singular feature of the Treasury's economic attitude is that nobody has ever clearly explained how economic recovery will take place. Ministers have been singing songs about recovery since the end of 1980. But the closest they have come to an answer to the question of how the recovery will come is the claim of Mr Leon Brittan, the Chief Secretary, as long ago as April 1981: it would come 'naturally', he said, 'just as day follows night'.[40] Unfortunately, night followed night for the next year and a half. Admittedly, for a brief period in April and May 1982 Mr Brittan thought day had dawned at last. 'Those who still refuse to see that the fruits of recovery are on the way', he said, 'should open their eyes and look again: the signs are all round them and this time recovery is going to last.' And a little later he said, 'the evidence of the start of a recovery is all about us. And not even the most blinkered pessimist could fail to see it.'[41] But the euphoria did not last. The night soon closed in again, and the day was always some way off. In general the speeches of economic Ministers were almost the same in 1982 as they were in 1981. Many of them could have been made just as well in one year as in the other. Recovery has been about to come since December 1980, much as with President Hoover it was always just around the corner. Indeed, we have often been told that it has begun, but it has not come, and nobody seems to know how it will come.

The question of whether or not the results of the Government's policy were intended is now academic. Certainly, if the Medium Term Financial Strategy envisaged more than 3 million unemployed, it should not have been adopted. And if it did not envisage 3 million unemployed, it should have been abandoned. But the Treasury's refusal to alter policy even when the unintended results — if they were unintended — became so unmistakeably injurious removed the options of pleading inadvertence or bad luck. Evidently everything that had happened was, in the Treasury view, either good or inevitable. Otherwise decisive alterations would have been made.

Almost all the tenets of monetarism have been destroyed. The Government proved unable to control the money supply. The inflation rate was about halved — a considerable achievement. Yet the Government's harshly deflationary policies had a much quicker and greater effect on output and employment than the theory had led it to expect. In 1980 Professor Friedman told the Treasury Committee that a successful policy of reducing inflation would have 'as an unavoidable side-effect a temporary retardation of economic growth'. The 'temporary retardation' would last less than three years.[42] Nobody could possibly describe what has happened as merely 'a temporary retardation of economic growth'. Growth has not merely been retarded. Output has fallen more than ever before, and unemployment has more than doubled. The claim that a change in the money supply would lead to a similar change in prices two years later has been decisively refuted, and the Rational Expectations Hypothesis has turned out to be as irrational as it always seemed. The theory of monetarism is in ruins, and experience of the last three years is there to prove it.

Monetarism as Ideology

Professor Friedman claims that his doctrine is 'scientific'[43] and that it has a sound empirical basis. Yet he and his followers believe that their assumptions need not be based on empirical evidence.[44] They can be quite unrealistic so long as the results seem good. That is to say the nature of the assumptions are not important provided they produce predictions which seem valid. Such a procedure is fully justified in the natural sciences because the experiments can be tested. But in economics it would be hard to imagine a more unscientific procedure. In economics everything is connected with everything else, and if the assumptions are carefully chosen, almost any result can be produced. And that result may be irrelevant or misleading because it is produced by some variable that the economist has not allowed for, or because it merely demonstrates a correlation and does not demonstrate cause and effect, or because the assumptions 'fix' the result. For example, Böhm-Bawerk said of Marx's method of 'proving' his labour theory of value that he acted like one, who, anxious to bring a white ball out of the urn, takes care to secure this result by putting in only white balls.[45] So contrary to what the Friedmanites maintain, the assumptions which economists make should be as realistic as possible and should be based on the available empirical evidence. Otherwise they cannot claim to be using 'scientific' methods or to be producing 'scientific' results. They may just be playing around with white balls.

Hence Friedman and his followers are slaves to what Schumpeter called 'the Ricardian vice'. That is, in Schumpeter's words, 'the habit of establishing simple relations between aggregates that then acquire a spurious role of causal importance whereas all the really important (and, unfortunately, complicated things) are being bundled away in or behind these aggregates'.[46] Friedman's belief that the immensely complicated process of inflation is always a purely monetary phenomenon is a classical example of Ricardo's 'vice'.

But monetarism's methodological flaws do not discomfort its devotees. Its appeal to many of them is ideological. For such adherents monetarism is much more than just a theory purporting to explain and predict some economic phenomena. It provides a whole attitude to politics and economics. It tells politicians how they should act − or rather how they should not act. It provides a reinforcement of the 'invisible hand', or perhaps one should say that it provides a glimpse of the 'invisible hand', but only a glimpse, for much of monetarism remains mystical − like the 'invisible hand'. Under Professor Friedman's persuasive advocacy monetarism has become identified with aggressively right-wing Conservative attitudes to politics and economics. The free market is all, and interference with it is both self-defeating and ill-intentioned. We have returned to early nineteenth-century *laissez-faire*. No wonder, then, that the explainer and propagandist of monetarism, Mr Tim Congdon, thought that many monetarists would be happier in the nineteenth century than in the twentieth.[47] What is dangerous is their apparent belief that economies do, and Governments can, behave in the twentieth century as they did in the nineteenth. In this century the problems are complex and intractable, and the economic setting is inhospitable to simple explanations and overarching theories.

We have seen that the synthesis of *laissez-faire* capitalism and revolutionary socialism, or the means of reforming the first in order to prevent the coming of the second, was political action by Governments. Tories and others who pressed for such reforms did not do so because they wanted to wreck the free market. They did so because they thought that economic efficiency was not the only proper end of government and that certain conditions were an affront to a civilized society. They agreed with Carlyle that the 'Mammon-gospel, of supply and demand, competition, *laissez-faire*, and Devil take the hindmost [was] one of the shabbiest gospels ever preached'.[48] There was, they believed, a higher aim of government and political action; and the state had a duty to try to make life tolerable for the least well-off and to give everybody the chance to develop his ability. Britain, in the Tory view, was a great nation, not a random collection of individuals. In that nation everybody had rights and duties, and those who were especially well endowed with rights had a duty to make a free economy bearable to all. The attitude of Tory and other reformers was that 'economic man' did not exist, and that Governments should not behave as though he did. In fact, the reforms brought about by government not only improved the living conditions of the poor and falsified most of the Marxian prophecies, but they helped the economy too. For the economy, after all, like 'economic man', is an abstraction, and anything that improves the health of the people or adds to social cohesion is likely to help the economy as well as the individuals most immediately affected.

Monetarism has brought back 'economic man' and the attitude to government that went with him. Only in the market can man find fulfilment. Elsewhere lies bureaucracy, blundering politicians, inflation, frustration and ignorance. The market, therefore, should not only be improved in the economic sphere by removing or crippling such hindrances as exist in the labour market or the housing market or elsewhere; it should also be extended to other fields such as education and health.

The economy, monetarists like their nineteenth-century predecessors believe, will balance itself if left alone. Whatever appearances to the contrary, its natural state is equilibrium and full employment. 'It may well be', wrote Keynes in *The General Theory*, 'that the classical theory represents the way in which we should like our economy to behave. But to assume that it actually does so is to assume our difficulties away.'[49] That, fifty years later, is precisely what the monetarists do. Hence, to them, politicians and anybody else who presumes to interfere are trespassers and should be prosecuted. With monetarism, then, we are back in the closed economic world and the pseudo-science of the classical and neo-classical economists. Governments should do almost nothing save control the money supply. The electorate, in its untutored way, may think that it elects Governments to do more than that. But it will soon learn better. This is classical economics and *laissez-faire* politics in modern, ill-fitting dress. Economic theory is all; social conditions are naught. Everything is for the best in the best of all possible worlds provided the market and the 'invisible hand' are left undisturbed to work their beneficent magic. Dr Pangloss is once more running our affairs, though the results make it seem that it is Dr Strangelove who is in charge.

11

Economic Recovery

There is in operation...a law of the deterioration of British economic policies. Like the 'average' Russian harvest ('worse than last year's, better than next year's') every government seems to have done more damage and to have succeeded in fewer things than the preceding one.

Sidney Pollard[1]

Frequent disappointments have taught me, that nothing need be despaired of, as well as that nothing can be depended upon.

David Hume[2]

In all transactions with the Treasury I am apt to suspect something of a trick.

Edmund Burke

Both the left-wing socialist, then, and the right-wing Manchester or neo-Liberal nostrums are inappropriate. Neither of them works or will work. Socialist economies abroad and the dismal years 1974–6 show that the Labour Party's mixture of extensive socialization with a dash of syndicalism would be disastrous. The only good thing about the so-called social contract was its name. And that was misleading: it was not 'social', since only the Labour Party and the trade unions were involved; and there was no con-tract, since it was not enforceable. The social contract exacerbated inflation and was heavily one-sided. 'The only give and take in the contract', wrote Labour's Chief Secretary, Joel Barnett, 'was that the Government gave and the unions took.'[3] Yet Labour seems to have learned nothing from its period of office and merely proposes a great deal more of a much stronger mixture. Once again the country is suffering from what Lecky called 'the unintelligent conservatism of English Radicalism'.[4]

Equally, the experience of the last three years in this country and of America under President Reagan shows that the consequences of monetarism are what its opponents always expected. The minimum requirement of any cure is that it should not be worse than the disease. Monetarism fails to pass that test. The eighteenth-century eccentric, John Mytton, in an attempt to cure his hiccoughs, set fire to his own nightshirt and burned himself to death.[5] Monetarism, likewise, is a self-inflicted wound rather than a cure for the nation's ills.

The nineteenth century does not provide solutions for twentieth-century problems. Pure economic theory, too, is more likely to hinder than to help. Economic theorizing, unless it is firmly anchored to the political and social needs and realities of the time, will probably be elegant rather than pertinent. Equilibrium economics is no doubt a useful conception for the lecture room. But many economists are not content to leave it safely there. They try to transfer it from their imaginary world to the real world, where of course it is a mirage. The real world is never in equilibrium; hence it is futile to formulate theories based on the idea and dangerous to act upon them. Algebra may be all right as a servant; it is no good as a master.

Besides, economists are not in agreement. 'As only one of them can be right,' Byron wrote of another profession, 'they may most of them be wrong.'[6] It would be odd if economists did all agree. But in the present state of wide divergence of opinion among them, it is wise for Tories to be eclectic and not to tie themselves to one particular economic doctrine.

Our salvation, then, lies not in doctrine of any kind. British difficulties, or the British disease, are neither solely economic nor solely political. There is no single explanation, and there is no single cure. That is indeed what a Tory would expect. He is profoundly aware of the complexity of things and, like Burke, deeply suspicious of the simplifiers. He distrusts those who try to reduce everything to one simple cause and who, having done so, then construct on that alleged cause an all-embracing explanation and remedy.

Two things, however, are clear. We have an old-fashioned slump, and we need to climb out of it. There is severe and chronic deficiency of aggregate demand: millions of people cannot get jobs at any wage, and firms in general cannot expand their sales because people cannot buy what they have to sell.

Like others, I have challenged the Government to explain what possible driving force there could be to bring about a sustained recovery in output and employment. No substantive response to this challenge has ever been given. The only reaction from the Government has been to make the dogmatic and increasingly fanciful claim that recovery is close at hand or, sometimes, that it has already started. As Mr Harold Macmillan said at the Carlton Club in the autumn of 1982: 'Now we are told that if we tighten our belts, the depression will simply go away. Nobody knows how. We are back in the age of witch doctors who tried to make the weather by making the right kind of speeches to their constituency.'[7] These claims are based, presumably, on the metaphysical belief that the economy is self-regulating. Metaphysical and religious statements cannot normally be falsified. But the claims about economic recovery are claims about how things work in the physical world, and thus they can be, and have been, dramatically falsified.

More of the same policies will produce more of the same results. Output may not fall nor unemployment rise as fast in the future as in the past. But the trends will continue so long as the policies remain as they are.

If we are to emerge from the slump, as we must, our economic policies must be drastically changed. 'There is only one argument for doing something,' wrote F. M. Cornford; 'the rest are arguments for doing nothing. The argument for doing something is that it is the right thing to do.'[8] The reasons why it is right to reduce unemployment were given in chapter 1. Nobody can claim that the economy is working properly if there are some 3 or 4 million unemployed, and nobody can reasonably say that a problem of that dimension does not concern everybody. The practical arguments are just as compelling. To do nothing damages the economy and damages the work force. We cannot allow our society to become permanently divided between a fortunate majority who can get work and an unfortunate minority for whom the unemployment prospects remain bleak; 'if we did, we would risk the creation of a "Clockwork Orange" society with all its attendant alienation and misery.'[9] Things have already gone pretty far when for those who are leaving a comprehensive school in Birmingham work is no longer mentioned as a possible option.[10] Unemployment can be likened to fever. Although a high fever is a symptom of some other condition, it is dangerous in itself and must be reduced by various means before the underlying cause is remedied. High unemployment is thus not the only reason for changing our policies. At present we are suffering a staggering loss of real income because of them.

Moreover, continued deflation will do yet more economic damage. It will further weaken the ability of the supply side of the economy to cope with any upturn in demand and thus make the return of high inflation not less but more likely. The leaders of the construction industry, for example, are arguing simultaneously that present conditions are intolerable and that any attempt to increase its work load must be cautious because the departure from the industry of a large part of the skilled labour force and the liquidation of many specialist suppliers has created the danger, if expansion is not gradual, of an explosion of pay and costs.

Finally, the extent of deflation which has been imposed is not God-given; it is Treasury-given. And to anybody who looks at the real economy instead of at the intermediate monetarist targets that have determined policy, it has clearly been excessive.

There must therefore be expansion, and there must be special measures to reduce unemployment; which brings us to what Henry James called 'the dear little deadly question of how to do it'.

For there to be a sustained economic recovery there must be a sustained increase in real demand. This emphatically does not mean that there should immediately be a substantial and indiscriminate expansion of *domestic* demand. If unemployment is to fall at all, real GNP will almost certainly have to rise by at least 2.5 per cent per annum. If unemployment were to fall by 250,000 (1 per cent of the work force) per annum, real GNP would almost certainly have to rise by 5 or 6 per cent per annum.* Hence real output would probably have to rise by more than

---

* These figures suggest that very dubious prospectuses are on offer from other parties.

20 per cent in four years to reduce unemployment from 3 million to 2 million over the same period. Up to now the biggest increase in real output over four years we have ever had was 15 per cent between 1962 and 1966.

These magnitudes suggest that if the attempt were made to achieve the relatively modest reduction in unemployment of 250,000 per annum through the expansion of domestic demand alone, starting from a position where the exchange rate is over-valued and foreign trade performance weak, our balance of payments on current account would be in deficit to the extent of something between £10 and £20 billion within two years. If the expansion of domestic demand were maintained, the deficit would continue to grow rapidly. The conclusion is inescapable. If policy were confined to a crude reflation, even quite a moderate one, there would be a balance of payments crisis even earlier than there has been in previous reflationary episodes. Almost certainly, therefore, an actual or threatened collapse of sterling would bring the whole enterprise to a standstill within two years of its inception.

This horror story has been told to dissociate this book from any notion that a significant and sustained recovery can be achieved through the mere expansion of domestic demand. But the story can also give us some guidance to the macro-economic conditions which any recovery programme must fulfil. They are the necessary conditions for recovery but may not be sufficient.

Leaving aside for the moment the danger of greatly increased inflation, the other major potential constraint on our ability to expand is our performance in international trade. As I mentioned earlier, all the previous episodes of reflation or 'go' have foundered on an emergent balance of payments crisis, which has led in turn to restrictive measures. Apart from the fact that the expansion of aggregate demand could not be sustained, the process had damaging consequences for the growth of the supply potential of the economy as well, because of the effect on investment and because no cumulative process, or virtuous circle, had time to get established.

The necessary conditions for sustained growth can be easily stated, though this is not often done. People too often think that the balance of payments constraint is brought about by our inability to borrow enough when we have a deficit. Admittedly, the emergence of a deficit with attendant financing difficulties is usually the manifestation of an inadequate trading performance. But ultimately the remedy does not lie in making borrowing easier; it lies in ensuring that right from the start exports contribute sufficiently to demand and that domestic as opposed to foreign output contributes sufficiently to supply.

Some hypothetical figures reveal the scale and nature of the problem. If the economy grows at 3 per cent and if there is no change in import penetration and no change in the terms of trade, then exports must obviously rise in volume by 3 per cent a year as well in order to maintain external balance.

If oil is excluded from the accounts,* the ratio of imports to domestic output has risen during the last ten years by an amount corresponding to 3 per cent of imports per annum. If this trend were now to continue, our 'minimum' growth rate could be sustained only if there were a rise of 6 per cent per annum in export volume. Yet the growth of export volume over the last ten years, partly because of the world recession, has been only 3 per cent. If import penetration were to rise faster (as it well might if output rises faster than in the past), or if the terms of trade were to deteriorate (as they well might if world industrial production were to recover), then the export requirement would be correspondingly larger still.

Our foreign trade performance is thus an even more serious constraint on growth than it has been in the past, for the following reasons. First, import penetration in manufactures has already reached a critical level. Secondly, our exchange rate is over-valued. Our measured competitiveness is still considerably lower than it was in 1978 — and we were far from being competitive even then. The high exchange rate has made our foreign trade performance worse than it would otherwise have been; and it is an impediment to an adequate trade performance in the future. Thirdly, apart from the direct effect on our exports of the world recession, there is a drift towards protectionism that is occasionally

* Oil cannot indefinitely grow as fast as imported manufactures, and our oil stocks will not last for ever. The analysis of the long-term predicament should therefore be based on the non-oil account.

overt but mostly of the insidious 'non'-tariff variety. It is not as though we have just been driving in the wrong direction and can now reach our destination a bit late simply by turning round and driving back. Our vehicle is now in worse condition, and the route we now have to take has been made much more difficult.

In summary, without measures to expand aggregate demand, unemployment will go on rising indefinitely.

But clearly we must abandon any hope that recovery can be rapid. We do not know how much destruction of capital (including human capital) has occurred. This argues for extreme caution. The first thing is to persuade people to put real recovery and lower unemployment at the top of their list of priorities. The next thing will be to make it clear to them that, not counting special employment measures, it will probably take seven or eight years, not four or five years, to reduce unemployment to 2 million. Perhaps it will be possible to do better than this; certainly we should try. But swings of opinion in this area can be so violent that, instead of an over-restrictive policy, we might be faced with proposals for an impossibly quick recovery. This would be no less damaging and should be strongly opposed.

What is to be done about foreign trade? If − despite the rising tide of protectionist sentiment in the United States, Europe and elsewhere, which has inevitably been produced by the beggar-my-self and beggar-my-neighbour deflationary policies pursued by many countries − we exclude import controls and export subsidies, there are broadly only two ways in which policy can improve our performance. The first is to channel the new resources made available in a reflationary package towards investment in our export industries and away from consumption. The second is devaluation.

So far as I am aware, no country has ever done well with an over-valued exchange rate, and sterling even after its recent fall is still greatly over-valued. Admittedly, the West German Deutsch Mark rose sharply in value in the late 1960s and in the early 1970s. But that rise was a consequence of the competitiveness of West Germany's economy and the resulting chronic surplus in her balance of payments. A currency which is high because of the competitiveness of a country's economy is a very different matter from a currency which, like the pound, is high because of domestic monetary policy and North Sea oil and not because of factors related to export performance. People go on buying German machines and components because of their quality. Similarly, there is all the difference in the world between the *fact* of a currency which is high because of success in foreign trade and the *hope* that a currency which is high because of the recession will somehow bring success. Dr Emminger, the former Governor of the Bundesbank, recently said that between 1978 and 1981 sterling had suffered 'by far the most excessive over-valuation...in recent monetary history'.[11]

Nevertheless, there are a number of difficulties with devaluation. Taken over a long period, it would have to be quite large, though gradual. A large and sudden devaluation, as advocated by the Labour Party, would be damaging, as would one caused by a balance of payments crisis. If we want balanced, sustainable growth, the devaluation should precede, not follow, the expansion.

Yet given the present organization of international capital markets with floating rates and free capital movements, it is not certain that the kind of devaluation which is needed could be successfully undertaken. The value of sterling is now largely determined by the view of the operators in international capital markets of what it ought to be, not by what a British Government wants it to be for reasons of economic strategy.

If, by reducing interest rates, by persuading the 'authorities' to sell sterling on a sufficient scale, we could somehow or other get the exchange rate to fall, we would then have to face the problem of revived inflation. But the dangers of this would be small if the policy were properly executed. When devaluation is the consequence of an external deficit and excess demand at home and therefore has to be accompanied by tax increases, it is indeed highly inflationary. But if a voluntary devaluation could be achieved at a time when the pound was over-valued, when we did not have a deficit and when we also had massive spare resources, indirect taxes could be lowered to offset the rise in prices caused by the devaluation. The inflationary effects could also be abated by other measures, which will be discussed shortly.

In any event, there is a limit to what we can do, acting by ourselves, to return to full employment. International co-operation will be necessary. Our industrial, trading and financial systems are inextricably intertwined with those of the rest of the world, which is itself in recession. At present there are neither the institutions nor the will to co-ordinate policies for a balanced world recovery. But we are faced with worldwide problems and should be searching for worldwide solutions.

It would not be appropriate to go into detail here about new institutions and how precisely they might operate. The problems they would have to deal with seem pretty clear. First, we need co-ordinated reflation. There is an intrinsic difficulty associated with this proposition because countries are depressed to different degrees and must therefore work towards full employment at different rates. Yet concerted reflation would not only help participating countries to avoid balance of payments crises by providing additional export markets but would also ensure that the public expenditure increases would not require higher taxation. If a country reflates unilaterally, the additional demand which it generates will be met, in part, by imports. To the extent that this is so, the reflation will create jobs abroad rather than at home. But if reflation is concerted, the waste of national resources spent on creating employment abroad can be offset by taking advantage of the job-creating opportunities offered by the reflationary expenditure of other Governments. As a result, the amount of additional resources which any individual Government has to pump into the economy in order to achieve a given reduction in domestic unemployment is reduced.

Secondly, we need co-ordinated trade policies. This is, or ought to be, the opposite of protectionism and 'trade warfare'. However executed, the principle must be to ensure that, preferably at a high level of international trade, countries help one another to achieve balanced trade at full employment. This, after all, is precisely what GATT is all about. Besides, in order to sustain the theorem that free trade is to the general advantage, you have to assume that there is full employment everywhere. We should not just assume that completely free trade is necessarily in every case the best way of organizing international trade. If, even with correlated fiscal policies, trade imbalances occur, there are ways consistent with GATT and the IMF in which countries can adjust. And the articles of GATT are far more concerned with non-discrimination than with free trade.

Thirdly, Governments should co-ordinate exchange rates and

also exercise some control over international capital movements, which are already sources of instability and could produce a far worse international crisis.

Fourthly, to avert the risk of renewed inflation if world production recovers, as well as to protect the interests of the less developed world, we should now adopt multinational policies towards commodities. However difficult it may be to achieve, all countries would gain in the long run from stable commodity prices and supplies. An international approach to energy conservation is also necessary to avoid inflation and other disruption whenever world recovery reveals another energy shortage. Today's glut is almost certainly temporary.

But we cannot merely wait to see what international arrangements are or are not made. There has to be some expansion in Britain anyway. And whatever the extent of the British devaluation, our industrial and trade performance will improve only if the additional resources made available to the economy are used for productive investment and are not drained away into increased pay and consumption. The deeply pessimistic view that unemployment now has to remain in the millions is inconsistent with the experience of the twenty-five years after the war. And the idea that expansion necessarily leads to increased inflation is quite unfounded. Certainly, if the economy were to expand beyond the limit of capacity, the expansion would undoubtedly lead to inflation. But with over 3 million unemployed there is plainly much slack in the economy, and there is no reason why a cautious expansion should produce a growth in inflation. Indeed, reflationary packages fed into the Treasury model in late 1981 and early 1982 by various people, including myself, indicated that they would produce increased output, lower unemployment *and* lower inflation.

Equally, an increase in the money supply as a result of additional bank lending does not necessarily lead to inflation. That the monetarist contention is wrong will not startle readers of earlier chapters of this book. Nor, on the other hand, does an increase in bank lending necessarily lead to growth. Everything depends, as Harold Lever and George Edwards explained in the *Sunday Times*,[12] on what is done with the new resources. If they are directed mainly to consumption, the results will be inflationary.

If they are directed largely into productive investment, the result will be growth with much less inflationary pressure because increased demand will be matched by increased supply.

Thus between 1974 and 1977 the Japanese money supply grew by 14.7 per cent a year, much as the British did. But in Japan the great bulk of the new money went into investment and did not lead to inflation.[13] Again, when the United States entered the war, the American Government massively increased the money supply by 30 per cent in 1942 and by over 25 per cent in 1943.[14] But by means of highly interventionist techniques of state planning it ensured that the increase was used mostly to finance the capital investment needed for the war effort. As a result, huge growth rates were achieved, accompanied by only modest inflation.

Government intervention in the economy and the spending of government money are inevitable. *Laissez-faire* is not an option. Indeed, even the *laissez-faire* state, as Sir Karl Popper has written, has to decide which freedom to protect:

> the freedom of the labour market, which amounts to the freedom of the rich to oppress the poor, or the freedom of the poor to unite? Whichever decision is taken, it leads to state intervention, to the use of organized political power, of the state as well as of unions, in the field of economic conditions. It leads, under all circumstances, to an extension of the economic responsibility of the state, whether or not this responsibility is consciously accepted.[15]

In other words, there is no escape from politics. Apparent reliance on the free market offers only the illusion of such an escape. Attempted control of the money supply, say, is just as much a political act as is a tax increase or a transport subsidy.[16]

Similarly, however strongly disposed a Government may be to adopt a hands-off industry policy, it finds intervention unavoidable. Talleyrand was talking about foreign affairs, but the definition of non-intervention that he submitted to the French Academy is equally applicable to the economy: '"Non-intervention"', he wrote, 'is a mystical and diplomatic word meaning much the same thing as "intervention".'[17] The present Government was temperamentally inclined to a hands-off industry policy, but instead of running down the Industry Department's budget, as it had intended, it soon found itself spending enormous sums of money.[18]

There are three other reasons why, whatever it may say, Government has little choice but to intervene. The first is social. If a large enterprise is about to collapse, the Government has to take some sort of action. Either it has to keep the company going, or it has to lessen the possibly devastating consequences to employment of the firm's demise. British Leyland and British Steel are obvious cases in point.

The second reason is economic. If the Government does not help industry, it will place British industry at a disadvantage with its competitors. Other countries help their industries, however much in theory they may be addicted to free-market economics. Thus West Germany has been giving increasing amounts of direct aid to her industry since the Promotion of Economic Growth and Stability Act was passed in 1967.[19] Switzerland too was compelled by the difficulties of her watch industry to encourage the spread of electronics technology.

The third reason is both economic and social. If areas of the country are becoming derelict, the Government cannot simply display the inertia of a President Coolidge, merely contenting itself every now and then with an attempt to adjust the money supply. Regional policies are a necessity. The process of deindustrialization has hit a number of regions particularly hard. They cannot be left in that state, and to restore them more will have to be done than was done in the past.

In fact, the present British Government has been giving assistance for high technology and other areas. It is providing £140 million support in 1982–3 for innovation in manufacturing industry and for the promotion of awareness of the new technologies – from flexible manufacturing to computer-aided design, from information technology to bio-technology.

But the objectives of industrial policy should, as far as possible, be kept separate. 'The core of industrial policy', as Dr Grant has said, 'should be concerned with measures which are designed to enhance the efficiency and international competitiveness of the industrial economy'.[20] The more efficient British industry is, the more jobs will be created in the rest of the economy.

Yet the social consequences of industrial change and decay cannot be neglected. Those who, through no fault of their own, have become what President Roosevelt once called 'industrial cannon fodder' have to be looked after, and devastated areas have to be renewed.

There can be no unchanging rules for either the method or the extent of government intervention. Both will be determined by circumstances. The first objective of achieving the greatest possible competitiveness is unlikely to be met unless the Government at least matches what other countries are doing, and most of them do much more than is readily apparent. The extent of intervention for social reasons depends on the size of the problem, and that at present is vast. Special employment measures are vital; we shall return to them at the end of this chapter.

An example of how much can be achieved when government and the private sector work together in the national interest is agriculture, which has been one of the outstanding successes in the British economy during the post-war years. Agriculture has enjoyed high investment, increased productivity and good labour relations. And through government-organized research and a government-organized service which communicates the results of that research to the farmer, new technology has been introduced to an extent which compares favourably with almost any other sector.

The Minister for Agriculture in the present Government, Mr Peter Walker, has pursued a series of policies which entail a sensible degree of government intervention, and the result has been that agriculture has performed considerably better than the rest of the economy. Agricultural production has increased every year, and productivity has improved. The proportion of the domestic market in temperate foodstuffs obtained by British produce has increased over three years from 67 per cent to 75 per cent, resulting in an improvement of our balance of payments of £1 billion. The volume of British food exports during the same period has increased: in 1982, compared with three years ago, probably by over £600 million. At the same time the food price index has risen by only 32 per cent, while the retail price index has gone up by 50 per cent. Farmgate prices have risen by even less.

Peter Walker has consistently refused to accept public expenditure cuts proposed by the Treasury. The Treasury wished to cut capital grants substantially, to reduce agricultural research, to reduce the agricultural advisory staff and to revalue the green pound so that the exchange rate would have the same adverse effects on agriculture as it did on industry. All of these proposals were successfully resisted by Mr Walker, and in consequence agriculture has survived the recession well and is in a position to defeat foreign competition. If the rest of British industry were in a similar state, there would be no difficulty in expanding the economy.

In order to ensure that additional resources produce growth rather than inflation, the Government should do four things. First, it should do all it can to reduce industry's costs. For example, the national insurance surcharge should be abolished, and possibly industry's ordinary national insurance contributions should be reduced.

Manufacturing industry is important not only because of the employment it provides but primarily because of its capacity for expanding output. If all manufacturing industry could be run by one man in a white coat, it would be more, not less, valuable to the economy. It is the dynamic potentiality for the sale of manufactured goods as productivity increases that alone makes possible the employment of people elsewhere in the economy (in the service industries, for example). Britain cannot exist, as a museum, on tourism alone.

Secondly, the Government must ensure that its own increases in spending are devoted to capital, not current, expenditure. High unemployment naturally produces considerable increases in social security, and capital expenditure has suffered. To make sure that the right capital projects are selected, the Government should choose them only after careful consultation with the private sector. The construction industry, which has been even harder hit than most and which is less import-intensive than most, should be helped. The massive fall in public investment which took place under the last Labour Government has continued. 'There appears to have been for many years', write Buiter and Miller, 'a firm and successful bipartisan commitment to reduce investment in social overhead capital. General government capital formation was

19 per cent lower in the first quarter of 1981 than it had been a year earlier.'[21] This long-term decline in public investment has done great damage to the economy and to the national infrastructure and must be gradually remedied. Investment is one of the main components of demand, but it also increases the supply capacity of the economy.

But increased spending by the Government is only one feature of a reflation. Once additional money has been disbursed from the Exchequer, it circulates throughout the economy in ways over which the Government has no direct control. In addition, any reduction in interest rates will also cause additional financial resources to flow through the economy, and the Government has no power directly to determine the use of these resources either. Where the Government has no direct powers, it should tilt our economic system so that resources flow in the right direction.

That brings us to the third and fourth measures which the Government should take to produce recovery: the reform of our financial system and the reform of what is called free collective bargaining.

For many years the City of London was the financial centre of the world, and it has a deserved reputation for unrivalled financial expertise. Its contribution to Britain's balance of payments is vast. The net overseas earnings of 'the City' in 1981 amounted to £3.5 billion.[22] Yet the City's financial supremacy has not benefited British industry. Owing to a relative disengagement between finance and industry in this country, Britain's financial success has been accompanied by economic failure. And other countries with a far less developed financial system have done far better than we have.

The disengagement goes back a long way. From about the 1860s onwards German and American banks were becoming more directly involved with industry;[23] indeed, in those countries and in France a prime objective of the banks was the support and furtherance of industrialization. In Britain by contrast, as local banks declined and banking was increasingly centralized in the City of London, the banks became not more but less involved with industry. Goschen, whom Lord Randolph Churchill 'forgot' and who succeeded him as Chancellor of the Exchequer, wrote in 1905 that 'the centripetal force' which brought 'our home capital to the city' was exceeded by 'the centrifugal force' which 'scattered' that capital all over the world instead of allowing it to be used at home.[24] The concentration of banking in London helped the City to secure its dominant international position in trade and finance. But, as Professor Glyn Davies has pointed out, industry was doubly hit. Local banks had been 'dependent on the locality for their success. No longer was this the case.' And the new banking structure was 'more appropriate to international lenders and less appropriate to local industrial lending'.[25]

In the inter-war years, as we have seen, Keynes condemned 'the flight of capital' abroad, and he thought that banks and bankers were 'by nature blind'.[26] Certainly, the banks, so far as British industry was concerned, were highly inactive,[27] and industrialists felt that they were not getting the help which their competitors abroad were receiving and that the British banks were wedded to obsolete patterns of investment.[28] In his last book, published just after his death in 1982, Lord Butler suggested that in the 1930s the City seemed 'remote from, and uninterested in, the problems of industry', which, he added, had 'a familiar ring at the moment'.[29]

Since the war British industry has suffered from a persistent shortage of investment. There has been the paradox that internationally Britain has probably had the best financial system in the world, while nationally the system has been gravely defective.

The debate about the role of the banks has been distorted by Labour's threat to nationalize them. The Wilson Committee, which was set up to review the functioning of financial institutions, reported in July 1980. Sir Harold Wilson recently explained the origin of his committee: 'After the collapse of the secondary banks and the property boom and subsequent crash there was great pressure from within the party to nationalize the banks and city institutions...and James Callaghan...decided to head off the pressure by setting up a committee....'[30] In view of its origin, the conclusion of the majority of the committee that there was 'no evidence of any general shortage of finance for industry at prevailing rates of interest and of levels of demand, and with present perceptions of the risks involved in real investment'[31] was scarcely surprising. But the committee made two qualifications. It stressed that it was not saying that the current cost of capital was acceptable; and it concluded that although there was no general shortage of finance, there was a lot of evidence of unsatisfied demand for long-term finance and that the difficulty of obtaining it was a considerable deterrent to long-term investment projects. It is no use the banks being ready to lend to industry if the terms they demand for the granting of loans are such that industry cannot afford to meet them.

It is less the availability of finance which is important than its cost. The fault has been that while other countries have had a policy of how savings should be used, Britain has not. Other countries have decided in favour of investment in industry; Britain has not. Decisions have been left to 'the market'. At the same time the market has been distorted by the giving of tax advantages to pension funds, to house buyers and to the purchasers of government stocks. In consequence, far too much of Britain's savings has gone to finance consumption and far too little to finance investment. The result has been lower growth and higher inflation than our competitors have experienced.

Thus only about half of British bank lending goes to industry, while in France, for example, the proportion is three-quarters.[32] In Germany and Japan the proportion going to industry is even higher. This misallocation of resources in Britain is explained partly by the reluctance of British banks to grant long-term loans to industry. British banks are perfectly willing to lend to companies but, compared with French, German and Japanese banks, they tend to insist on relatively short repayment periods. This inhibits British companies from borrowing for investment because repayment puts a severe strain on their cash flow. Indeed, 'a lengthening in the term of the loan usually reduces the repayment rates more significantly than a change in interest rate.'[33] In 1982 Mr George Edwards calculated that the average annual cash flow costs of loans in the UK — that is to say, the amount a company has to pay each year in principal and interest — was 38 per cent of the loan compared with 23 per cent in Germany and 7 per cent in Japan.*

* The clearing banks have claimed in reply that 'there is very little difference in total lending figures between France, Germany and the UK.' But this conclusion can be reached only by adding in the lending by the National Loans Fund to the nationalized industries, which is of doubtful relevance to an argument which concerns bank lending to private industry.

Clearly, the banks should lend for longer terms — as, indeed, they are beginning to do.

Meanwhile the best way to redress the disadvantage suffered by British industry would be to adopt the suggestion of the committee set up by Mr Michael Grylls, MP. This was that instead of paying to the banks the whole of the interest payable on their loans and then receiving corporation tax relief on those payments at a later date, industrial companies should be allowed to pay their interest to the banks net of corporation tax, and then the interest so paid would not rank as eligible for tax relief. The effect of the 'Grylls proposal' would be effectively to halve the immediate cost to industry of interest payments.

However, more needs to be done if Britain's industrial decline is to be reversed and if the resources and the expertise of the City are properly to be exploited to strengthen our industry. No Tory wants to substitute the judgement of civil servants or politicians as to the viability of investment projects for that of bankers and other professionals. Therefore the banks and the other financial institutions should be encouraged to be involved more directly in British industry. Indeed, as the financial relationship between the banks and industry became closer, a greater involvement on the part of the banks would inevitably follow. They would be anxious to ensure that their investments were successful.

It is even more important to increase the proportion of lending which goes to investment. This could best be done without great bureaucratic interference by imposing, as George Edwards and Harold Lever suggested,[34] a ceiling on total bank lending. As they pointed out, 'we already have an implicit ceiling.' But within the overall ceiling there would be a distinction between lending for investment and lending for consumption, and the one would be related to the other. The banks' access to profitable consumption credit business would be made dependent on their success in lending to industry by means of the introduction of a fixed ratio between the ceilings for both kinds of lending. In other words, in order to win opportunities for additional consumer lending, the banks would first have to find ways of lending more to companies.

This seems an excellent blend of government guidance and free enterprise and incentives. The banking and financial systems should so operate as to promote the national interest. Their prosperity should not be separated from that of the rest of the economy. The forces of the market, even when they are not distorted, do not necessarily lead the financial system towards the best possible furtherance of the public good. Therefore there has to be guidance from the state. But within that guidance the banks and the institutions should be left to run their own affairs. They know how to do that better than anybody else.

Yet if expansion is to result in increased production and not renewed inflation, it is not only the financial system that will need reform. Every Government since the war has been plagued by two intractable problems: low productivity and inflationary wage claims by trade unions. They have not been our only problems, however, and they are not independent of other considerations. In economics everything is connected with everything else, and much the same is true of politics. Low investment, for example, has contributed to low productivity, which in turn has contributed to low investment. And both have made wage claims much more inflationary than they would otherwise have been. Until the mid-1960s the claims by British unions were not larger than those made by unions elsewhere. But productivity, and hence growth, were much lower. And in the 1970s, as Treasury Ministers rightly point out, we paid ourselves some 300 per cent more for an increase in output of about 15 per cent.

Unfortunately, nothing has been done under this Government to improve the way in which wage bargains are made. Monetarism is supposed to make worries about wage bargaining unnecessary. The pure monetarist doctrine is that inflation cannot be influenced by trade unions or indirect taxes. Certainly, there has been a welcome decline in the size of wage settlements, because the unions have been greatly weakened by mass unemployment. But what is supposed to happen when unemployment declines? Union militancy has not quite disappeared even with the present level of unemployment, and it is surely likely to increase if more people are working. Presumably, the adapted theory is that the unions will have been chastened by the events of the last few years and will, therefore, decide to be co-operative. In doing so, they will be influenced by the improvements in trade-union law which have been made and will be made over the next few years. Obviously, this is possible. A moderate trade-union leadership

might emerge, and it might be supported by a rank and file intent
above all on keeping what they might well regard as fairly pre-
carious jobs. The trade-union leadership remained moderate from
1945 to 1957 (and to a lesser extent until the late 1960s) at least
partly because Governments of both parties consulted the unions
and passed legislation that took account of their views. This
moderation was only partly induced by memories of the 1920s
and 1930s — and those hard memories probably had more bad
consequences than good.

But even in the 1930s wages started to rise again once unemployment had stopped rising, and they continued to rise even
though unemployment remained high.[35] If employment revives,
therefore, the trade unions are unlikely to behave like poodles
of monetarism. There will be much pent-up bitterness among the
rank and file as well as among the leaders, and revenge will probably be taken. Much of management will be tougher than in the
past, and trade-union law will be less biased in favour of the
unions, but British industrial relations will probably worsen.
Inflationary wage claims will succeed each other, and we shall
be back where we were, except that Britain's industrial capacity
will have shrunk considerably in the meantime, and Britain will
have fallen even further behind her competitors.

This may well happen in any case, even if mass unemployment
continues at more or less the present level. It is not at all certain
that in the long run stringent fiscal and monetary policies would
continue to be successful in dealing with inflation. Indeed, Mr
Tylecote has vigorously argued that unemployment is likely to
reduce inflation in the short term and raise it in the long term.[36]

Either way, therefore, monetarism does not seem to be a
satisfactory solution to the pay problem. If unemployment stays
up, the remedy will have proved, yet again, to be worse than
the disease. If it comes down, inflation will probably move up
again. In either event there will be a legacy of bitterness and an
inheritance of industrial strife. Finally, as was seen earlier, the
Government has not been able to rely solely on monetarism. It
has interfered arbitrarily in the wage-bargaining process in the
public sector.

There is no purely economic solution to the wages problem that
is tolerable. The only one that might work would be constantly

rising unemployment, which would be disastrous. Under all other conditions the unions are able to bid up wages far beyond the growth of productivity. That has always been the result of so-called free collective bargaining, which Mr Callaghan once called 'free collective vandalism'. In any case, the large public sector means that the Government cannot avoid taking a view of what the employees there should be paid.

Hence all recent Governments, despite their previous protestations when in opposition that they would never resort to such an unspeakable device, have sooner or later adopted an incomes policy of one kind or another. And indeed nearly all democratic Governments abroad, though their 'free collective bargaining' has usually worked better than ours, also have arrangements which seek to reduce the level of wage claims. So whether we call it like Mr Patten 'the reform of pay bargaining',[37] or like Mr Waldegrave 'incomes leadership',[38] or like Sir Geoffrey Howe when in Opposition 'a policy for incomes', or like Professor Meade 'wage-fixing',[39] we shall need an incomes policy. Keynes saw during the war that the problem of collective bargaining under full employment was a political and not an economic one. We are a long way from full employment, but we are still faced with a political, not an economic, problem.

There are, broadly, three objections to incomes policies. The first is that they constitute intolerable interference with market forces. This need not detain us. A Tory should have no objection to interfering with market forces. And anyway, even in the absence of an incomes policy, large companies and unions interfere with market forces.

The second objection, put forward by Professor Hayek, Professor Usher and others, is that an incomes policy is incompatible with the maintenance of a free society. Hayek has argued that such policies are necessarily arbitrary and contrary to the rule of law and will lead to an authoritarian state.[40] Professor Usher believes that a democratic Government cannot decide incomes 'without at the same time destroying the consensus required for the preservation [of democracy]'.[41] Undeniably, there is a connection between economic liberty and political liberty. If all economic power lies in the state, there will be no political liberty. And if a Government imposed an incomes policy which purported by permanent rigid control to determine precisely the incomes of everybody in the country, that would almost certainly be the end of democracy. We can thus travel that part of the way with Professors Hayek and Usher but, in my view, no further.

Political liberty does not depend upon the existence of the degree of economic liberty advocated by Professor Hayek. Indeed, as we saw earlier, political liberty was preserved by abandoning full economic liberalism. The idea that democracy can be preserved only through adherence to minimum government is false. Of course, in a democracy it is vital that not all matters fall within the political sphere. But if an issue is already in the political sphere, nothing is gained by pretending that it is not, or by claiming that political liberty will be ended by its being treated as a political matter. Incomes policy, after all, has been in the political arena for more than a quarter of a century. There is no fixed frontier for the activities of the state. The arbitrary limits of the liberal state in the nineteenth century were burst long ago, and a Tory, at least, believes that the economic system has continually to be modified to make it acceptable to the majority of the population. Finally, higher unemployment and/or inflation is surely a far bigger threat to the maintenance of democratic government than an incomes policy, and those are the alternatives.

The third argument is that incomes policies do not work. Certainly they have always broken down after a comparatively short time. Equally, they have been imposed only in times of crisis, when the system of free collective bargaining was producing unacceptable results, and they have usually been irresponsibly opposed by the Opposition of the day — the Conservative Opposition of 1974—9 was an honourable exception — whatever its practice when last in power. Britain's decentralized system of pay bargaining and the diffusion of power within the unions makes an incomes policy both more necessary than in most other countries and, at the same time, less likely to be successful. But the conclusion should not be that we should never try to have an incomes policy again. That is not feasible. Every recent Government, as we have seen, has had some kind of incomes policy. The conclusion should be that we should try to avoid the mistakes of the past and go on trying. After all, the argument for an incomes policy is that there is no alternative. Even the alternative of mass unemployment does not avert the necessity of an incomes policy.

The object of an incomes policy or of improving the system of pay bargaining is to persuade people to behave responsibly in their own interests. While each group of workers may have an interest in pushing up its own wages, higher wages all round mean higher prices all round, and nobody is better off. On the other hand, if a group of workers is the only one not to push up its own wages, it will plainly be worse off. Hence it is not necessarily in a group's interest to behave responsibly unless it knows that other people are also going to behave responsibly.

A nineteenth-century Italian village was regularly flooded by the river Ticino because the peasants would not join together to build an embankment high up the valley. Instead, each proprietor built 'a bit of low embankment' round his own field. So whenever the Ticino rose high, it swept away all the embankments and flooded everybody's fields.[42] The aim of an incomes policy is to build an embankment which helps everybody by preventing each from being flooded as a result of the actions of other people.

The first need, then, is to provide information. The Government has to outline the economic prospects, indicate what its fiscal and monetary proposals are and set out the implications for wages and prices. But if that is all the Government does, it will not affect behaviour except by creating high unemployment. If the Government wishes to affect behaviour, it must consult both sides of industry. That is the second need. Otherwise everybody will go his own way. And if those consultations are going to lead to any result, they must be genuine. In other words, the Government must pay attention to the views of those whom it is consulting. That is the third need. Of course, there are other factors, such as the nature of the Government's economic and social policies, the degree of union militancy and the nature of the country's institutions, which will determine whether the incomes policy has any effect. That is why an incomes policy, except under conditions of high unemployment, is a political matter. In a crisis a compulsory freeze may be necessary; otherwise the law should be kept out.

Recently some interesting ideas have been advanced about the form an incomes policy should take. Professor Layard has put forward proposals for taxing employers who give their workers more than the norm.[43] Sir Henry Phelps Brown, using the

Australian precedent, has suggested a 'national award' to every worker, the amount of which would be decided by an independent commission. After that there would be arbitration if employer and workers did not agree, and if that was not accepted, there would be no limitation on striking.[44] And Professor Meade has proposed 'not quite compulsory arbitration', when the arbitral body would make its award according to whether the management's or the workers' case was more likely to promote increased employment.[45] I would not rule out these proposals.

But in introducing an incomes policy the important thing is to get the principles right. It should not be produced at a time of crisis, and arrangements should be made and announced in advance to ensure that no workers will suffer by the timing of its introduction. In the past, too much has depended on the date of a policy's introduction, and its efficacy has been undermined by the sense of unfairness that has resulted from the fact that some groups of workers have just slipped through by an accident of timing while others have not.

An incomes policy should not be used, either deliberately or inadvertently, to interfere with differentials. People have a strong sense of fairness and of custom,* and if an incomes policy alters differentials, it will not last long; moreover, when it has been wrecked, the differentials will be restored.

The public and private sectors work under different conditions, and therefore different arrangements have to be made for them. But the exclusion of the private sector will ensure that the public sector will break the policy. Similarly, there should be no discrimination against the weak groups in the public sector. Despite Professor Meade's strong advocacy, an incomes policy should not be used to allocate labour 'appropriately' to different industries: 'Growth industries have been able to expand their employment without offering above average increases in earnings.'[47] Similarly, an incomes policy should not be used to redistribute income. If such an attempt is made, the policy will break down. Redistribution is the function of the tax system, not of an incomes policy.

Finally, an incomes policy should not be used on its own. It

---

* Differentials were broadly the same in 1960 as in 1913.[46]

should be used in conjunction with the appropriate fiscal and monetary policies.

The three general principles therefore are, first, that an incomes policy should be seen to be fair or at least not demonstrably unfair; secondly, that an incomes policy is about the control of inflation and not about the distribution of income or anything else; and, thirdly, that it should not be used by itself — an incomes policy is a fragile thing, and if other functions are given to it, or if it is not supported by other instruments of policy, it will not be able to stand the strain.

However, there is going to be high unemployment for some time. The important principle here is that the unemployed are part of society. And they may not remain part of society if the rest of us think that our obligations to them are met merely by paying them the lowest possible level of unemployment benefit. Or, to put it another way, it is indefensible to talk about the house-wife's budget and then treat the unemployed as though they were not part of the family. Yet that is what has happened. In the USA the third generation of blacks is now out of work, with all the inevitable consequences of poverty, crime and alienation from society. There must be a bridge between the unemployed and the rest of the country. Those whom Byron once described as guilty of 'the capital crime of poverty' have to be helped. And the best way of helping them is to provide as many as possible of them with jobs. There is also the compelling argument of common sense: it is much more sensible to pay people for working than for not working. And since a cautious expansion of the economy will not greatly reduce unemployment for a number of years, there must be a variety of special employment measures.

A number of proposals for reducing unemployment have been put forward. In 1981 Professor Layard made two suggestions.[48] These are, first, that employers should receive a weekly subsidy of £70 for employing anybody who has been unemployed for more than six months. This measure would last for one year, and each worker would be paid the full rate for the job. (Obviously, work forces would have to be monitored to see that those taken on under this scheme were additional and not substitutes for those already employed.) This should create some 250,000 jobs at the cost of £500 million.

In addition, any worker who has been unemployed for more than six months should have the right to be employed on a publicly supported project at a wage that is 20 per cent higher than his benefit entitlement. Housing renovation is one area where this scheme would have great attractions, as is the Community Programme. This also would cost about £2,000 a job, and probably about 250,000 would take advantage of the scheme.

The House of Lords Select Committee on Unemployment does not favour the Layard proposals, but it is its 'firm view' that the Government 'must positively assist the creation of jobs'. It believes that this can be done 'without fuelling inflation'.[49] The Committee put forward a variety of proposals, including the long-term creation of 100,000 jobs in the voluntary sector and of 300,000 jobs in the public sector (which includes contracting to the private sector) and of 90,000 jobs by investment-led creation. In total the Committee estimates that its proposals would have a net Exchequer cost building up to about £1.95 billion per year, though '[since that] figure takes no account of either savings or the social costs of unemployment or the value of work done through new jobs, the cost should in fact be considerably lower than this.' The Committee believes that its proposals would lead to a reduction in unemployment of approximately 1 million over two to three years.[50]

Various suggestions for work sharing have been made by the Government and other bodies. These are useful provided, of course, they do not lead to a loss of efficiency. An imaginative scheme has been put forward by a former industrialist, Mr Leonard Stone, in an unpublished paper 'Is Unemployment Inevitable?'. After pointing out that disillusion will soon set in unless training can be seen to be leading to reliable employment, Mr Stone suggests that 'firms with more than a hundred employees should volunteer to reduce their working month from twenty to nineteen days and take on sufficient additional workers to permit the business to continue with its normal twenty-day routine.' This would amount to 5 per cent more people being employed; and the additional 5 per cent on wage costs would be met partly by the employer's debiting the Department of Health and Social Security with what the additional workers had been receiving in benefit. The employer would have to pay the rest, although it is not impossible, adds Mr Stone 'that a small...contribution might be made by other workers who would benefit by an additional twelve free days a year' and who would be aware that they were 'participating in a real effort to solve the most pressing of today's problems'. Finally Mr Stone emphasizes that such arrangements would have to be voluntary.

One method of reducing unemployment is to allow or encourage people to retire early. This should be used with great care or not at all. Sickness and ill health often influence the decision to accept early retirement, and these are often associated with financial problems. 'This suggests', says a recent Government study, 'that workers are generally forced into early retirement and not that they opt for it voluntarily'.[51] As Professor Sinfield points out, 'the danger for the older workers unemployed for five or ten years, and for the early retired is that these people will be entering a stage of greater poverty in their sixties rather than later.'[52] In other words, we shall be creating more poverty among old people.

Exactly which mix of policies should be adopted is a matter for argument. Britain's long-term recovery must not be hampered. That means that nothing must be allowed to reduce competitiveness. But, subject to that qualification, everything possible should be done to reduce unemployment. The political, social and economic arguments for doing so are all overwhelming. The only arguments against are 'foggy' ones connected with discredited economic dogma. But if there is mass unemployment for any length of time, plainly the alleged self-equilibrating forces in the economy have gone to sleep or gone abroad. Monetarists are then, presumably, reduced to arguing that mass unemployment is all the fault of the unions, who are keeping the so-called natural rate of unemployment, if the phrase may be forgiven, unnaturally high.

That these methods of reducing unemployment are artificial or 'unnatural' is of no consequence. 'Natural' and 'unnatural' are words best avoided in politics and particularly in economics. The word 'natural' is usually used when the writer happens to approve of what is being done and the word 'unnatural' when he happens to disapprove. Ruskin derided Ricardo for talking about the 'natural price of labour' as 'that which will maintain the labourer'. 'Maintain him!' exclaimed Ruskin, 'yes but how?...Will you arrange their maintenance so as to kill them early...or so as to enable them to live out a natural life?' Again, Ruskin pointed out that land which would support only ten idle and ignorant people would support thirty industrious and intelligent ones. 'Which of these', he asked, 'is their natural state, and to which of them belongs the natural rate of wages?'[53]

There is nothing especially natural about well over 3 million unemployed, and nothing especially artificial in taking steps to reduce that number. So-called market forces are no more 'natural' than the efforts of human beings to improve the human lot. 'Art', as Burke said, 'is man's nature.'[54] Finally, deflation is no more 'natural' than reflation.

Anyway, unemployment is not going to reduce itself by some mystical process. Indeed, it shows every sign of continuing to increase by a process which is all too obvious. *Laissez-faire* is an especially inappropriate attitude to unemployment. The state is responsible for its citizens, and it has a duty to act.

12

Political Recovery

Nothing in progression can rest on its original plan. We may as well think of rocking a grown man in the cradle of an infant.

Edmund Burke[1]

Wise venturing is the most commendable part of human prudence. It is the upper storey of prudence, whereas perpetual caution is a kind of underground wisdom that doth not care to see the light.

Halifax[2]

A 'consensus', that is to say a policy which accorded with the general views of intelligent but not very far-sighted men of affairs and with the material advantage of the politically effective spiritual and economic interests of the country.

Robert Blake[3]

Economic policy is only an element of politics, and it should not be considered in isolation. No economic creed, even if it is by chance more or less suitable for the circumstances of the time, can eliminate the need for the exercise of the political arts. In governing a country there are no automatic pilots. There is no substitute for politics.

For years in this country the quality of the political dialogue has been declining in step with the performance of the economy. An improvement in one would probably lead to an improvement in the other. There are internal and international constraints on all Governments, and these tend to be underestimated by politicians in Opposition. In consequence, they raise hopes of what they would be able to achieve if only they were elected: once in power, the constraints they have been ignoring ensure that those hopes are dashed. This breeds cynicism. Our troubles are both political and economic. Had our economic performance been considerably better, we would probably have muddled through with our old political arrangements. Equally, had our political institutions been more fitted to post-war conditions, the economy would probably have grown faster. Be that as it may, we now need both political and economic change if Britain is to survive as a free and reasonably prosperous country.

There will be no sustained economic recovery without a political recovery too. The relative British economic failure since the war cannot be laid merely at the door of businessmen and trade unionists. Successive Governments have sought and gained the votes of the electorate with promises to do one thing, improve another or abolish a third. But whether they have carried out these promises or not, the British economic performance has not improved; rather, it has deteriorated. Hence the judgement of Professor Sidney Pollard printed at the head of the previous chapter. Politicians, too, have been culpable. Indeed, many would lay the chief blame upon them.

But it is unlikely that the political element in our economic failure has been due solely to the inadequacy of our politicians. We have had inadequate politicians before, and there is little reason to believe that, taken as a whole, the post-war batch has been worse than that of previous eras. Arguably, indeed, it has been better. More probable explanations for our political failure are either that the problems the country has faced have been more difficult than in the past or that our political and constitutional arrangements have been out of tune with the times. Of course, if our political arrangements have been at fault, that does not shift the blame from our politicians; if the system needed alteration, it was their responsibility to alter it. But the inadequacy of our political arrangements provides a more hopeful hypothesis than the mere inadequacy of our politicians, since it is almost certainly easier to improve the quality of our system of government than to improve the quality of our politicians.

The constitution, or the politicians, used to have a talent for gradual, almost imperceptible, innovation. 'In politics, as in everything else,' Derby said when Prime Minister in 1858, 'the same course must be pursued — constant progress...adapting our institutions to the altered purposes they are intended to serve, and by judicious changes meeting the demands of society....'[4] And indeed that capacity for adaptation continued for many years after Derby spoke.

The British political system weathered the storms of the First World War, the greatly enhanced power of the trade-union movement, the rise of the Labour Party, the country's diminished economic and international standing and the Great Depression astonishingly well. The chief constitutional problem was that British institutions had evolved during a period when individualism, modified *laissez-faire* and small government were the key features of the economic and political systems. They were not designed to deal with large concentrations of what are now called corporate power or with the greatly enhanced functions of the state.

Lloyd George, Baldwin and MacDonald dealt with this new situation in different styles but with great skill. Beatrice Webb scoffed that in the First War Lloyd George handed each government Department over to the relevant interest to run. 'In that way,' she wrote, 'our little Welsh Attorney thinks, you combine the least political opposition with the maximum of technical knowledge.'[5] Lloyd George himself was clear that government could not be carried on during war or peace 'without...the co-operation of Labour'.[6] His successors came to the same conclusion. There was thus introduced into the governance of the country what Mr Keith Middlemas has called 'corporate bias'. The 'triangle between government, employers and unions was not a system...but a tendency or bias central to the evolution of modern government'.[7]

The political leaders realized that they had to deal directly with both sides of industry and that Parliament alone could not settle the industrial affairs of the nation. Similarly, the trade-union leaders recognized that they had great power but preferred to use it in conjunction with the political leaders of the state rather than in conflict with them. Even on the occasion when the relationship most obviously broke down — the General Strike — the TUC leaders were distinctly unhappy in their new militant role and called off the strike at the first opportunity. This 'corporate bias' did not become explicit.* Parliament's place at the heart of the constitution was not disturbed, but Parliament was bypassed. It still seemed the centre of decisions, and it enjoyed more prestige and attracted more attention than the bypass. But the heavy traffic went round it, not to it.

Regrettably, the new state of affairs was not institutionalized. It could have been. But when Citrine, the remarkably accommodating Secretary of the TUC, suggested to Neville Chamberlain in 1937 that he set up a Council of State on which trade-union leaders would serve, Chamberlain ruled it out as a 'dangerous innovation'.[8] Yet Chamberlain's constitutional prudery did not alter the facts. The Chairman of the Conservative Party in the following year admitted that 'we cannot defend the nation against the will of the unions....it is part of the price we have to pay for this alleged democracy.'[9]

By the end of the war, Mr Middlemas believes, 'a new order' had been established. What he calls 'the governing institutions', which were the bodies representing business and labour interests, had become 'part of the extended state', and this 'corporate bias had replaced, for all practical purposes, classical democratic theory as that had been understood in 1911'.[10] Despite this, in the post-war period there were few constitutional innovations, dangerous or otherwise, even though social, industrial, economic and political change made them even more necessary than they had been in 1937. As a result of the war and of Ernest Bevin's dominating role at the Ministry of Labour, the trade unions were far more influential and powerful than they had been before it. British industry became steadily more concentrated. And the 'Keynesian revolution' placed far greater responsibilities on Governments for guiding the economy and maintaining full employment than they had accepted before.

Yet British political and constitutional theory largely ignored this new complex reality in much the same way as did a large

---

* Mr Middlemas has made a considerable contribution to knowledge. But his phrase 'corporate bias' is surely misleading. There was no 'corporate bias' on the part of politicians or anyone else. There was a corporate phenomenon, which the political leaders could not ignore and to which they had to react. All the same, Mr Middlemas's phrase has entered the language and cannot be avoided.

part of economic theory. Before the important changes to the Committee system of the House of Commons introduced by Mr Norman St John-Stevas and the present Government, almost the o only major innovation since the war was the setting up of the National Economic Development Council (NEDC) in 1961. 'The practice and knowledge of the world', said Burke, 'will not suffer us to be ignorant that the constitution on paper is one thing, and in fact and experience is another.'[11] But after 1945 the politicians, unlike those in other countries who were making changes, seemingly lost the ability to bring the constitution on paper more into line with the constitution in fact. Parliamentary democracy was presumed to function as it had done in the days when unions were not powerful, most firms were not large and the Government did not intervene in the economy. Indeed, British constitutional theory was the counterpart of *laissez-faire* theory, with which it had grown up.

Neither the contemporary theory of *laissez-faire* nor the theory of British parliamentary democracy properly accommodates powerful corporations. Both tend to assume them away because they did not exist when the theories were formulated. But as they are in fact very much with us and show no signs of going away, it is worth trying to define what is meant by corporations and corporatism. Corporate forces are both sides of industry and all the other interests in society.

> Faced with the prospect of increasingly ungovernable societies, and with the ultimate threat of national disintegration [Professor Ionescu has written], the representative Governments relinquish their positions as unique national policy makers and seek 'partnerships' or 'contracts' with each of those corporate forces in modern society without which that society would cease to function.[12]

There is a long and reputable corporatist tradition in this country. But corporatism today is something of a dirty word because of its associations with Italian and Spanish Fascism. The philosopher of Fascism, Giovanni Gentile, claimed that 'in the corporative system the Italian genius was once again leading the world for the first time since the Renaissance', and Mussolini made equally high claims for it. 'The Fascist state', he announced, 'is

corporative or it is nothing.'[13] The answer seems to have been
that it was nothing. For although Mussolini talked much about
the corporative system, he did virtually nothing to make it effective. It did not become properly organized until 1936, by which
time there were twenty-two corporations. But 'whether they
performed any genuine function, which had not been done before'
is, in the view of Mr Mack Smith, 'still a mystery'.[14] The so-called
representatives of the workers were not elected but appointed
from above, and in reality the system was designed to keep the
workers quiet, while leaving the employers a free hand. According
to the Italian communist historian, Giuliano Procacci, the corporations were 'the means by which the major monopolistic groups
…managed to silence every remnant of working-class protest and
demands, and to put pressure on the state to strengthen their
position'.[15]

Unlike Mussolini, Franco was not an enthusiastic corporatist,
but the results in Spain were much the same as they were in Italy.
The *sindicatos* were the means by which the workers were placed
under the control of the Government,[16] while the large employers
were usually able to bypass them and to deal directly with government departments. As well as controlling the workers, corporatism
was a useful propaganda device in both Italy and Spain. It implied
to the unwary that the Mussolini and Franco regimes embodied
some principle of political philosophy that provided an alternative
to democracy. But of course it provided nothing of the sort.
'Organic democracy' was in both countries merely a propaganda
fraud. Neither of them was any more corporate than they were
democratic.

Mr Tony Benn, whose usage of the word is mysterious, even
believes that Stalin's Russia was corporatist.[17] Maybe he thinks
that the corporations were the Communist Party, the Army and
the secret police.

In fact, of course, since corporatism implies a partnership
between the state and the corporate forces or interest groups, a
dictatorship cannot be corporatist. Indeed, writes Ionescu, 'it
is not the state which should be described as corporate but
society…. The more society tends to be corporate, the less authoritative and powerful is the state.'[18]

Hence for authoritarians of the left and the right, interest groups are anathema. They believe that they themselves embody the public interest, and therefore interest groups can only distort that interest and thwart the wishes of the ruler. Thus Hobbes complained that corporations in the state were 'worms in the body politic'.[19] And Rousseau believed that, if 'the general will' was to be truly expressed, it was 'essential that there be no subsidiary groups within the state....'[20] The Abbé Sieyès followed Rousseau in repudiating pluralism and maintained that 'corporate interest' led to 'conspiracy and collusion'; therefore social order inflexibly required that 'no citizens must be allowed to organize themselves in guilds.'[21]

Conservatives are on the other side. They are aware of the corporatist tradition in England. The historian Maitland thought it 'only a little too definite to say' that the members of the medieval House of Commons 'represented corporations aggregate'.[22] Burke regarded 'the ancient corporations of the kingdom' as some of the buttresses of English freedom. 'The perennial existence of bodies corporate and their fortunes', he wrote in 1790, 'are particularly suited to a man who has long views', but the French had rashly destroyed them.[23] Like Burke, Disraeli was something of a corporatist. It was our 'great national institutions', he wrote, that made us a nation. Among these were 'our universities, our great municipal and commercial Corporations, our Magistracy, and its dependent scheme of provincial polity', and without them 'the inhabitants of England, instead of being a nation, would present only a mass of individuals governed by a metropolis, whence an arbitrary senate would issue the stern decrees of its harsh and heartless despotism.'[24]

The Liberal Acton took much the same view. The strength of local corporations, the many religious sects, the landed and the commercial interests and the great number of voluntary groups were buffers between the individual and the state. Liberty implied diversity, and diversity implied groups.[25]

To return to the Conservatives, L. S. Amery thought in 1947 that 'our geographico-arithmetical constituencies' had largely 'lost their justification as the basis of a representative system', and he advocated a new Reform Act, which would create a 'separate House of Industry' or 'Sub-Parliament'. 'The new principle of functional representation' could thus be tried, 'without destroying the existing geographical principle'.[26]

Earlier, in 1930, Winston Churchill, after wondering 'whether institutions based on adult suffrage could possibly arrive at the right decision upon the intricate propositions of modern business and finance', suggested an 'Economic Sub-Parliament, debating day after day with fearless detachment from public opinion... without caring a halfpenny who won the general election'.[27] The Economic Council recommended by Harold Macmillan in 1938 would have been 'the keystone of the structure of a planned economy'.[28] So Churchill, Macmillan, Amery and Citrine were all thinking along much the same lines.

Notwithstanding this distinguished ancestry, corporatism is also suspect today because the power of big industry and of the trade unions is resented. But this power is simply a product of the fact that if either capital or labour goes on strike, the economy slows down or comes to a stop. Industrialists may refuse to co-operate and to invest because the unions strike too much or will not use the new investment properly. The unions may refuse to co-operate because there has been inadequate investment and their members suffer as a result. Either way the public usually suffers too.

Let us start with the unions. The trade unions' part in helping to prove Marx wrong was largely unintentional. It was none the less beneficial for that. Outside Britain, after all, many of the trade-union leaders in the late nineteenth and early twentieth century were Marxists. Nevertheless, the role that the trade unions played in shoring up the capitalist system was, from the point of view of trade unions as opposed to that of their leaders, highly sensible even if it ran contrary to their avowed aims. The reason, of course, is that however opposed trade unionism may be to capitalism, trade unions can exist only in a free democratic society. Poland has most recently demonstrated that truth. In a socialist society unions immediately become part of the apparatus of the state, or they are a threat to it. Trade unions in the Soviet Union are merely what Lenin at the Tenth Congress called 'transmission belts', and there is therefore nothing particularly surprising in a former luminary of the secret police becoming their head. Next time it may be a former ambassador or a retired general. They are all employees of the state, and in this sense, if in no other, the division of labour in Russia has been abolished, as in the Marxian myth.

Free trade unions, then, can exist only in free societies. The withering away of the state under socialism is a Marxist dream; the withering away of free trade unions under socialism is a Marxist fact. And in seeking to end free enterprise and to substitute full socialism, Marxist trade-union leaders in this country share the predicament of bees: if they succeeded in stinging, they would themselves be killed. The analogy is inexact, of course, as while their organizations would effectively be abolished, they themselves would prosper as ambassadors, generals or even policemen.

The leftward trend among some trade-union leaders coincided with economic decline and the deterioration of trade-union behaviour. The latter was not all the fault of the unions. The inadequacies of Governments and of businessmen have spurred on, or at least have connived at, trade unionism's destructive conduct. Nevertheless, the unions here have behaved more obtusely than unions in other countries. Furthermore, in doing so the unions have not even enjoyed the support of their own members. All the surveys show that most trade unionists themselves deplore union behaviour and that the great majority of them believe that the unions have too much power – or at least that other unions do.

Yet the unpopularity of the unions among their own members demonstrates a political and industrial failure. In an ideal world, no doubt, institutions would reform themselves when they saw that their activities were at variance with their objectives and contrary to the interests of their members. In our world they seldom do. So the politicians and the industrialists should have helped either to reform the unions or to create a situation in which reform was unnecessary.

But the position has been little better on the other side of industry. Capital did not perform well, though that was more the fault of 'finance' than of industry. In any event, there was too little industrial investment. At the same time much of British management was gravely inadequate. It was often weak and unimaginative and tried, with damaging results, to be authoritarian.

Besides the CBI is in no better condition than the TUC. 'Only

in a partnership independent of politics, between the great partners
— the Government, the trade unions and the employers — ', Iain
Macleod told the Conservative Party Conference in 1958, 'is there
any real lasting hope of good, sound industrial relations.' That is
still true, but the partnership cannot work today as it did sometimes in the past. There is now, regrettably, no question of the
partnership being 'independent of politics'. The TUC has become
even more enmeshed in Labour Party politics than ever. The days
of the partial disengagement of the Woodcock era are long past.
Similarly, though with far less excuse, since it has no formal ties
with the party, the CBI despite the efforts of those who run it
has become little more than an adjunct of the Conservatives. And
neither the CBI nor the TUC can rely on being able to lead its
members.

Broadly, there are four ways of dealing with the problem of the
industrial interests. The first is to create a fully-fledged socialist
state. That would remove the difficulty by coercing industry
and by removing genuine trade unions. As Schumpeter once said,
'only Russia has solved the problem of industrial discipline.'[29] But
here, once again, the remedy would be worse than the disease. The
second is the syndico-socialism of the present Labour Party. But
the incoherence and inconsistency of *Labour's Programme 1982*
and of Bennism offer no possibility of a successful outcome. The
third possible solution is one which is currently being attempted:
monetarism, combined with the gradual reform of the law relating
to trade unions. That option has been discussed in chapter 11.
Many other European countries have been more fertile than
we have in introducing devices and institutions to promote co-
operation. And the fourth way is to acknowledge the necessity
of consent and the limits of political and economic coercion and
to try to supplement the limited apparatus of one-party executive
government which was well suited to dealing with a very different
world. That entails constitutional reform. The reform of the constitution would have other purposes besides mitigating the problem
of the industrial 'interests', but here its purpose would be to make
the Government stronger in relation to the corporate forces,
while at the same time seeking a more co-operative and less
destructive role for them.

The suggestion that there is something wrong with our political arrangements is resisted by the constitutional conservatives of all parties. Is it not well known, they ask, that our British constitution is the best in the world? Many once thought so, but while it patently still has many virtues, our constitution must be judged not by its majesty and beauty or by its previous great achievements but by its results over a recent period of time. The second line of defence is to say that it would be taking great risks to alter the British constitution when we already possess a constitution of proven and historic worth. This is to ignore the fact that the British constitution has often been altered in the last 300 years. even if we look back no further than the revolution of 1688. Those alterations have not merely been organic or unconscious. Much of the British constitution has certainly been unintended, but its unintended parts have not always been better than the intended ones. In any case, many drastic reforms of the constitution have taken place from the Septennial Act to the Reform Bills to the Parliament Act. The constitution has never been treated as something too sacred to be touched. Recently, however, it seems to have been frozen into immobility. Mr Nevil Johnson has argued that 'much of the traditional language of the British constitution …has lost its vitality' and become 'formal'.[30] This helps to explain why the process of adaptation seems to have faltered.

Paradoxically, the economic radicals in all parties also tend to be constitutional conservatives. This is truer of the Conservative than of the Labour Party. Although Mr Michael Foot is an economic radical who has no wish for constitutional reform except in peripheral matters, the far left of the Labour Party wants not so much the reform of the constitution as its abolition.

The Conservative monetarist right is opposed to constitutional reform, while the non-monetarist constitutional left is inclined to favour it. The reason is clear, if inadequate. The monetarists believe that British failure has been due to the refusal of previous Governments to follow their particular nostrum and that failure will be turned into success now that the correct economic doctrines are being carried out. The Tory left, finding these doctrines unconvincing, looks for deeper causes for our current malaise than the inability of successive Governments to hit upon the right economic theory. Yet monetarists should surely see the danger posed to their panaceas by the current British system. Even if monetarism should be thought to work triumphantly, there is no certainty that the British voters would show due and proper gratitude. And if they did not, the Labour Party would then set about dismantling the monetarist triumph. Be that as it may, attachment to rigid economic doctrines and attachment to the current political arrangements tend to go together.

Twenty-five or thirty years ago many teachers of politics held up the British system as an outstanding example of how a country should be governed, and nobody does that today. To appreciate the reasons, it is necessary to look at the peculiarities of the British system and the premises on which it is based. The most important feature of the British form of government was the two-party system. That operated well in Britain for many years, and I still think that a two-party system which works is the best form of government. But the British two-party system worked only because it included a number of essential features. The most important of these was the closeness of the parties to each other. 'Democracy', as John Mackintosh wrote, 'is not a machinery for conducting abrupt about-turns....'[31] A country cannot possibly be well governed if its policies are subject to major fluctuations every five years. Not only do such fluctuations make it virtually impossible for industry to plan and run its affairs efficiently, they are damaging to social cohesion and cause intense political strife. If the parties are close together, they will necessarily be moderate. To be close together, they both have to be centrist, and centrism entails moderation. Similarly, they both have to be relatively free of ideology. Ideology is by its nature extremist, and parties in the grip of it move towards the wings. These conditions held good, with only an occasional bout of extremism, while the Liberals and the Conservatives were the two major parties in the state. And despite the emergence in the 1920s of the Labour Party, with an avowedly socialist constitution, as one of the two major parties, there was still no fundamental divergence between the Conservatives and Labour during the inter-war period. This was due largely to the good sense of Baldwin and MacDonald.

Churchill's wartime coalition Government laid down the post-war consensus based on Keynesian economic policies and the Beveridge Report. This consensus did not include the question of nationalization, and the parties differed on many other matters as well. But they were not far apart, and during the thirteen Conservative years drew even closer together. Indeed, even in the 1970 election, which took place shortly after the famous conference of the Conservative leadership at Selsdon Park and Sir Harold Wilson's subsequent coinage of the phrase 'Selsdon man', there was only a small difference between the parties, as the Nuffield study makes clear.[32] But after he had lost the election, Sir Harold reversed himself on three of the principal policies he had pursued in office — Europe, prices and incomes policy and the reform of industrial relations — and the post-war consensus was ended. Labour moved sharply to the left; a few years later the Conservatives moved to the right. And today the two parties are farther apart than they have ever been.

The essential conditions for a two-party system have therefore disappeared. Now the two parties are usually on the flanks of the political spectrum instead of in the centre. Britain used to be one of the least dogmatic countries in Europe. Probably both left and right are now more doctrinaire than their counterparts on the Continent. In one vital respect, however, the movement of the two parties has not been reciprocal. However far some of its leading members have moved to the right, the whole of the Conservative Party remains within the democratic tradition. The same is not true of the Labour Party. There have also been other causes or effects of the decay of the two-party system. New parties have arisen or gained in strength, and save for 1979 there has over the last twenty-five years been a fairly steady decline in the proportion of the electorate voting for the two main parties.*

The effective ending of the two-party system is all the more important because of the peculiarities of the British constitution.†
That constitution places the whole executive power in the hands

---

* I have written about many of the matters discussed in this chapter in my previous books. This creates a dilemma. It would be absurdly unrealistic to assume that the reader had read those books and intolerably repetitious to say again all that I have previously said. I have tried to resolve it by including only the bare bones of an argument that I have advanced before.

† With the exception of New Zealand, Britain is now just about the only democratic country in the world that does not enjoy the constitutional protection of proportional representation, a federal system or a separation of powers. In other words there is less constitutional restraint on a government in Britain than in other democracies.

of the party which wins a majority of seats in the House of Commons, even though that party almost never wins a majority of votes in the country. This did not matter until well after the Second World War. Only in 1929 did Britain attain universal suffrage, and only then did talk of a majority of the electorate have much meaning. Moreover, up to 1914 so many seats were left uncontested that calculations of the popular vote won by the parties were unprofitable. And 1931 and 1935 were the only two elections which have ever produced a Government based on a majority of the popular vote under universal suffrage.

After the war Parliament and the constitution enjoyed great prestige. Though Governments never won a majority of the votes, their right to govern was unquestioned. There was conflict, but the conflict took place within a framework of order. There was no shortage of consent. But as Britain's economic difficulties intensified, the authority of the Government has weakened and Governments have won a smaller proportion of the popular vote. Thus the Labour Government in October 1974 won only 39.2 per cent of the votes cast, and even the Conservative Government of 1979, which had a decisive majority in the House of Commons, gained only 43.9 per cent.

Neither the fact that their popular electoral support had weakened nor that there was a lack of consent in the country seemed to have affected the conduct or the policies of successive Governments. They appeared to think that they had the same right to govern with the support of only 39 per cent of the electorate as they would have had if they had gained the support of 60 per cent of the vote. This was an abuse of the spirit of the constitution, though not of its letter. Indeed, the less support Governments enjoyed, the more extreme they became. This would not have mattered too much if their various policies had worked. After all, a successful policy based on a popular vote of 38 per cent would be preferable to a failed policy based on a popular vote of 54 per cent. But the policies failed.

If the party leaders think their authority is not impaired by their low popular vote, their view is not shared by everybody else. Since Parliament nearly always upholds the Government when it has a majority, it cannot supply the legitimacy which a Government based upon a small popular vote lacks. This is because in always supporting the Government the majority party in Parliament is acting on plebiscitary rather than on parliamentary principles: it supports the Government not because all its members agree with what the Government is doing but because the Government won the last general election and it does not want to precipitate another one. But the plebiscitary principle is just the one which, in the circumstances we are discussing, does not give the Government legitimacy. The Government has not won a popular majority, only a parliamentary one; it has not won a plebiscite. In acting as it does, therefore, Parliament — which here effectively means the governing party — does not add to the Government's authority. Its actions are evidently controlled or pre-ordained.

Not surprisingly, this governmental process has not been impressive. And groups, above all, of course, the trade unions, have felt free to decide whether or not they should obey this law. However inexcusable this behaviour is, the guilt is mitigated by the behaviour of Governments. Under our present arrangements, Governments lack authority because they do not generate adequate consent and because they espouse extremist policies; they promise too much and achieve too little. The British tradition of compromise has been lost just when it is most needed.

Constitutional reform is therefore long overdue. The first step should be a more proportional voting system. The system of government which the present method of voting sustains has broken down. A constitution which places all executive power in the hands of the larger of the two minorities could be defended only on the grounds that it worked. Similarly, in my view, it can be unanswerably attacked only on the ground that it does not work. There are, of course, many other arguments for electoral reform, such as fairness of representation and the fact that, when there are three large parties, our first-past-the-post system becomes a casino, but they are all subsidiary to the issue of whether or not the current system is working, and they are all well known.

Broadly, there are three possible proportional systems. There is the additional-member system used in Germany, which is favoured by many people in this country. There is the single transferable vote, which is favoured by the Social Democratic–Liberal Alliance. And there is the list system, which seems to be favoured by nobody here, though it works well enough in many European countries. The single transferable vote is the 'purest' form of proportional representation, but it is used only by Ireland, Malta and the World Health Authority. Experience of it is limited, therefore, and it is a very far cry from what we have now. The additional-member system has worked well in Germany, and its adoption in Britain would cause the smallest break with the past. That is why I favour it, with the variations proposed by the Hansard Society.[33]

The principal objection to electoral reform is the claim that it would lead to ineffective coalition government. It is certainly likely to lead to a coalition, but there is no reason to suppose that a coalition would be less effective than the Governments thrown up by our present system. Coalition Governments on the Continent have not in general been less successful than British Governments, and British coalition Governments have not been weaker than British single-party Governments. Disraeli's remark that 'England does not love coalitions' is often quoted, but the circumstances in which it was made are usually forgotten. First Disraeli had, shortly before making his remark, proposed a coalition with Cobden and Bright.[34] And, secondly, he was talking about not a coalition Government but a coalition of opposition.[35] In any case, since the eighteenth century there has been no evidence that the voters do not like coalitions. Indeed, all the evidence points the other way.

Not surprisingly, most conservatives have favoured the first-past-the-post system.* After all, for many years it worked well, and it suited the Conservative Party. But Birkenhead favoured proportional representation, and in 1930 Hoare, then Party Treasurer and later both Foreign and Home Secretary, also favoured PR to check any future socialist majority. 'We should really obtain security', he wrote, and would know that there 'would be a continuous policy on which all commercial and industrial interests might work as an established fact, and on which they might base their economic plans....'[37] In the same year Churchill wrote to Beaverbrook, 'I do not think there will be a Government capable

---

* As Mr Nevil Johnson has pointed out, the British relative majority, or first-past-the-post system is a relic from the pre-party era, when it was 'the fairest way of enabling voters to choose particular men'. It is out of date in the age of parties, however.[36]

of restoring the position, which has not got behind it a real majority of the nation.'[38] In the 1950s, too, Churchill favoured electoral reform.[39]

The arguments used by Churchill and Hoare sum up the chief advantages of electoral reform. It would help to produce continuity. Adversary politics, or the two-party system, tends to manufacture or intensify conflict; a more proportional system would tend to lessen it. Electoral reform would ensure that we could have full-blooded socialism, with all its incalculable consequences, only if it were the wish of a majority of the electorate. Without electoral reform we may get it against the wishes of the majority of the people merely because of the quirks of the present electoral system. And electoral reform would strengthen the Government's hand against the industrial interests because the Government would have the backing of what Churchill called 'a real majority of the nation'. In other words, it would be much easier for a Government to mobilize consent. 'We must persuade', wrote Harold Macmillan after much experience; 'we cannot compel.'[40] A Government representing, say, 60 per cent of the country would be much more persuasive than one representing 40 per cent, and its need to resort to compulsion would be correspondingly less.

But electoral reform would take us only part of the way. Universal suffrage every five years and largely formalized parliamentary debates would still not be sufficient to bear the whole public weight of the political process. The interests would become less destructive because they would no longer be able to line up behind the Opposition in the virtual certainty that they would in time be able to undo the legislative or governmental activities to which they objected. They would in consequence become more controllable and more controlled.

Nevertheless, we need in addition better arrangements than we have at present. The multinationals pose problems, though, as John Mackintosh has pointed out, they are not to blame for our troubles.[41] The multinationals provide much-needed capital. But they present dangers because they can come and go. They may also so apportion the international division of labour that certain host countries gain the less skilled parts of the operation and are deprived of the more advanced technology. As no single state can control the multinationals, however, they must be dealt with through the European Community. Oligopoly has been growing in Britian. In twenty major industries surveyed in 1969, three firms on average controlled between 50 per cent and 90 per cent of each market.[42] But since then the tendency towards concentration seems to have slowed.[43] Professional corporate bodies, such as those of doctors and lawyers, are also important in their respective spheres, and their independence must be preserved. But it is because of the trade unions' power and their political activities that they are the most conspicuous interests, and it is they who cause the most pressing political problems.

There are some who would like to deal with these problems by means of attrition and conflict. But Tories have a prejudice against compulsion and a bias towards agreement.* The Tory disposition is above all to accept facts. Tories recognize that the nineteenth-century economy has gone and that oligopoly and powerful trade unions have taken its place. Those are the facts. In twenty years' time new technology may have brought new facts, and large companies and trade unions may be things of the past. But that is not the case yet, and, as Lord Randolph Churchill once said, the Tory instinct is 'to legislate rather for the moment than for the dim and distant future, gratefully leaving that job to posterity'.[45] Tories were, in any case, never enthusiasts for *laissez-faire* with its glorification of individual self-interest and its distrust of groups. They want to preserve as many of the beneficent features of a free market as possible while preventing its ideologists from destroying it altogether.

Moreover, the Tory is mindful of the corporatist history of this country. And he is strongly aware of the immense amount of good which has been done by individuals coming together to produce a communal effort: whether in churches, school and charitable societies; in companies, partnerships and trade unions; in political parties and other political organizations; in tennis club and other

---

* This is partly because, shunning ideology, a Tory is not as certain that he is right as, say, a Manchester Liberal. Burke, as usual, put the point best: 'I will not', he said, 'enter into the question how much truth is preferable to peace. Perhaps truth may be far better. But as we scarcely have the same certainty in the one we have in the other, I would — unless the truth were evident indeed — hold fast to peace which has in her company charity, the highest of the virtues'.[44]

sporting and social activities; or, above all, in the armed forces, which are the highest embodiment of the group or corporate spirit. Indeed, Sir Denis Brogan was being more than half-serious when he affirmed that 'the Englishman who is not a member of any society...is not a true born Englishman.'[46]

A Tory, then, rejects the simple idea that individuals are selfish and good and groups selfish and bad. Bernard Shaw once said that trade unionism is the capitalism of the proletariat.[47] Many trade unionists today are far from being proletarian, but Shaw's remark is a useful insight. Trade unionism is a natural result of industrialism, and until some better method is found of protecting the 'proletariat', it must be permitted to indulge in its own capitalism if it so chooses. Of course, ordinary capitalists and trade-union capitalists have different objects and different functions and so are likely not to agree; hence some machinery and special efforts are needed to weave them together. But right-wingers and monetarists who deplore trade unionism should remember that it is only in communist countries and other dictatorships that free trade unions have been abolished.

Where does this leave us with the corporate bodies in general and the trade unions in particular? Clearly, the trade unions still need further reform. Mr Prior's and Mr Tebbit's Bills have been cautious and sensible. There is a limit to the usefulness of the law in industrial relations. It can be employed successfully only if it enjoys strong popular support. The unions must be democratized. This will not necessarily make them more moderate. It is often thought, said Iain Macleod when Minister of Labour in 1956, that 'the workers are less militant than their leaders. All I can tell you, speaking quite frankly, is that this is not my experience, nor is it the experience of any Minister of Labour.'[48] After his recent experiences, Mr Scargill would probably disagree. Since Ian Macleod's day, many of the union leaders have become politically more extreme, and, owing to high unemployment, the rank and file has become more cautious. In any case, for the reasons given in chapter 8, further democratization of the unions is essential. And further measures, such as the introduction of legally enforceable agreements and the making of the continuance of union immunities dependent upon the observance of the agreements and of proper procedures, will be necessary in due course.* Reform is in the interests of the unions themselves — they are not, after all, the only people who now break agreements — and it should be part of a wider package. Yet that will not necessarily make its acceptance easy.

Like most groups of people, the trade unions do not take readily to reformation; no one likes losing his privileges. So union reform should be gradual, and it should leave the unions with quite enough power to do their job. It should be implemented, as far as possible in a spirit of co-operation; after all, reform will have the support of most of the union membership. And, as well as being the proper Conservative method, co-operation is far more likely to be successful than an all-out attack.

The trade-union leaders are often likened to the medieval barons. But it is worth remembering that the only successful medieval kings were those who co-operated with their barons. That was how the barons were little by little brought under control. William the Conqueror is the outstanding example of such co-operation. Henry I co-operated in a different way. He effectively created a new baronage, an expedient probably not open to a modern Government. Stephen showed the folly of confrontation. He arbitrarily arrested such great potentates as the Earl of Chester and Geoffrey de Mandeville, who indulged in mayhem as soon as they were released. Henry II was one of the most successful of English medieval kings and, contrary to what used to be thought, was not anti-feudal. He made extensive use of the nobility in government. John and Henry III, on the other hand, both became alienated from the baronage and used foreigners in an attempt to build up an alternative governing class. Both as a result suffered appalling baronial wars.

Bringing the baronage under control was thus not a competition between the king and his nobles for power but the attempted resolution of a relatively narrow range of problems over which the interest of crown and nobles conflicted. And this was usually achieved by the crown's acquisition of new instruments of government.

In his essay 'Taming the Barons' John Mackintosh suggested that interest-group leaders should be brought into a transformed

---

* In 1910 two Labour leaders, Arthur Henderson and George Barnes, introduced a bill to make strikes illegal unless thirty days' advance notice were given.[49] We have come a long way in the wrong direction since then.

House of Lords. Existing peers would keep their titles but would no longer be Members of Parliament. And to prevent both proletarian and aristocratic hackles from rising, the new members would be called not peers but something on the lines of 'Members of the Upper House'. Out of, say, 200 members appointed for each Parliament, industry and the trade unions would have 40 nominations each, the Government 20 (which would include of course, Ministers), and the remaining 100 would be given to other interest groups. The powers of the new Second Chamber would be the same as those of the old; the Prime Minister and the Government would be determined, as now, by the composition of the House of Commons and would not be affected by the second chamber.[50]

This is an attractive proposal. It would bring 'corporate bias' into the open, and it would be modernizing an ancient institution rather than creating a wholly new one. Above all, it would be bringing 'the interests' into Parliament. Disraeli would probably have approved. 'The great art in creating an efficient Representative government', he wrote, 'is to secure its representation of those interests of the country, which are at the same time not only considerable but in their nature permanent.' 'And to bind up with our form of polity the feelings of vast and influential classes of the nation', he added, 'obviously tends to the perpetuity of the State....'[51]

Unfortunately, the proposal is probably too radical to gain support. A surprisingly large number of people are opposed to any reform of the House of Lords, even though its present composition lays it wide open to attack by the Labour Party. Those who have great experience of the House strongly favour reform; it is only those who admire it from afar who are able to magnify its virtues. But even the reformers tend to favour an elected Second Chamber and would probably draw the line at a new baronial one. So both reformers and the ultra-conservatives of all parties would be offended by the prospect of active trade unionists entering the sacred portals. Safely retired trade-union leaders are, of course, warmly welcomed.

'At the highest level in our national life,' the Employment Secretary, Mr Maurice Macmillan said in 1972, 'we are seeking to complement power with responsibility by offering the TUC and

CBI, as representative bodies, a say in the management of the economy.'[52] The CBI and TUC are now too party-political to carry out such a task even if they were offered it. When the leaders of the CBI pointed out in August 1982 that industry was facing great difficulties, the cry went up from its membership that it should be optimistic, not pessimistic, and that it was letting down the Government. The fact that it has a duty to industry to tell the truth and that it is not an organ of the Conservative Party was forgotten. In reality, as Mr C. Gordon Tether commented, there is nothing virtuous about always looking on the bright side; 'as Britain's own story over the past year testifies, there may be a high price to pay for indulgence in false optimism.'[53] As it turned out, the CBI was right and its critics wrong.

At about the same time the Director-General of the CBI, Mr Beckett, met Labour's Shadow Chancellor, Mr Shore. The only surprising thing about that meeting was that they had not met regularly before. Yet the meeting evoked an absurd outcry from some of the CBI, and one prominent firm resigned. The level of political intelligence and sophistication in the CBI is evidently not high. Both the TUC and the CBI, therefore, are in the grip of ideology. For ideology to have taken over the parties is bad enough; for it to have spread to bodies which should be essentially practical in their approach is deplorable.

The 'governing institutions' are not only too party-political to be partners with the Government; they are also too weak. The CBI is hopelessly divided. Politics is only partly to blame. Employers' organizations in this country always have been weak. Unlike in Germany, for example, firms have not been prepared to hand over power to a central body. At present the membership of the CBI is diffuse, and some large firms do not belong to it. There is no power at the centre. If the centre gave a lead, the members would not follow; and if it made an agreement with the Government, it would be unlikely to be able to keep its side of the bargain.

The TUC has long been in the same position. Britain suffers from the most ramshackle trade-union structure in the civilized world. As a result of the legal privileges and their structure, the trade unions are both over-mighty and impotent. They can sometimes control Governments; they cannot control themselves. The union chieftains may seem like Robespierres to the rest of the country; too often they are like Ledru-Rollins to their own unions: 'I must follow them since I am their leader.'

Thus if they try to co-operate with the Government, the likelihood is that they will soon lose their influence with their rank and file. This happened in the First War. The more the TUC collaborated with the Government, the more powerful the shop stewards became.[54] Today there is more power on the shop floor than there was then, and the union leaders are correspondingly weaker. Only when there is an outstanding trade-union leader does power remain at the centre, and then only for a time.

Hence both the TUC and CBI are insufficiently 'representative' to be able to contribute much to the sort of consensus that the Heath Government sought. Until or unless they are given much more power by their members, 'tripartism' will have only limited usefulness.[55]

Instead of shaky and secretive tripartism or, worse, bipartism as during the so-called social contract or (what may be worse still) government trying to do everything on its own, ignoring or rejecting industry and the trade unions, we need to bring the corporations into the light of day and to seek their co-operation in the open. The aim is not to give them more power and influence; the aim is to bring their interests into line with other interests and to exert some democratic influence over them.

The only way to do that is to set up a public, preferably televised, forum in which all the main interests can take part. That is the second necessary institutional reform. Since, regrettably, John Mackintosh's idea of turning the House of Lords into such a body is probably too ambitious, the new body, which would be only advisory, has either to be an enlargement and extension of the NEDC or a completely new institution. In it, the Government, the unions, industry (including small businesses) and representatives of the consumer would all be brought together.

A great benefit of this institution would be that the interests would have to argue their cases against each other. One of the causes and results of inflation is that most interests are trying to take more out of the economy than is in total available. They tend to think their quarrel is with the Government, which is arbitrarily denying them their rightful due. But in reality each one's claim to national resources can usually be granted in full only if another interest's claim is either rigorously scaled down or rejected altogether. The forum would make this truth clear; the present system obscures it by giving the impression that the struggles are merely between the Government and particular interests.

Another great advantage is that in this forum it should be possible to discuss issues on their merits, stripped of their ideological uniforms, as indeed has happened in the 'little Neddies'. No doubt some of the political partisanship which at present infects the CBI and the TUC would penetrate the new 'House of Industry'. But those who used it as a rostrum for party propaganda would enhance their reputations neither with those whom they represented nor with their fellow members. After all, most unions now have many Conservative or other non-Labour supporters, and most large companies have many non-Conservative shareholders. More important, the participants in the forum would not want to waste their time listening to party propagandist speeches. They get enough of that elsewhere. Electoral reform would probably tend to diminish the 'political' element in the forum.

The Government would explain its plans for the coming year, and the various interests would put forward their proposals and objectives. Clearly, prices and incomes would be only part of the discussion, but their relationship to other factors in the economy would be more clearly demonstrated than is usually possible today. The impact of wages not only on inflation but also on employment and investment would be made plain. The unions have a greater interest than anybody else in securing investment which generates employment.[56] Since 1966 there has been an increasing tendency for investment in manufacturing industry to be labour-saving, which has created little new capacity, rather than labour-using, which would increase capacity and provide more not fewer jobs.[57] Workers have every incentive to reverse that trend, and investment that produces jobs is much more likely if the employers have some assurance that they are not going to face a wages explosion. All in all, the forum should help to promote, as Selwyn Lloyd said of the NEDC, 'a greater sense of national purpose in the conduct of our economic policy'.[58]

A further advantage would be that the great producers groups would be face to face with consumer interests.* That is the third element of reform. Of course, producers are all consumers, too, but they are liable to forget it when wholeheartedly pursuing their sectional interest. 'The facts', as Keynes once put it, 'that a man is a cannibal at home and eaten abroad do not cancel out to render him innocuous and safe.'[59] So contact with people who specifically represented consumers and taxpayers – though they in their turn would, of course, mostly be producers as well – could not fail to be salutary. Like other people, consumers' and taxpayers' groups can get infected by ideology, but in the new forum they would be likely to be fairly immune and to play a politically neutral and positive role. In any case, trade unionists would be enabled to see that their interests as consumers are different from their interests as producers, and that even in their capacity as producers they are damaged by high inflation.

Taxpayers, incidentally, should be consulted outside the forum. Nearly everybody is afflicted with a tax return. A useful fourth reform would be to include questions on that form asking how money should be spent and how it should be raised. Much ritual obeisance is paid to HM taxpayer. This would be a way of genuinely consulting the taxpayers and finding out their wishes.

Through the new House, then, the trade unions, as well as industry and commerce, could be given a more responsible role to play in the economy. The forum would legitimate the corporate forces, and, in Disraeli's phrase, the feelings of their members would be further bound up with 'our form of polity'. Both sides of industry would be subject to public scrutiny. No longer could they rely on getting away with the easy assumptions or obvious contradictions which can pass unchallenged in the trade-union conference hall or in the directors' boardroom. Activities which might have a damaging effect on the public or on particular areas would have to be backed by serious argument. The Government, too, would have to explain its fiscal, monetary and other policies without the hindrance or the protection of the gladiatorial conventions of the House of Commons. Finally, by clearly revealing the limitations on governmental action, the forum would help to downgrade the expectations of Government. At present

---

* Consumer interests are represented on the NEDC, but that meets in private.

Governments do this themselves by performing consistently badly. The forum, however, should improve performance while lowering expectations. This would be altogether preferable.

'But will they come when you do call for them?', as Hotspur asked Glendower.[60] Would the leaders of the great interests be prepared to attend the new body, or would they have the reluctance of some medieval MPs to come to Westminster, though no town of any size deliberately avoided representation?[61] When Glendower said he knew how to 'command the devil', Hotspur replied that he knew how to 'shame the devil'.[62] And it would be more a matter of 'shaming' than 'commanding'. Some group leaders might be reluctant to face their 'peers' when they were pursuing a particularly extreme course of action. And some trade-union leaders dislike democracy and the whole democratic process. Yet if they failed to appear, they would be demonstrating the weakness of their case, and they might have difficulty in explaining their action to their members. (This is yet another reason for democratizing the unions.) Besides, the Government could more or less ensure attendance by laying down that the consultative process between groups and the Government could take place only in the forum and the institutions surrounding it.[63] Hence not only would those, in the French saying, who absented themselves be wrong, they would be excluding themselves from consultation with the Government. And that, too, would be unpopular with their members.

Of course, there would not always, or even often, be full agreement. Some of the members of the 'House of Industry' would be determined not to agree. But it is hard to believe that the forum would not diminish the area and intensity of disagreement or that the process would not be educational to those taking part, to the public and to the Government. Hence the achievement of more coherent and consistent policy-making would be assisted. Just as with 'corporate bias', the forum and its institutional appendages would be an attempt to separate industrial affairs from the struggle for power. But the new institution would certainly fail if the Government always believed that it knew best and treated the forum just as a talking shop. A piece of constitutional machinery is no substitute for the wish to achieve consensus and the attempt to pursue consensus policies. Ultimately, no doubt, when there was conflict the Government's view, if it was supported by Parliament, would have to prevail. But if the Government were not prepared to make concessions and to acknowledge that not all wisdom in these matters was to be found at Whitehall and Westminster, the whole exercise would be abortive, and those taking part would lose all influence with those whom they represented. In fact, as Daniel Bell has argued:

> there cannot be *one* overriding interest whose claims take precedence at all times — neither the individual, his property or his rights; nor the State, with its claim to direct and control economic and social activities...nor the plural groups with their claims for redress and protection.[64]

No Tory should disagree with that. And those who do not like the 'nanny state' should not believe in 'nanny government'.

A Select Committee of the House of Commons should be set up to maintain parliamentary as opposed to governmental contact with the new body, and there should be nothing in it to offend even the most old-fashioned of constitutional purists. To those to whom 'corporatism' is still a dirty word it would be pointed out that the new body would not increase the amount of corporatism in this country. That is determined by the degree of corporate power, not by the presence or absence of corporate institutions.* In any case, as has been shown, the idea has a distinguished Conservative pedigree. It is akin, too, to the rule of 'the concurrent majority', put forward in the last century by the American Conservative John C. Calhoun. According to Calhoun, there were two different ways in which the sense of the community could be taken: one regarded numbers only; 'the other, on the contrary, regards interests as well as numbers....' The first was the numerical and the second 'the concurrent, or constitutional majority'.[65] Calhoun conceded that government by a numerical majority had 'the major advantage of simplicity'.[66] But simplicity in these matters is not an advantage, and in suggesting that government by numerical majority needs to be supplemented and that 'interests'

---

* It might be better to use the term 'power sharing', except that because of its association with Northern Ireland it might be even more pejorative with some people than would 'corporatism'.

are not something evil to be despised, Calhoun was thinking on the same lines as many British Conservatives.

'Concerted action' has been tried by most of our European partners at one time or other, and their economies have been more successful than ours. Admittedly, for various reasons concerted action is today mostly in the doldrums. In Germany, for instance, the then president of the employers' organization, Herr Schleyer, took the Government to court over the Co-determination Act in 1976, and since then, apart from a short period in 1979, there have been only informal procedures. Chancellor Schmidt used to spend many hours meeting each side of industry jointly or separately. Austria is the great exception. 'Concerted action' still flourishes there, and Austria's economic performance during the last few years can bear comparison with that of any other country.

'Concerted action', then, would not solve all our difficulties, but it would help. It would help to depoliticize part of our economic life or would at least make the leaders of both sides of industry less partisan. And it would help to spread awareness of the truth that while competition is necessary for both an efficient economy and a free society, co-operation and consensus are no less necessary both for the attainment of that efficiency and for the preservation of that society.

Such an institution and the attitude which lay behind it would bring us nearer to full employment without inflation. It would be pointless even to try to draw up a blue print of how this might be achieved. Everything would depend upon the circumstances of the time. Politics is diplomacy, and moves cannot be worked out in advance when it is not known how the other people and interests involved will react. But it would be easier in the 'House of Industry' than elsewhere to demonstrate to the trade-union leaders that an employment policy demanded wage restraint or an incomes policy (or whatever phrase was then in vogue). And it would be easier for the trade-union leaders to outline in that setting what would be needed to gain the consent of their members without overstating their case. Politics is also bargaining, and there would seem to be plenty of scope for bargains.

Of course, other measures would be needed as well. There should be increased share ownership by employees, increased profit-sharing and increased consultation and participation. Again, there is far more of this on the Continent than there is here. We live in a participating society, in which small groups of people, by withdrawing their participation, can create loss or chaos; it is foolish not to recognize this. Some people, because of the nature of their job and of the conditions they work under, have not the slightest wish to 'participate'. They merely want to do their work, get their pay and go home. But the great majority do wish to be consulted and to be involved, and they should be given those rights. Mr Nevil Johnson seems to me to be correct in saying that the concept of political democracy is not applicable to industry.[67] Nevertheless, a property-owning democracy entails the belief that labour is a form of property. Carlyle long ago looked forward to the principle of 'permanent contract instead of temporary' and of the employer granting his workers 'permanent interest in his enterprise and theirs'.[68] That principle may be utopian, though the Japanese come near to it. But the worker does have an interest in his firm that goes far beyond just being paid for his work, and progress in giving proper recognition to that interest has been made in the last two decades. It is less than thirty years ago that a car company sacked 6,000 workers without consultation and without notice.

Again, it will be the easier to make more satisfactory arrangements the less ideology and partisan politics contaminate industry. The divisions between industry, Government and unions at the top have been mirrored on the shop floor. Our industrialization in the nineteenth century and the theories of the utilitarians produced a pernicious philosophy of work. In accordance with the ideas of the political economists about economic man, it was assumed that people worked for two reasons only: the love of gain and the fear of destitution and starvation.

Workers were seldom, if ever, given a fixed contract. Their wages varied with the state of the market. They were treated as aliens by the owners, who hired them at the lowest price, doubted their loyalty, distrusted their ability to take responsibility and in general believed them to be futile and idle. This industrial psychology, erroneous though it was, was a self-fulfilling prophecy. It tended to produce the attitudes it expected to find, and it led to embittered divisions between the classes. This was one of the reasons — the promptings of Arnold were another — why many of the middle classes abandoned the industrial life for the more cultured worlds of medicine, the law, the Empire and even finance.

The fear-and-greed school of management reached its apotheosis in the American Bethlehem steel works in the 1880s, when so-called scientific management treated workers as though they were unreliable machines, clocking on and off, and every job was measured to a fraction of a second, leaving no scope for individual initiative. But, also in America, Elton Mayo at the Bell works in Chicago in the early 1920s showed that the earlier ideas of management were wrong and that the motives of workers were quite different from what the crude ideas of Manchester Liberalism had assumed. Mayo showed that work is basic to people's self-respect, and that workers wanted to be given responsibility and that they performed far better when they were trusted and involved. Job satisfaction was at least as important as money.

If managers want increased productivity, they are much more likely to attain it if they make their work forces feel that they are wanted and are doing a worthwhile job. British management has fatally underused the talent at its disposal.

Trade-union leaders tend to distrust schemes for wider partici-pation as a threat to their own position. Collective bargaining, at least as practised in Britain, is an outcome of the old system, under which it was thought that the only things which concerned the workers were pay and conditions.

Share ownership is one way of encouraging the feeling of 'belonging'. But the Government should do more to secure wider involvement at work: a code of practice on good participation techniques; a government purchasing policy to favour those adopting a code of practice; a Queen's Award to those who are outstanding; and, most important, insistence by the Government that its own employees are consulted and involved on all matters which closely affect them.

The British people have never taken kindly to authoritarian control. Yet that is the style which most British management has tried for more than a hundred years. Not surprisingly, it has largely failed. If the British public is responsible enough to be consulted about the choice of its own Government, it is responsible enough to be consulted at the place where it spends most of its conscious life: at work.

There should also be more consultation on local issues. This matter falls largely outside the scope of this book. But to many people and to many areas local issues are of greater interest than national issues; and a greater public involvement would strengthen local government, which is one of the important 'interests' of the country and one which a Tory should be especially concerned to foster. Again, Professor Dahrendorf has recently advocated that we should have directly elected mayors who combined 'the functions of the present mayor with those of the town clerk and to some extent the majority leader'.[69] I made a similar proposal in 1969, and I still think it would do much to increase public interest and to revive local authorities.[70] It would also prevent the sort of chicanery which took place after the last GLC election, when the respected Labour leader was immediately removed and Mr Ken Livingstone put in his place.

If we have not paid sufficient attention to local feelings, we have been too parochial in our national policies. The seventh element of reform should be that our policies are trans-national. If the promises and plans put forward by the parties do not take account of the international constraints on any Government, they will turn out to be deceptions. When I was concerned in the Foreign Office with the European Community from 1979 to 1981, it did not seem to me to be functioning well. Nor, however, were many national Governments. The Community is the only one we have, and we should work to improve it while getting the best out of it — something we have hitherto failed to do. Isolationists who wish us to leave the Community are about as sensible as were the American isolationists, Colonel Lindbergh and Colonel MacCormack, in 1940. No state is now an island, and international co-operation is an imperative. The Labour Party should look at the socialist parties in Europe. Socialism in one country is unattainable. Equally, for the economy to be wholly at the mercy of international market forces is, or should be, unthinkable. Hence interventionist national policies in a sensible international framework is the only feasible objective.

Conclusion

My argument is that the Tory approach, as outlined in this book, offers the best chance of reversing Britain's decline. Of course, it does not provide a complete or a permanent solution. There are no complete solutions in politics: nothing is acceptable to everybody, and anyway nothing works out exactly as intended. There are no permanent solutions either. As the problems change, so too should the solutions — though, as we have seen, they frequently don't.

For a Tory, politics comes before economics. That is largely because he does not believe that in economics everything is for the best in all possible worlds provided the government does not intervene. In other words, he rejects *laissez-faire* and the idea that the economy is self-regulating. *Laissez-faire* had its origins in the limited capacity of late eighteenth-century and early nineteenth-century British Governments to act effectively and in the rationalizations of the political economists. Those rationalizations ignored the welfare of the majority of the population and were based on dogma, not fact. The dogma and the suffering of the labouring classes produced the counter-dogma of Marxist socialism.

Although the conditions which *laissez-faire* and Marxism were meant to explain or justify have long since passed away, we are still lumbered with the rival ideologies. Nearly fifty years ago Stanley Baldwin said that *laissez-faire* was as dead as the slave trade.[71] Yet now we evidently need a new Wilberforce. *Laissez-faire* or Manchester Liberalism, in the guise of Friedmanite monetarism, has crept out again and once more dominates people's minds. As early as 1819 Sismondi found the English *laissez-faire* doctrine of economic science 'so speculative' that it was 'divorced from all practice'. And even in its heyday in the nineteenth century, when conditions of perfect competition were optimistically assumed, *laissez-faire* theoretically led to the best outcome for all only if the existing distribution of incomes were taken for granted.[72] Now we have nothing approaching perfect competition, and many people do not accept the existing distribution of wealth. At the same time there has been abundant evidence in this century that the economy is not self-regulating. In fact, the policies of the present Government have had a powerful 'regulating' effect on the economy, but they have operated in a perverse direction.

Yet many economists go on teaching neo-classical economics as though nothing had changed. They are like the professors in Samuel Butler's *Erewhon*, who, believing that to teach a boy 'the nature of the things which exist in the world around him...would be giving him a narrow and shallow conception of the universe', taught him 'hypothetics'. This was 'originally composed at a time when the country was in a different state of civilization to what it is at present, a state which has long since disappeared and been superseded'.[73] Neo-classical economics today is 'hypothetics'.

So the revival of *laissez-faire* is just about as astounding as the revival of Marxism despite the failure of the Marxist prophecies to come true. Both are 'self-sealing' systems. When *laissez-faire* goes wrong, its adherents ascribe its failure to government intervention, like arsonists blaming the fire brigade, and when Marxism goes wrong, the fault similarly never lies with the doctrine but is due to the past, to bad leadership or to sabotage.[74] Tories can leave Marxism to wither away or to be destroyed by others. But they have a duty to kill off *laissez-faire* again, and in doing so they will probably damage Marxism, since the two doctrines thrive and wane together.

The Conservative monetarists thought that the post-war years had been a failure because of too much 'Keynesian' government interference. The socialists now think capitalism has broken down at last. Both ignore what happened abroad. In other countries there was more effective government intervention and there were policies and institutions to promote a degree of industrial consensus. Here we carried on with adversary politics and did not further free enterprise in a way that our competitors did. Because of our *laissez-faire* and free trade tradition and because of fear or love of socialism, we have failed to produce a viable partnership between government and industry. Instead we have retreated from the real world into ideology.

Ideology is not confined to economics. The fog of Manchester Liberalism has swirled into the realm of political and constitutional ideas. Ideology simplifies. And, in politics and constitutional matters, to the Tory at least, simplicity is misleading and dangerous.

What does the constitution in fact as opposed to paper now amount to? This is the process: a party in opposition thinks up a parcel of policies which it hopes will improve the national fortunes and which it believes will enable it to secure election, and then, having won the support of much less than half the electorate, it proceeds to carry out those policies irrespective of their effects, while the new party in opposition is beginning the same process so that, if and when it is elected, it can reverse nearly everything that its predecessor has done. This cannot be dignified by the description 'constitutional'; it is mere self-indulgence. In the absence of reform, we are not far off Disraeli's 'arbitrary senate'. Of course, the process is not quite as arbitrary as it looks. There is still some underground separation of powers. Nevertheless, the process is far too simple, peremptory and random, and not surprisingly it works badly. Ideology is no substitute for institutions. 'The simple governments', as Burke said, 'are fundamentally defective, to say no worse of them.'[75] Parliament must remain supreme, and universal suffrage must remain the final arbiter. But both need to be supplemented and adapted in ways suggested earlier.

Maybe Britain's recent constitutional sterility will soon come to an end. Even if it does not, what Professor Dahrendorf has called 'the imagination of reality', which is greater than that of politicians and professors, may come to our rescue.[76] But it has left it pretty late.

The Tory approach is to be more concerned with practice than with theory. There is no point in pretending that everything is or should be solved by the market. Even economic life is not just a market place, still less is it a market place presided over by a Walrasian auctioneer constantly clearing each and every market. Groups and the Government, as well as individuals, are inextricably involved in the economy, and many decisions are made by power and not by the market.

Nevertheless, Tories fully agree with Manchester Liberals about the necessity of competition. If the British economy is not competitive, Britain's relative economic decline will soon become absolute. They do not accept Ruskin's remark that 'Government and co-operation are in all things the Laws of Life; Anarchy and competition the Laws of Death.'[77] But while Ruskin excluded competition, Manchester Liberals exclude co-operation. Tories know that competition and co-operation are both indispensable, as is the intervention of government; and they aim to build a synthesis, just as they built a synthesis in the nineteenth century. Similarly, Tories reject the naive socialist belief that the coming of socialism will in some way bring competition to an end. In every social order there will be competition between individuals.[78]

If we are to get back to anywhere near full employment, there will have to be a combination of both co-operation and competition. Otherwise not only the economy but the state too may fall apart. At present there is a mis-match between *laissez-faire* ideas and present-day economic facts. There is a further mis-match between our ancient political institutions, which are geared to a modified *laissez-faire* economy, and the political activities which are necessary both to deal with the 'interests' and to guide the economic affairs of the nation.

Monetarists try to alter the facts to bring them into line with their doctrine. Tories repudiate the doctrine. To them economics, when it claims as in the case of monetarism to be scientific, is a pseudo-science; and when it is empirical, it is part of politics. But it is only a part, and like algebra it should be servant, not master. Hence Tories throw off the tyranny of theory. They seek to recognize the facts and aim to adapt our institutions to fit them. By judicious change they try to preserve political stability.[79]

That stability is unlikely to last unless serious attempts are made to deal with unemployment and to improve our system of government. Britain can work both in the sense that her ancient institutions can be revived and in the sense that unemployment can be brought down to a tolerable level. Otherwise the future will be bleak and the national decline will continue. The Tory approach may lead to many mistakes. But the mistakes will be fewer and smaller than if the alternative approaches are followed. That is so because one thing is certain. We are far more likely to take the right road if we can see where we are going than if we are engulfed in ideological fog.

Appendix

Past Words

Cobbett thought that 'the doctrine of consistency, as now in vogue, is the most absurd that ever was broached.'[1] Without going as far as Cobbett, I think that consistency is a boring virtue, if indeed it is one at all. I have not been consistent on electoral reform. I changed my mind on it in the mid-1970s. But in case anybody should think that I have only very recently come to hold the views on economics expressed in this book, it may be relevant to indicate what I have said in the past on these matters.

The Body Politic (1969)

The British Tory party has been the most successful right-wing party in the world because it has not been right-wing. The party has nearly always governed itself from the left and the country from the centre. (p. 90)

More competition and efficiency are of course essential. But a party which gets half its votes from the workers and which believes in authority and security cannot sensibly make a religion out of the uncontrolled forces of the market. The devotees of that supreme being are a select band. (p. 92)

Speech at Cambridge, 19 February 1971

On incomes policy there is a difference between the parties and it can be summed up in one sentence. Conservatives often imply they have not got an incomes policy but in fact have got one; the Labour Government said they had got an incomes policy but in fact did not have one.

Speech at Amersham, 30 January 1975

In politics an intellectual credit balance is not built up by chunks of dogma....The summons to return to what are alleged to be Tory first principles comes mainly from the wing of the party that looks back to the liberal nineteenth-century *laissez-faire* tradition. But that tradition represents only one strand — and not the main one — in the Tory Party's history and philosophy....

'Economic man' was the creation of the classical economists and the utilitarians, and he also exists in the Marxist order of things. He is no part of the Conservative universe.

If economics were all that we were concerned with, it might be sufficient to dip into the text books of American professors to discover our political philosophy, to find out not only what we should be thinking but what we should be doing. But then politics is a good deal more than an aspect of banking.

Obviously the whole question of economic management in general and inflation in particular lies at the heart of the political debate. And naturally any prudent Conservative will pay great attention to demand management which must involve sensible control of the money supply. But even if all that the monetarists said was true (and even if they all said the same thing), that for a Conservative would not be the end of the matter. A Tory would have to examine the political and economic consequences of a monetarist policy. He might for instance come to the conclusion that such a policy would produce an unacceptable level of un-employment, or he might think that the pursuit of such a policy would be likely to lead to civil disturbance....

I am at a loss to understand why such a policy should be con-sidered suitable for the Tory party. It may be inevitable, or it may be better than the alternatives. But it has not yet been shown to be either of those things. And unless it is, it can hardly be considered a fundamentally Tory policy.

Yet in any event the monetarist case is far from proved, and until it is, the Tory with his traditional distrust of simple solutions and economic panaceas will remain agnostic....

Our approach has to be non-doctrinaire. A Tory Party with a Clause 4 would be a contradiction in terms. It follows that the slogans of *laissez-faire* are not enough. Emphasis on freedom, the free market and the rights of property is valuable, but it is only part of the truth. And to mistake the part for the whole is of course the essence of heresy. Having fought that heresy in the past, the Tory party would be foolish now to espouse it. *Laissez-faire* in fact provides no adequate basis for governing the country, nor indeed for winning the support of the majority of the electors.

This [Labour] Government and the trade-union leaders have preferred unemployment to acting seriously against inflation.... The system of electing union leaders by postal ballot should be extended, and public money should be used to help cover the cost....There is no reason in logic, history, philosophy or expediency why the Tory Party should join the Labour Party in moving towards the extreme. Indeed there are compelling reasons why it should not....

Inside Right (1977)

Nobody but the most bovine party hack believes that all the policies and actions of his party have always been right, or that all the actions and policies of other parties have always been wrong. Yet an admission of occasional error is a very different thing from the suggestion that almost the whole Tory Party has been marching in the wrong direction for thirty years. And certainly the allegation that Toryism has been betrayed does raise some apparently awkward problems.

For one thing it implies that Churchill, Eden, Macmillan, Butler, Douglas-Home, Heath and Macleod were all either grossly misguided or were not true Tories. This seems improbable. For another there is some incongruity in a party which gives intellectual speculation a lower place in politics than do its opponents and which believes that policies grow out of the needs, fears, hopes and wishes of the people and out of the demands of the time, coming to the conclusion that it has been intellectually in error since 1945. (p. 12)

The Conservative political stance since 1945 may be summarized as: general welcome of the welfare state, though such acceptance does not preclude alteration, improvement or pruning; full employment, however defined, as a prime aim of economic policy; the encouragement of ownership of property; the acceptance of trade unions as an important estate of the realm coupled with the recognition that many of the activities of trade unionism are economically damaging, and, lately, constitutionally unjustifiable; the conviction that Britain must play her proper part both militarily and diplomatically in the defence of the West; the belief that the mixed economy is a condition both of political freedom and of social stability; the judgement that private enterprise is not only essential to the preservation of political freedom but also when applicable to the most efficient form of economic organization, coupled with the recognition that here as in other countries the state is bound to play an important part in the economy. (p. 19)

Conservatives agree that competition is indispensable to a free society. But they do not make a god of it, and even if they did they would not agree that it was the one and only god. In economics, Conservatives are not monotheists. (p. 117)

Accordingly, in a period of competing theories, the wise Tory will... use whatever aid is at hand, and with many theoretical doubts he will proceed with cautious empiricism. In economics as in politics, abstraction is the Tory enemy. (p. 232)

Lecture on Conservatism at the Cambridge Union,
7 February 1980

A free state will not survive unless its people feel loyalty to it. And they will not feel loyalty unless they gain from the state protection and other benefits. Lectures on the ultimate beneficence of competition and on the dangers of interfering with market forces will not satisfy people who are in trouble. If the state is not interested in them, why should they be interested in the state?

In the Conservative view, therefore, economic liberalism, *à la* Professor Hayek, because of its starkness and its failure to create a sense of community, is not a safeguard of political freedom but a threat to it....

Indeed the Welfare State is a thoroughly Conservative institution — which is why Conservatives did so much to bring it into existence — and its roots go deep in British history....

The interventionist state and the welfare state are not going to go away. That is something, as I have indicated, which I welcome. Those who believe otherwise have, in my view, fallen into the trap of ideology and dogma — which is or should be to Conservatives the unpardonable sin.

Speech in Cambridge on 'R. A. B. Butler and the Continuity of Post-War Conservatism', 8 November 1980

But economics, like politics, is not a science. It cannot be, because the human element is too large. One is always unwise, therefore, to take the current wisdom of economists as gospel truth. After all we have seen that wisdom alter often enough. And it is anybody's guess when the economic fashion will change. I would guess that it won't last half as long as blue jeans or beards....

I think it was Harold Macmillan who said the economy was not a motor car; it was more like a horse. And that is why economic sages are necessarily more like racing tipsters than scientists and their views should be treated with sceptical attention rather than with pious agreement or enthusiastic support....

Just as politically we believe in authority but believe in liberty as well, so we realize that, while there are rules of economics to be observed, they do not all point infallibly in one direction with no deviation to right or left. There are always choices open to us and there are always choices to be made. We are not an economically determinist party, still less a financially determinist one....

But we shall have to find an answer to the problem of unemployment. We all know that unemployment doubled under the last Labour Government. Michael Foot and other socialist Ministers continually said that the current level of unemployment was 'intolerable'. And what did they do? They tolerated it.

We also know that, had Labour won the last election, unemployment would have sharply increased. Yet neither the deficiencies of our opponents nor the world recession absolve us from trying to deal with what the Prime Minister has rightly called a 'human tragedy'. As she said, 'Human dignity and self-respect are undermined when men and women are condemned to idleness. The waste of a country's most precious assets — the talent and energy of its people — make it the bounden duty of government to seek a real and lasting cure....

There has been a temptation in some quarters to go back to the nineteenth century in search of allegedly eternal truths instead of seeking to adjust our ideas to take account of changing economic and political realities....

The legitimate boast of every Conservative Government since the war has been that we looked after those who had been hardest hit by economic and social forces beyond their control. We have done so for the sake of national solidarity and because of our Conservative sense of community....

References

1 *Unemployment*

1   Carlyle, *Past and Present*, p. 168.
2   Viner, in Boulding, *Economic Analysis*, p. 3.
3   Macmillan, *The Middle Way*, p. 372.
4   Deane, *The Evolution of Economic Ideas*, p. 156.
5   ibid., p. 156.
6   Galbraith, *Economics, Peace and Laughter*, pp. 7–9.
7   Hirschman, *Essays in Trespassing*, pp. 287–8.
8   Samuel Butler, *Erewhon*, ch. 22.
9   Orwell, *The Road to Wigan Pier*, p. 87.
10 First Report of the Social Security Advisory Committee, 1981, p. 33.
11 D. J. Smith, *Unemployment and Racial Minorities*, quoted in A. Walker, *The Poverty of Taxation*, p. 19.
12 ibid., pp. 19–20.
13 A. Walker, *The Poverty of Taxation*, pp. 25–6.
14 Supplementary Benefits Commission, *Annual Report 1979*, Cmnd 8033, pp. 8–9.
15 *European Economy*, no. 10, November 1981, pp. 112–14 (published by the Commission of the European Community).
16 Donnison, *The Politics of Poverty*, p. 69; A. Walker, *The Poverty of Taxation*, p. 21.
17 Minford and Peel, 'Is the Government's Economic Strategy on Course?', pp. 15–17. For a slightly fuller discussion of this, see chapter 10 below.
18 *Annual Report 1979*, Cmnd 8033, p. 41.
19 Donnison, *The Politics of Poverty*, p. 71.
20 See chapter 11 below.
21 HL, 1982, 142, p. 51.
22 Hinde, *Castlereagh*, p. 244.
23 Feiling, *The Second Tory Party, 1714–1832*, p. 293.
24 HL, 1982, 142, pp. 57–9.
25 Kapo, *A Savage Culture*, p. 145.

26 HL, 1982, 142, pp. 57–9.

27 Seabrook, *Unemployment*, pp. 212, 111.

28 HL, 1982, 142, p. 59.

29 Sinfield, *What Unemployment Means*, p. 105.

30 ibid., p. 150.

31 Donnison, *The Politics of Poverty*, p. 64.

32 Hansard, Standing Committee E, 26 February 1980, col. 1180, quoted in Supplementary Benefits Commission, *Annual Report 1979*, Cmnd 8033, p. 84.

33 Supplementary Benefits Commission, *Annual Report 1979*, Cmnd 8033, p. 86.

34 Report of the Social Service Advisory Committee, p. 26.

35 Coleridge, *A Lay Sermon*, p. 230.

36 Coleridge, *On the Constitution of the Church and State*, p. 7.

37 Speech in Birmingham Town Hall, 19 April 1979.

38 This passage is not in either of the *Alice* books. It appeared in Jonathan Miller's television production of *Alice*.

39 Skidelsky, *Politicians and the Slump*, p. 52.

40 Pinto-Duschinsky, *The Political Thought of Lord Salisbury, 1854–1868*, pp. 78–9.

2   Political Economy

1   Ricardo, *The Principles of Political Economy and Taxation*, p. 81.

2   Carlyle, *Past and Present*, pp. 1–3.

3   Disraeli, *Sybil*, bk 1, ch. 5.

4   Coleridge, *On the Constitution of the Church and State*, p. 156.

5   S. E. Finer, *The Life and Times of Sir Edwin Chadwick*, pp. 20–1.

6   Halévy, *The Growth of Philosophy Radicalism*, p. 104.

7   Cruikshank, *Charles Dickens and Early Victorian England*, p. 46.

8   Quoted in Rubin, *A History of Economic Thought*, p. 336, and in Halévy, *The Growth of Philosophic Radicalism*, p. 318.

9   E. Johnson, *Sir Walter Scott: The Great Unknown*, p. 1253.

10 Lockhart, *Life of Scott*, vol. 4, pp. 85–7.

11 E. Johnson, *Sir Walter Scott*, pp. 1157, 1253.

12 Lockhart, *Life of Scott*, vol. 4, pp. 73–4.

13 Coleridge, *Table Talk*, p. 198.

14 R. J. White, Introduction to Coleridge's *Lay Sermon*, p. xlii.

15 Coleridge, *Table Talk*, p. 318.

16 Coleridge, *On the Constitution of the Church and State*, p. 7.

17 Coleridge, *The Friend*, vol. 2, pp. 138–9.

18 Brinton, *Political Ideas of the English Romanticists*, p. 75.
19 Coleridge, *A Lay Sermon*, p. 229.
20 Coleridge, *Table Talk*, p. 318.
21 Coleridge, *A Lay Sermon*, p. 229.
22 Coleridge, *Table Talk*, pp. 198—9.
23 Coleridge, *A Lay Sermon*, pp. xli, 156—62; *On the Constitution of the Church and State*, p. 50.
24 R. Southey, *Essays*, vol. 2, p. 224; Cobban, *Edmund Burke and the Revolt against the Eighteenth Century*, p. 209.
25 R. Southey, *Colloquies*, vol. 1, p. 193; *Essays*, vol. 2, pp. 28—9.
26 C. C. Southey, *Life and Correspondence of Robert Southey*, vol. 6, p. 200.
27 R. Southey, *Essays*, vol. 1, p. 224.
28 R. Southey, *Colloquies*, vol. 1, p. 29.
29 Brinton, *Political Ideas of the English Romanticists*, p. 102.
30 R. Southey, Essays, vol. 2, p. 210; *Colloquies*, vol. 1, p. 195.
31 *The Excursion*, VIII, lines 167—85.
32 Moorman, *William Wordsworth*, vol. 2, p. 338.
33 ibid., p. 472.
34 E. Johnson, *Sir Walter Scott*, p. 975.
35 Cruikshank, *Charles Dickens and Early Victorian England*, p. 178.
36 Best, *Shaftesbury*, p. 125.
37 Coleridge, *A Lay Sermon*, p. 140; *On the Constitution of the Church and State*, p. 52.
38 Lord Robbins, *Political Economy, Past and Present*, p. 153.
39 Adam Smith, *The Wealth of Nations*, bk 4, ch. 2.
40 Ruskin, *The Stones of Venice*, vol. 3, p. 115.
41 Brinton, *Political Ideas of the English Romanticists*, p. 133.
42 Ricardo, *The Principles of Political Economy and Taxation*, ch. 5, pp. 52, 61.
43 Adam Smith, *The Wealth of Nations*, bk 1, ch. 8.
44 Gray and Thompson, *The Development of Economic Doctrine*, p. 267.
45 J. S. Mill, *Principles of Political Economy*, p. 992.
46 Hirschman, *Essays in Trespassing*, pp. 169—70.
47 Mitchell, *Alexander Hamilton*, p. 104.
48 Maccunn, *Six Radical Thinkers*, p. 188.
49 J. M. Keynes, *The General Theory of Employment, Interest and Money*, p. 32.
50 Adam Smith, *The Wealth of Nations*, bk 4, ch. 5.
51 Adam Smith, *A Theory of Moral Sentiments*, quoted in Deane, *The Evolution of Economic Ideas*, p. 7.
52 Carlyle, *Past and Present*, ch. 3, p. 18.

53 Maccunn, *The Political Philosophy of Edmund Burke*, p. 9.
54 See Halévy, *A History of the English People in the Nineteenth Century*, vol. 1, pp. 579—83.
55 James Mill, *An Essay on Government*, p. 17.
56 Coleridge, *Table Talk*, pp. 226—7.
57 Ruskin, *Unto This Last*, p. 2.
58 Sismondi — see n. 8 above.
59 *Peter Bell the Third*, pt II, XIV.
60 Schumpeter, *History of Economic Analysis*, p. 725.
61 Gray and Thompson, *The Development of Economic Doctrine*, pp. 270—1.
62 Carlyle, *Past and Present*, p. 16.
63 ibid.
64 Gray and Thompson, *The Development of Economic Doctrine*, p. 3.

3   *The Socialist Antithesis*

1 Engels, *Condition of the Working Class in England*, ch. 12, quoted in Hobsbawm, *The Age of Revolution*, p. 182.
2 Hume, *Essays*, p. 48.
3 Troyat, *Tolstoy*, p. 591.
4 Berlin, *Karl Marx*, p. 21.
5 Popper, *The Open Society and its Enemies*, vol. 2, p. 166.
6 Stewart, *Keynes and After*, p. 31; Popper, vol. 2, *The Open Society and its Enemies*, pp. 168—9, 184.
7 Dumont, *From Mandeville to Marx*, pp. 147, 84.
8 Marx, *The Poverty of Philosophy*, quoted in Barber, *A History of Economic Thought*, p. 120.
9 Gray, *The Socialist Tradition*, p. 322.
10 Preface to the *Critique of Political Economy*.
11 Carr, *The Bolshevik Revolution 1917—1923*, vol. 2, p. 5.
12 Marx, *The Civil War in France*, p. 44.
13 Engels, Introduction to *The Civil War in France*, p. 19.
14 Carr, *The Bolshevik Revolution 1917—1923*, vol. 1, p. 77; Conquest, *Lenin*, p. 83.
15 Ulam, *Lenin and the Bolsheviks*, p. 430.
16 Hook, *Revolution, Reform and Social Justice*, pp. 52, 77.
17 Berlin, *Karl Marx*, p. 18.
18 Popper, *The Open Society and its Enemies*, vol. 2, p. 133.
19 Baechler, *The Origins of Capitalism*, p. 40.
20 Steiner, *Tolstoy or Dostoyevsky*, p. 259.

21 Hook, *Revolution, Reform and Social Justice*, p. 170.
22 Beevor, *The Spanish Civil War*, p. 19.
23 Quoted in Ionescu, 'Lenin, the Commune and the State', p. 155.

4 *The Synthesis and the Tory Tradition*

1 Carlyle, *Past and Present*, p. 19.
2 Coleridge, *Biographia Literaria*, p. 112.
3 Montesquieu, *De l'Esprit des Lois*, Introduction to vol. 1.
4 Woodward, *The Age of Reform 1815–1870*, pp. 12–13.
5 Perkin, *The Origins of Modern English Society*, p. 237.
6 Southey, *Essays*, vol. 2, p. 211.
7 Perkin, *The Origins of Modern English Society*, pp. 241–2.
8 Cobban, *Edmund Burke and the Revolt against the Eighteenth Century*, p. 209.
9 Perkin, *The Origins of Modern English Society*, p. 243.
10 ibid., pp. 248–9.
11 ibid., pp. 248–51.
12 Woodward, *The Age of Reform 1815–1870*, p. 453.
13 Carlyle, *Past and Present*, p. 2.
14 Woodward, *The Age of Reform 1815–1870*, pp. 449–56; Halévy, *A History of the English People in the Nineteenth Century*, vol. 3, pp. 119–29.
15 *The Age of Bronze*, lines 572–3.
16 Brinton, *English Political Thought in the Nineteenth Century*, p. 49.
17 Pelling, *A History of British Trade Unionism*, pp. 16–23.
18 Harrison, *Before the Socialists*, pp. 2, 12.
19 Pelling, *A History of British Trade Unionism*, pp. 66–7.
20 R. J. White, *The Conservative Tradition*, pp. 208–9.
21 Baring Pemberton, *William Cobbett*, pp. 169–70.
22 Best, *Shaftesbury*, p. 89; Rubin, *A History of Economic Thought*, p. 324.
23 Halévy, *A History of the English People in the Nineteenth Century*, vol. 4, p. 138.
24 Best, *Shaftesbury*, p. 105.
25 ibid., p. 118.
26 ibid., pp. 124–5.
27 Bellairs, *Conservative Social and Industrial Reform*, p. 13.
28 Preface to the first German edition of *Capital*, Marx–Engels, *Selected Works*, vol. 1, p. 408.
29 Woodward, *The Age of Reform 1815–1870*, pp. 610–11.

30 Gash, *Mr Secretary Peel*, pp. 621—2.
31 Gash, *Sir Robert Peel*, pp. 318—19, 322.
32 ibid., pp. 589—90.
33 Lord Butler, *The Conservatives*, p. 97.
34 'Not a Middle Party but a Middle Government', *Collected Works of Bagehot*, ed. St John-Stevas, vol. 7, p. 198.
35 Woodward, *The Age of Reform 1815—1870*, pp. 150, 610.
36 *The Wisdom of Disraeli*, ed. Comyn-Platt, p. 62.
37 Carlyle, *Past and Present*, p. 29.
38 Disraeli, *Lord George Bentinck*, p. 557.
39 R. J. White, *The Conservative Tradition*, p. 26.
40 Ward, in Southgate, *The Conservative Leadership 1832—1932*, pp. 99, 90.
41 Blake, *Disraeli*, p. 553.
42 Moneypenny and Buckle, *The Life of Benjamin Disraeli*, vol. 2, p. 712.
43 Crystal Palace speech, 1872, *Tory Democrat*, pp. 46—7.
44 Southgate, *The Conservative Leadership 1832—1932*, p. 202.
45 P. Smith, *Lord Salisbury on Politics*, p. 49.
46 Kennedy, *Salisbury 1830—1903*, pp. 147, 297.
47 Boothby, *I Fight to Live*, p. 382.
48 Lewis and Maude, *The English Middle Classes*, quoted in Beer, *Modern British Politics*, p. 273.
49 Thornton, *The Habit of Authority*, p. 287.
50 Brogan, *The American Political System*, pp. 23—4.
51 Halévy, *The Growth of Philosophic Radicalism*, pp. 205—7, 225.
52 Burn, *The Age of Equipoise*, p. 153.
53 Robbins, *Political Economy, Past and Present*, p. 59.

5   *The Retreat from Political Economy (or the Neo-Classicals)*

1 Quoted in Thomas, *The White Hotel*, p. 111n.
2 Dostoevsky, *The House of the Dead*, p. 257.
3 *The Works of George Savile*, ed. Raleigh, p. 242.
4 Schumpeter, *History of Economic Analysis*, p. 76.
5 Blaug, *Economic Theory in Retrospect*, p. 127.
6 Schumpeter, *History of Economic Analysis*, p. 540.
7 Gray and Thompson, *The Development of Economic Doctrine*, p. 326.
8 Lord Balogh, *The Irrelevance of Conventional Economics*, pp. 32—3, 78—9.
9 Schumpeter, *History of Economic Analysis*, p. 888.
10 Marshall, *Principles of Economics*, pp. 92—3.

11 Gray and Thompson, *The Development of Economic Doctrine*, p. 268.

12 Schumpeter, *History of Economic Analysis*, pp. 545, 886, 892.

13 ibid., p. 919, n. 23.

14 Adam Smith, *The Wealth of Nations*, p. 232.

15 ibid., p. 169.

16 Deane, *The Evolution of Economic Ideas*, p. 121.

17 Blaug, *Economic Theory in Retrospect*, pp. 406, 416, 290.

18 Stewart, *Keynes and After*, pp. 40—1.

19 Quoted in Balogh, *The Irrelevance of Conventional Economics*, p. 12.

20 Ensor, *England 1870—1914*, p. 501.

21 Harrod, *The Life of John Maynard Keynes*, p. 143.

22 Marshall, *Principles of Economics*, pp. 315—16.

23 Joan Robinson, 'What has Become of the Keynesian Revolution?', in Milo Keynes (ed.), *Essays on John Maynard Keynes*, p. 124.

24 Schumpeter, *History of Economic Analysis*, pp. 827, 242, 1021.

25 Tobin, *Asset Accumulation and Economic Activity*, p. 34.

26 *Lecture on Political Economy*, quoted in Robinson, *Economic Philosophy*, p. 54.

27 Schumpeter, *History of Economic Analysis*, pp. 1021, 1015.

28 Gray and Thompson, *The Development of Economic Doctrine*, p. xvii.

29 Blaug, *Economic Theory in Retrospect*, p. 495.

30 Schumpeter, *History of Economic Analysis*, pp. 986—8.

31 Mises, *A Critique of Interventionism*, p. 20.

32 ibid., pp. 21—2, 48, 18, 32—4.

33 ibid., p. 26.

34 Faulkner, *From Versailles to the New Deal*, p. 205.

35 Cooke, *The Vintage Mencken*, pp. 222—3.

36 *Reflections on the Revolution in France.*

37 Maccunn, *The Political Philosophy of Edmund Burke*, p. 42.

38 Speech on the Reform of Representation in the Commons, 1782.

39 *Reflections on the Revolution in France.*

40 Maccunn, *The Political Philosophy of Edmund Burke*, p. 9.

41 Deane, *The Evolution of Economic Ideas*, pp. 84—5.

42 *Principles of Political Economy*, pp. 4, 8.

43 ibid., p. 8.

44 For an excellent discussion of this point, see Professor Preece's 'The Political Economy of Edmund Burke', *Modern Age*, Summer 1980, pp. 266—73; see also Gilmour, *Inside Right*, pp. 66—7.

45 Dostoevsky, *Letters from the Underworld*, trs. C. J. Hogarth, pp. 25—40.

46 Dumont, *From Mandeville to Marx*, pp. 61—2.

47 Ruskin, *Unto this Last*, p. 60.

48 Robinson, *Economic Philosophy*, p. 74.

6   *Keynes and the Inter-War Years*

1   Harrod, *The Life of John Maynard Keynes*, p. 143.
2   Gilbert, *Winston Churchill*, vol. 5, pp. 97—8.
3   Macmillan, *The Middle Way*, p. 369.
4   Stewart, *Keynes and After*, p. 13.
5   Skidelsky, *Politicians and the Slump*, pp. 11—12, 60.
6   Blake, *The Conservative Party from Peel to Churchill*, p. 228.
7   Brittan, *Left or Right: the Bogus Dilemma*, p. 69.
8   Skidelsky, *Politicians and the Slump*, p. 59.
9   J. M. Keynes, *The Economic Consequences of Mr Churchill*, p. 8.
10   Skidelsky, *Politicians and the Slump*, p. 276.
11   Skidelsky (ed.), *The End of the Keynesian Era*, pp. 19—22; Gilbert, *Winston Churchill*, vol. 5, p. 51.
12   Gilbert, *Winston Churchill*, vol. 5, p. 97.
13   J. M. Keynes, *A Tract on Monetary Reform*, p. 68.
14   Harrod, *The Life of John Maynard Keynes*, p. 346.
15   U. K. Hicks, *The Finance of British Government, 1920—1936*, p. 279.
16   Harrod, *The Life of John Maynard Keynes*, p. 352.
17   Deane, *The Evolution of Economic Ideas*, pp. 176—7.
18   ibid., p. 179.
19   Hansard, 15 April 1929, col. 54.
20   Skidelsky, *Politicians and the Slump*, pp. 40—1; Moggridge, *Keynes*, p. 184.
21   J. M. Keynes, *Essays in Persuasion*, pp. 118—19.
22   Skidelsky, 'The Revolt against the Victorians' in Skidelsky (ed.), *The End of the Keynesian Era*, p. 9.
23   Harrod, *The Life of John Maynard Keynes*, p. 348.
24   ibid., pp. 346—50.
25   Gilbert, *Winston Churchill*, vol. 5, pp. 92—100.
26   J. M. Keynes, *The Economic Consequences of Mr Churchill*, pp. 6, 22, 23.
27   Gilbert, *Winston Churchill*, p. 98.
28   Skidelsky, *Politicians and the Slump*, p. 68.
29   J. M. Keynes, *Essays in Persuasion*, pp. 132—7.
30   Stewart, *Keynes and After*, p. 72.
31   J. M. Keynes, *Essays in Persuasion*, p. 165.
32   Hayek, *The Road to Serfdom*, p. 9.
33   *The Middle Way*, p. 198.
34   Feiling, *The Life of Neville Chamberlain*, p. 229.
35   Clarke, *The Conservative Party*, p. 63; Beer, *Modern British Politics*, pp. 292—7.

36 Stewart, *Keynes and After*, p. 176.
37 14 February 1935, quoted in ibid., p. 75.
38 Moggridge, *Keynes*, pp. 108—9, 118—19.
39 Middlemas and Barnes, *Stanley Baldwin*, p. 931.
40 Skidelsky, 'The Political Meaning of the Keynesian Revolution', in Skidelsky (ed.), *The End of the Keynesian Era*, p. 36.
41 Hayek, *Full Employment at Any Price?*, p. 15.
42 J. M. Roberts, *The Pelican History of the World*, p. 207.
43 J. M. Keynes, *The General Theory of Employment, Interest and Money*, pp. xxi, xxiii.
44 Dostoevsky, *Crime and Punishment*, Epilogue.
45 Marcello de Cecco, 'The Last of the Romans', in Skidelsky (ed.), *The End of the Keynesian Era*, pp. 22—3.
46 J. M. Keynes, *The General Theory of Employment, Interest and Money*, p. 378.
47 ibid., pp. 378—9.
48 M. Keynes, *Essays on John Maynard Keynes*, p. 127.
49 Moggridge, *Keynes*, p. 187.
50 ibid., pp. 30, 137.
51 Harrod, *The Life of John Maynard Keynes*, p. 465.
52 ibid., p. 466.

7 *The Post-War Years and How Monetarism Captured the Conservatives*

1 Lines 3—4.
2 Montaigne, 'That a man ought soberly to meddle with judging of divine laws', *Essays*, Bk 1, ch. 31.
3 On the promulgation of Papal Infallibility in 1870.
4 Cmnd 6524.
5 Pliatsky, *Getting and Spending*, p. 10.
6 Lord Robbins, quoted in Harrod, *The Life of John Maynard Keynes*, p. 584.
7 Kahn, 'Mr Eltis and the Keynesians', p. 5.
8 Pollard, *The Wasting of the British Economy*, pp. 2—3.
9 Eltis, 'The Failure of the Keynesian Conventional Wisdom', p. 1.
10 Speech at Preston, 5 September 1974.
11 Brittan, *How to End the Monetarist Controversy*, p. 19.
12 Matthews, 'Why has Britain had Full Employment since the War?'.
13 ibid., pp. 556—7.
14 Scott, *Can We Get Back to Full Employment?*, p. 3.
15 ibid., pp. 20—1.

16 Beer, *Britain Against Itself*, p. 38.
17 Scott, *Can We Get Back to Full Employment?*, pp. 68—9.
18 Pollard, *The Wasting of the British Economy*, pp. 1, 23, 22, 39, 47—51.
19 Harrod, *Towards a New Economic Policy*, p. 30; quoted in Pollard, op. cit, p. 50.
20 Brittan, *The Treasury under the Tories*, p. 288.
21 Deane, *The Evolution of Economic Ideas*, p. 187.
22 Schonfield, *Modern Capitalism*, pp. 272—4, 287—8.
23 ibid., pp. 275, 282, 296, 438.
24 ibid., pp. 292—3.
25 Hirschman, *Essays in Trespassing*, p. 6.
26 Friedman, *The Optimum Quantity of Money*, p. 96. But the words quoted here were first spoken in 1967.
27 Galbraith, *Economics, Peace and Laughter*, pp. 47—8.
28 Stewart, *Keynes and After*, pp. 285—7.
29 Wigham, *Strikes and the Government, 1893—1974*, p. 106.
30 Tapsell, *Monetarism in Practice*, pp. 18—21.
31 Joseph, *Reversing the Trend*, p. 4; quoted in Butler and Kavanagh, *The British General Election of 1974*, p. 64.
32 Paul Smith (ed.), *Lord Salisbury on Politics*, p. 24.
33 Joseph, *Monetarism is not Enough*, p. 7.
34 ibid., pp. 7—8.
35 Clarke, *The Conservative Party*, p. 63.
36 Crosland, *Socialism Now*, p. 18.
37 Wand, *The Four Great Heresies*, p. 57.

8   *The Socialist Alternative*

1 Bell, *The Cultural Contradictions of Capitalism*, p. 245.
2 Runciman, *Social Science and Political Theory*, p. 47.
3 *The Complete Writings of William Blake*, ed. G. Keynes, p. 667.
4 *Labour's Programme 1982*, pp. 7—8, 17, 23, 19, 191.
5 Hook, *Revolution, Reform and Social Justice*, p. 1.
6 The process is well described in Kogan and Kogan, *The Battle for the Labour Party*, passim and p. 12.
7 *Labour's Programme 1982*, pp. 93—9, 18—19, 21, 24, 36, 8, 9.
8 ibid., pp. 229, 247—8, 205—6, 120, 126—7, 179, 206, 211—12, 216, 215, 249, 51, 7.
9 Pliatsky, *Getting and Spending*, p. 130.

10 Ninth Report from the Committee of Public Accounts, 1981–2, 17 March 1981.
11 Barnett, *Inside the Treasury*, p. 128.
12 Benn, *Arguments for Democracy*, pp. 3–17.
13 Crouch, in Kavanagh (ed.), *The Politics of the Labour Party*, pp. 176, 181.
14 Butler and Kavanagh, *The British General Election of 1979*, p. 343.
15 Benn, *Arguments for Democracy*, p. 166.
16 *Labour's Programme 1982*, pp. 4, 39, 44, 69, 284, 179, 209.
17 ibid., p. 35.
18 ibid., p. 244.
19 R. A. Butler, *Our Way Ahead*, p. 10.
20 Hayek, *The Road to Serfdom*, p. 89.
21 Montesquieu, *De l'Esprit des Lois*, vol. 2, 4.
22 Crewe, in Kavanagh (ed.), *The Politics of the Labour Party*, p. 13.
23 ibid., pp. 37, 26.
24 Rodgers, *The Politics of Change*, p. 166.
25 Crewe, in Kavanagh (ed.), *The Politics of the Labour Party*, p. 45.
26 Benn, *Arguments for Democracy*, pp. 223–4.
27 Crewe, in Kavanagh (ed.), *The Politics of the Labour Party*, p. 41.
28 Kogan and Kogan, *The Battle for the Labour Party*, p. 105.
29 Benn, *Arguments for Democracy*, p. 101.
30 Mackintosh, *Parliament and Social Democracy*, p. 161.
31 Speech in Huyton, 17 September 1982.

9 *The Monetarist Diagnosis*

1 Friedman, *The Optimum Quantity of Money*, p. v.
2 Bacon and Eltis, *Britain's Economic Problem: Too Few Producers*, p. 89.
3 Hicks, in *Crisis '75*, ed. Seldon, p. 17.
4 Congdon, *Monetarism: An Essay in Definition*, p. 1.
5 ibid., p. 18.
6 Friedman, *The Counter-Revolution in Monetary Theory*, pp. 22–6.
7 Congdon, *Monetarism: An Essay in Definition*, pp. 23–5.
8 Friedman, *The Counter-Revolution in Monetary Theory*, pp. 22–6.
9 ibid.
10 ibid.
11 Lawson, *The New Conservatism*, p. 4.
12 Friedman, *The Counter-Revolution in Monetary Theory*, pp. 22–6.
13 ibid.
14 F. A. Hayek, letter to *The Times*, 8 June 1980.

15 Friedman, Treasury and Civil Service Committee 1979–80, *Memoranda on Monetary Policy*, p. 56.

16 Friedman, *Unemployment versus Inflation?*, p. 30; Friedman, in *Inflation: Causes, Consequences, Cures*, pp. 44–7.

17 Congdon, *Monetarism: An Essay in Definition*, pp. 23–5.

18 Friedman, *The Optimum Quantity of Money*, pp. 105, 102–4.

19 Congdon, *Monetarism: An Essay in Definition*, pp. 23–5.

20 Friedman, Treasury and Civil Service Committee 1979–80, *Memoranda on Monetary Policy*, p. 56.

21 Friedman, 'Monetarism: A Reply to the Critics', *The Times*, 3 March 1980.

22 Schumpeter, *History of Economic Analysis*, pp. 312–15, 702–5.

23 Blaug, *Economic Theory in Retrospect*, pp. 557–8; Schumpeter, *History of Economic Analysis*, p. 1101.

24 Tobin, *Asset Accumulation and Economic Activity*, p. 9.

25 J. M. Keynes, *A Tract on Monetary Reform*, p. 80.

26 Lord Kahn, letter to *The Times*, 14 April 1977.

27 Quoted in J. M. Keynes, *A Tract on Monetary Reform*, p. 74.

28 Friedman, quoted in Balogh, *The Irrelevance of Conventional Economics*, p. 174.

29 Friedman, *The Counter-Revolution in Monetary Theory*, p. 17.

30 Friedman, *The Optimum Quantity of Money*, p. 265.

31 Friedman, 'The New Monetarism, Comment', p. 53.

32 Friedman, *The Optimum Quantity of Money*, p. 97.

33 Kaldor, 'The New Monetarism', p. 13.

34 This seems, for example, to be the argument of David Laidler in his essay 'A Survey of Some Current Problems', pp. 101–3, in Clayton *et al.*, *Monetary Theory and Monetary Policy in the 1970s*.

35 HC, 1979–80, 720, p. 60.

36 Cramp, 'Does Money Matter?', p. 31.

37 HC, 1979–80, 720, pp. 57–8.

38 Friedman, *The Optimum Quantity of Money*, p. 269.

39 Tobin, 'Money and Income: Post Hoc Ergo Propter Hoc?', p. 301.

40 ibid., pp. 318–27.

41 Hahn, 'Professor Friedman's View on Money', p. 394.

42 Friedman, *The Optimum Quantity of Money*, p. 174, n. 6.

43 Walters, *Money in Boom and Slump*, p. 41.

44 *The Times*, 13 July 1976.

45 ibid., 23 August 1976.

46 ibid., 14 July 1976.

47 Congdon, *Monetarism: An Essay in Definition*, p. 6.

48 *The Times*, 8 May 1977.

49 ibid., 24 May 1980.
50 Richardson, *Reflections on the Conduct of Monetary Policy*, p. 12.
51 Friedman, 'The New Monetarism, Comment', p. 53.
52 ibid., p. 55.
53 Reprinted in *Essays on Economic Policy*, vol. 1, pp. 128–53.
54 ibid., p. 129.
55 Kaldor, *The Scourge of Monetarism*, pp. 26–7.
56 See Frank Hahn's review of *The Optimum Quantity of Money* in *Economica* (1971), reprinted in Surrey, *Macroeconomic Theory*, p. 400.
57 Friedman, *Unemployment versus Inflation*, p. 35.
58 Parkin, 'Where is Britain's Inflation Going?', p. 4; see also Friedman, *Unemployment versus Inflation*, pp. 30–5, and in *Inflation: Causes, Consequences, Cures*, pp. 45-7.
59 Hayek, *Full Employment at any Price?*, p. 46; and *Inflation: Causes, Consequences, Cures*, p. 118; see also Peter Jay in the same volume, pp. 27–34.
60 Robbins, *Political Economy, Past and Present*, p. 93.
61 Hicks, 'What is Wrong with Monetarism?', pp. 5, 7.
62 See, for example, Hayek in *Inflation: Causes, Consequences, Cures*, p. 118; Friedman, *The Counter-Revolution in Monetary Theory*.
63 See Kahn, 'Thoughts on the Behaviour of Wages and Monetarism', p. 2.
64 Tylecote, *The Causes of the Present Inflation*, p. 18.
65 ibid., pp. 13–18; Scott, *Can we Get Back to Full Employment?*, p. 4.
66 Henry Phelps Brown, 'A Non-Monetarist View of the Recent Pay Explosion'.
67 Friedman, *The Counter-Revolution in Monetary Theory*, p. 24.
68 I am greatly indebted to Dr Brian Outhwaite, the second edition of whose book *Inflation in Tudor and Early Stuart England* was published in the autumn of 1982.
69 Friedman, *The Optimum Quantity of Money*, p. 101.
70 ibid., p. 102.
71 Tobin, *Asset Accumulation and Economic Activity*, p. 41.
72 Minford and Peel, 'Is the Government's Economic Strategy on Course?', p. 2.
73 ibid., p. 1.
74 'Preposterous Claims of the Monetarists', *The Times*, 28 April 1981.
75 M. Keynes, *Essays on John Maynard Keynes*, p. 126.

10 *The Monetarist Cure*

1 Friedman, *The Optimum Quantity of Money*, p. 172.

2   Letter to *The Times*, 3 March 1980.

3   Speech at Upminster, 22 June 1974; quoted in Norton and Aughey, *Conservatives and Conservatism*, p. 87.

4   Letter to *The Times*, 4 March 1980.

5   Lord Cockfield, HL, 2 April 1980, col. 1362.

6   Treasury and Civil Service Committee, Monetary Policy, *Minutes of Evidence*, pp. 208—9.

7   Ford, *Monetary Aggregates and Economic Policy*, p. 1.

8   Richardson, *Reflections on the Conduct of Monetary Policy*, p. 14.

9   ibid., pp. 8—9.

10 Ford, *Monetary Aggregates and Economic Policy*, p. 1.

11 Minford and Peel, 'Is the Government's Economic Strategy on Course?', p.1.

12 Mr John Biffen, Hansard, 1 July 1980, cols. 1397, 1396.

13 HC, 1979—80, 720, pp. 8—9.

14 Lawson, *The New Conservatism*, pp. 4—5.

15 Richardson, *Reflections on the Conduct of Monetary Policy*, pp. 12—13.

16 Lord Cockfield, HL, 2 April 1980, col. 1362.

17 *Sunday Telegraph*, 2 May 1982.

18 Minford, 'A Return to Sound Money', p. 31.

19 Patrick Minford, Evidence to the Treasury and Civil Service Committee 1980—1, HC, 163—11.

20 HC, 1981—2, 270, para. 30.

21 J. M. Keynes, *The Economic Consequences of Mr Churchill*, p. 19.

22 Barnett, *Inside the Treasury*, pp. 22, 124.

23 *Financial Statement and Budget Report, 1980—81*, p. 16.

24 HC, 1979—80, 720, Table 6, p. 116, and Lord Kaldor's *Memorandum*, paras, 87—96.

25 *Financial Statistics*, May 1982.

26 *Budget Financing and Monetary Control* (OECD, 1982), Tables 1 and 3.

27 J. M. Keynes, *Essays in Persuasion*, p. 281.

28 Department of Employment Press Notices, 26 October and 2 December 1982.

29 Preliminary results of the 1981 *General Household Survey — OPCS Monitor*, GHS 82/1, table 14, and the 1981 *Labour Force Survey*, OPCS Series LF3, no. 3 table 4.14.

30 HC, 1979—80, 163—11, p. 212.

31 J. M. Keynes, *The Economic Consequences of Mr Churchill*, p. 9.

32 Buiter and Miller, *The Thatcher Experiment*, p. 23.

33 Hansard, vol. 29, col. 284.

34 Buiter and Miller, *The Thatcher Experiment*, p. 77.

35 See, for example, Professor Tobin's evidence, Treasury and Civil Service Committee, Monetary Policy, *Minutes of Evidence*, p. 210; Ford, *Money*

Aggregates and Economic Policy, p. 13.
36 *Observer*, 11 July 1982.
37 *Financial Times*, 9 November 1982.
38 Written reply from Mr David Waddington to Mr David Knox, Hansard, 6 July 1982.
39 From 'Verses on the Death of Dr Swift'.
40 At Thornaby, 24 April 1981.
41 Leon Brittan, speeches to the Brigg and Scunthorpe Conservative Association, 2 April 1982, and at the opening of Cutler's Gardens, 17 May 1982.
42 HC, 1979—80, 720, pp. 56, 60.
43 *The Times*, 31 March 1980.
44 Friedman, *Essays in Positive Economics*, quoted in Tylecote, *The Causes of the Present Inflation*, p. 200; Balogh, *The Irrelevance of Conventional Economics*, pp. 14, 216, 178; Minford and Pell, 'Is the Government's Economic Strategy on Course?', p. 122.
45 Gray and Thompson, *The Development of Economic Doctrine*, p. 294.
46 Schumpeter, *History of Economic Analysis*, p. 668.
47 Congdon, *Monetarism: An Essay in Definition*, p. 13.
48 Carlyle, *Past and Present*, p. 158.
49 J. M. Keynes, *The General Theory of Employment, Interest and Money*, p. 34.

11 *Economic Recovery*

1 Pollard, *The Wasting of the British Economy*, p. 165.
2 Letwin, *The Pursuit of Certainty*, p. 14.
3 Barnett, *Inside the Treasury*, p. 49.
4 Kirk, *The Conservative Mind*, p. 292.
5 T. H. White, *The Age of Scandal*, p. 80.
6 Note to stanza III of Canto II of *Childe Harold's Pilgrimage*.
7 Quoted by Mr Christopher Patten, MP, Hansard, 9 November 1982, col. 469.
8 Cornford, *Microcosmographia Academica*, p. 14.
9 Speech by the writer on 'R. A. Butler and the Continuity of Post-War Conservatism', 8 November 1980.
10 *Guardian*, 19 October 1982.
11 Group of Thirty, *Exchange Rate Policy Reconsidered*, p. 4.
12 Lever and Edwards, *Banking on Britain*, pp. 7—8.
13 ibid., p. 11.

14   I am indebted to Mr George Edwards for these figures.

15   Popper, *The Open Society and its Enemies*, vol. 2, p. 167.

16   See Cawson, *Corporatism and Welfare*, pp. 59—60, 65.

17   Schenk, *The Aftermath of the Napoleonic Wars*, p. 192.

18   Grant, *The Political Economy of Industrial Policy*, p. 97.

19   ibid., pp. 75, 24.

20   ibid., p. 144.

21   Buiter and Miller, *The Thatcher Experiment*, p. 16.

22   *United Kingdom Balance of Payments*, 1982, Table 6.1.

23   Middlemas, *Politics in Industrial Society*, p. 180.

24   Lord Goschen, *Essays on Economic Questions* (1905), p. 17, quoted by Professor Glyn Davies in his first submission to the Wilson Committee, p. 6.

25   Professor Davies, first submission to the Wilson Committee, p. 8.

26   J. M. Keynes, *Essays in Persuasion*, p. 176.

27   Skidelsky, *Politicians and the Slump*, p. 28.

28   Middlemas, *Politics in Industrial Society*, p. 180.

29   Lord Butler, *The Art of Memory*, p. 17.

30   *Property Monthly*, August 1982.

31   Cmnd 7937, para. 257.

32   George Edwards, *Bank Lending and Industrial Investment*, 1979, a response to the British Clearing Banks' paper of the same title. In what follows I am greatly indebted to Mr. Edwards.

33   Carrington and Edwards, *Financing Industrial Investment*, p. 183.

34   Lever and Edwards, *Banking on Britain*, pp. 15—16.

35   Henry Phelps Brown, *Incomes Policy, a Modest Proposal*, p. 3.

36   Tylecote, *The Causes of the Present Inflation*, pp. 110—16.

37   Patten, *The Tory Case*, p. 127.

38   Waldegrave, *The Binding of Leviathan*, p. 68.

39   Meade, *Wage-Fixing*, vol. 1, *Stagflation*.

40   Hayek, *The Constitution of Liberty*, pp. 220, 228—30, 282—3.

41   Usher, *The Economic Prerequisite to Democracy*, pp. 50—1, 136.

42   Ruskin, *Unto this Last*, pp. 141—2.

43   Layard, *Is Incomes Policy the Answer to Unemployment?*

44   Henry Phelps Brown, *Incomes Policy, a Modest Proposal*, pp. 8—10.

45   Meade, *Wage-Fixing*, vol. 1, *Stagflation*, p. 109.

46   Norris, 'Differentials in Pay', p. 31.

47   ibid., p. 37.

48   Layard, *A New Deal for the Unemployed*.

49   HL, 1982, 142, pp. 70, 155, 150, 146.

50   ibid., pp. 161—3.

51   *Employment Gazette*, April 1980, p. 386, quoted in Sinfield, *What Unemployment Means*, p. 82.

52 ibid., pp. 82—3.
53 Ruskin, *Unto this Last*, pp. 164—5.
54 Burke, *Appeal from the New to the Old Whigs.*

12 *Political Recovery*

1 Letter to the Sheriffs of Bristol, 1777.
2 *The Works of George Savile*, ed. Raleigh, p. 245.
3 Blake, *The Conservative Party from Peel to Churchill*, p. 37.
4 Lord Butler (ed.), *The Conservatives*, p. 142.
5 Guttsman, *The English Political Elite*, p. 213.
6 Lloyd George, *War Memoirs*, p. 627.
7 Middlemas, *Politics in Industrial Society*, pp. 20, 243.
8 Addison, *The Road to 1945*, p. 55.
9 ibid., p. 56.
10 Middlemass, *Politics in Industrial Society*, pp. 371—4.
11 Speech on 'The Duration of Parliament', 1780.
12 Ionescu, *Centripetal Politics*, pp. 1—2.
13 Mack Smith, *Mussolini*, pp. 271, 414.
14 Mack Smith, *Italy*, p. 395.
15 Procacci, *History of the Italian People*, p. 430.
16 Tamames, *La República: La Era de Franco*, p. 441.
17 Benn, *Arguments for Democracy*, p. 137.
18 Ionescu, *Centripetal Politics*, p. 27.
19 Herman Finer, *The Major Governments of Modern Europe*, p. 9.
20 Rousseau, *Social Contract*, p. 275.
21 Sieyès, pp. 158—9.
22 Maitland, *The Constitutional History of England*, p. 85.
23 Burke, *Reflections on the Revolution in France.*
24 Disraeli, *Vindication of the English Constitution*, pp. 181—2; see also Robert Blake, *Disraeli*, p. 282.
25 Brinton, *English Political Thought in the Nineteenth Century*, pp. 207—9.
26 Amery, *Thoughts on the Constitution*, pp. 64—7.
27 Romanes Lecture, quoted in Gilbert, *Winston S. Churchill*, vol. 5, pp. 361—2.
28 Macmillan, *The Middle Way*, pp. 291, 293.
29 Schumpeter, *Capitalism, Socialism and Democracy*, p. 380.
30 Nevil Johnson, *In Search of the Constitution*, p. 26.
31 Mackintosh, *Parliament and Social Democracy*, p. 213.
32 Butler and Pinto-Duschinsky, *The British General Election of 1970*, pp. xiv, 92.

33 *Report of the Commission on Electoral Reform*, 1976.
34 Trevelyan, *The Life of John Bright*, pp. 205—7.
35 Robert Blake, in David Butler (ed.), *Coalitions in British Politics*, p. 1.
36 Nevil Johnson, *In Search of the Constitution*, p. 218.
37 Middlemas, *Politics in Industrial Society*, p. 317.
38 Gilbert, *Winston S. Churchill*, vol. 5, pp. 365—6.
39 David Butler, *The Electoral System in Britain since 1918*, p. 209; Lakeman, *How Democracies Vote*, p. 301.
40 Macmillan, *The Past Masters*, p. 237.
41 Mackintosh, *Parliament and Social Democracy*, pp. 172—3.
42 Middlemas, *Politics in Industrial Society*, p. 433 and 433n.
43 *Trade and Industry*, 17 November 1978, pp. 358—60.
44 Burke, speech, 6 February 1772.
45 Churchill, *Lord Randolph Churchill*, pp. 65—6.
46 Brogan, *Citizenship Today*, p. 14.
47 Bell, *The Cultural Contradictions of Capitalism*, p. 78n.
48 Nigel Harris, *Competition and the Corporate Society*, p. 172.
49 Macdonald, *The State and the Trade Unions*, p. 75.
50 'Taming the Barons', reprinted in Mackintosh, *Parliament and Social Democracy*, pp. 112—35.
51 Disraeli, *Vindication of the English Constitution*, p. 134.
52 Coombes, *Representative Government and Economic Power*, pp. 86—7.
53 *The Times*, 17 August 1982.
54 Middlemas, *Politics in Industrial Society*, p. 98.
55 See Coombes, *Representative Government and Economic Power*, pp. 78—93, for a useful discussion.
56 Crouch, 'Varieties of Trade Union Weakness', pp. 87—104.
57 Scott, *Can We Get Back to Full Employment?*, pp. 4, 43—67.
58 Coombes, *Representative Government and Economic Power*, p. 141.
59 J. M. Keynes, *A Tract on Monetary Reform*, p. 34.
60 William Shakespeare, *King Henry IV, Part I*, Act III, sc. i.
61 *Parliament through Seven Centuries*, p. 9.
62 *King Henry IV, Part I*, Act III, sc. i.
63 See Mackintosh, *Parliament and Social Democracy*, p. 132.
64 Bell, *The Cultural Contradictions of Capitalism*, p. 259.
65 Kirk, *The Conservative Mind*, p. 157.
66 Coit, *John C. Calhoun*, p. 529.
67 Nevil Johnson, *In Search of the Constitution*, p. 228.
68 Carlyle, *Past and Present*, pp. 237, 241.
69 Dahrendorf, *On Britain*, p. 107.
70 Gilmour, *The Body Politic*, p. 333.

71 Cowling, *The Impact of Hitler*, pp. 52, 436.

72 Deane, *The Evolution of Economic Ideas*, p. 121; C. B. Macpherson, *The Real World of Democracy*, p. 58.

73 Samuel Butler, *Erewhon*, ch. 21.

74 See Hook, *Revolution, Reform and Social Justice*, p. 45.

75 *Reflections on the Revolution in France.*

76 Dahrendorf, 'Effectiveness and Legitimacy', p. 407.

77 Ruskin, *Unto this Last*, p. 102. The words first appeared in *Modern Painters*.

78 See von Mises, *A Critique of Intervention*, p. 60.

79 See Norton and Aughey, *Conservatives and Conservatism*, pp. 280–6.

Appendix

1 Brinton, *English Political Thought*, p. 64.

Bibliography

Adison, Paul, *The Road to 1945*, London, 1975

Agar, Herbert, *The United States*, London, 1950

Amery, L. S., *Thoughts on the Constitution*, 2nd ed., Oxford, 1953

Bacon, Robert, and Eltis, Walter, *Britian's Economic Problem: Too Few Producers*, London, 1976

Baechler, Jean, *The Origins of Capitalism*, Oxford, 1975

Ball, R. J., *Money and Employment*, London, 1982

Balogh, Lord, *The Irrelevance of Conventional Economics*, London, 1982

Barber, William J., *A History of Economic Thought*, London, 1967

Baring Pemberton, W., *William Cobbett*, London, 1949

Barnett, Joel, *Inside the Treasury*, London, 1982

Beer, Samuel H., *Modern British Politics*, London, 1965

Beer, Samuel H., *Britain Against Itself*, London, 1982

Beer, S. H., and Ulam, A. D. (eds.), *Patterns of Government*, 2nd ed., New York, 1962

Beevor, Anthony, *The Spanish Civil War*, London,1982

Behrens, Robert, *The Conservative Party from Heath to Thatcher*, London, 1980

Bell, Daniel, *The Coming of Post-Industrial Society*, London, 1973

Bell, Daniel, *The Cultural Contradictions of Capitalism*, London, 1976

Bellairs, Charles, E., *Conservative Social and Industrial Reform*, London, 1977

Benn, Tony, *Arguments for Democracy*, London, 1981

Berlin, Isaiah, *Montesquieu*, London, 1955

Berlin, Isaiah, *Karl Marx*, 2nd ed., London, 1948

Best, C. F. A., *Shaftesbury*, London, 1964

Birch, A. H., *Representative and Responsible Government*, London, 1964

Blake, Robert, *Disraeli*, London, 1966

Blake, Robert, *The Conservative Party from Peel to Churchill*, London, 1970

Blaug, M., *Economic Theory in Retrospect*, London, 1964

Block, Geoffrey, *A Source Book of Conservatism*, London 1964

Böhm-Bawerk, Eugen von, *Karl Marx and the Close of his System*, London, 1898

Boothby, Robert, *I Fight to Live*, London, 1947

Boulding, Kenneth E., *Economic Analysis*, 3rd ed., London, 1955

Brinton, Crane, *Political Ideas of the English Romanticists*, Oxford, 1926

Brinton, Crane, *English Political Thought in the Nineteenth Century*, London, 1933

Brittan, Samuel, *The Treasury under the Tories, 1951—1964*, London, 1964

Brittan, Samuel, *Left or Right, the Bogus Dilemma*, London, 1968

Brittan, Samuel, *Steering the Economy*, London, 1971

Brittan, Samuel, *Capitalism and the Permissive Society*, London, 1973

Brittan, Samuel, *How to End the Monetarist Controversy*, 2nd ed., London, 1982

Brittan, Samuel, and Lilley, Peter, *The Delusion of Incomes Policy*, London, 1977

Brogan, D. W., *The American Political System*, London 1943

Brogan, D. W., *The Price of Revolution*, London, 1951

Brogan, D. W., *Citizenship Today*, North Carolina, 1960

Brown, A. J., 'Inflation and the British Sickness', *Economic Journal*, March 1979

Brown, Henry Phelps, 'A Non-Monetarist View of the Recent Pay Explosion', *Three Banks Review*, March 1975

Brown, Henry Phelps, *Incomes Policy, A Modest Proposal*, London, N. D.

Brown, Henry Phelps, 'The Underdevelopment of Economics', *Economic Journal*, March 1972

Buck, Philip W. (ed.), *How Conservatives Think*, London, 1975

Buiter, Willem H., and Miller, Marcus, *The Thatcher Experiment: An Interim Report*, London, 1981

Bullock, Alan, and Shock, M. (eds.), *The Liberal Tradition*, London, 1956

Burke, Edmund, *Works*, 16 vols., 1826—7

Burn, W. L., *The Age of Equipoise*, London, 1964

Butler, R. A., *Our Way Ahead*, London, 1956

Butler, R. A., *The Art of the Possible*, London, 1971

Butler, Lord (ed.), *The Conservatives*, London, 1977

Butler, Lord, *The Art of Memory*, London, 1982

Butler, D. E., *The British General Election of 1951*, London, 1952

Butler, D. E., *The Electoral System in Britain 1918—51*, 2nd ed., Oxford, 1963

Butler, D. E., and Rose, Richard, *The British General Election of 1959*, London, 1960

Butler, David (ed.), *Coalitions in British Politics*, London, 1978

Butler, David, and Kavanagh, Dennis, *The British General Election of February 1974*, London, 1974

Butler, David and Kavanagh, Dennis, *The British General Election of 1979*, London, 1980

Butler, David, and Kitzinger, Uwe, *The 1975 Referendum*, London, 1976

Butler, David and Pinto-Duschinsky, Michael, *The British General Election of 1970*, London, 1971

Butler, David, and Stokes, Donald, *Political Change in Britain*, London, 1969

Butler, Samuel, *Erewhon*, 1872

Campbell, Peter, *French Electoral Systems*, London 1958

Carlyle, Thomas, *Past and Present*, 1843

Carr, E. H., *The Bolshevik Revolution, 1917–1923*, 3 vols., London, 1950–3

Carrington, J. C., and Edwards, George, *Financing Industrial Investment*, London, 1979

Carrington, J. C., and Edwards, George, *Reversing Economic Decline*, London, 1981

Cawson, Alan, *Corporatism and Welfare*, London, 1982

Churchill, Winston, *Lord Randolph Churchill*, London, 1907

Citrine, Lord, *Men and Work*, London, 1964

Clarke, David, *The Conservative Party*, London, n.d.

Clayton, G., *et al.*, *Monetary Theory and Monetary Policy in the 1970s*, London, 1971

Cobban, Alfred, *Edmund Burke and the Revolt against the Eighteenth Century*, London, 1929

Coit, M., *John C. Calhoun*, London, 1950

Coleridge, S. T., *The Friend*, 2 vols., 1812

Coleridge, S. T., *A Lay Sermon*, ed. R. J. White, London, 1972

Coleridge, S. T., *Table Talk*, 1835

Coleridge, S. T., *Biographia Literaria*, Everyman ed., London, 1965

Coleridge, S. T., *On the Constitution of the Church and State*, Everyman ed., London, 1972

Congdon, Tim, *Monetarism: An Essay in Definition*, London, 1978

Conquest, Robert, *Lenin*, London, 1972

Cooke, Alistair (ed.), *The Vintage Mencken*, New York, 1955

Coombes, David, *Representative Government and Economic Power*, London, 1982

Cornford, F. M., *Microcosmographia Academica*, 5th ed., Cambridge, 1953

Courtney, C. P., *Montesquieu and Burke*, Oxford, 1963

Cowling, Maurice, *The Impact of Hitler*, Cambridge, 1975

Cowling, Maurice (ed.), *Conservative Essays*, London, 1978

Cramp, A. B., 'Does Money Matter?', *Lloyds Bank Review*, October 1970

Crosland, C. A. R., *The Future of Socialism*, London, 1956

Crosland, C. A. R., *Socialism Now*, London, 1975

Crosland, C. A. R., *Social Democracy in Europe*, London, 1975

Crouch, Colin, 'Varieties of Trade Union Weakness', *West European Politics*, vol. 3, no. 1, January 1980
Cruikshank, R. J., *Charles Dickens and Early Victorian England*, London, 1949
Dahrendorf, Ralf, *The New Liberty*, London, 1975
Dahrendorf, Ralf, 'Effectiveness and Legitimacy', *Political Quarterly*, vol. 51, 1980
Dahrendorf, Ralf, *After Social Democracy*, London, 1981
Dahrendorf, Ralf, *On Britain*, London, 1982
Deane, Phyllis, *The Evolution of Economic Ideas*, Cambridge, 1978
Desai, Meghnad, *Testing Monetarism*, London, 1981
Dickens, Charles, *Bleak House*, 1852–3
Dickens, Charles, *Hard Times*, 1854
Disraeli, Benjamin, *Popanilla*, 1827
Disraeli, Benjamin, *Vindication of the English Constitution*, 1835
Disraeli, Benjamin, *Coningsby*, 1844
Disraeli, Benjamin, *Sybil*, 1845
Disraeli, Benjamin, *Tory Democrat* (Disraeli's Manchester and Crystal Palace Speeches), 1950
Disraeli, Benjamin, *Lord George Bentinck*, 1852
Disraeli, The Wisdom of, ed. T. Comyn-Platt, London, 1920
Donnison, David, *The Politics of Poverty*, Oxford, 1982
Douglas, James, 'The Overloaded Crown', *British Journal of Political Science*, October 1976
Dostoevsky, *The House of the Dead*, 1861–2
Dostoevsky, *Crime and Punishment*, 1866
Dostoevsky, *Letters from the Underworld*, trs. C. J. Hogarth, London, 1968
Drucker, H. M., *Doctrine and Ethos in the Labour Party*, London, 1979
Dumont, Louis, *From Mandeville to Marx*, Chicago, 1977
Eatwell, John, *Whatever Happened to Britain?*, London, 1982
Eichner, Alfred S., (ed.), *A Guide to Post-Keynesian Economics*, London, 1979
Eltis, Walter, 'The Failure of the Keynesian Conventional Wisdom', *Lloyds Bank Review*, no. 122, October 1976
Ensor, R. C. K., *England 1870–1914*, London, 1936
Faulkner, Harold U., *From Versailles to the New Deal*, New Haven, 1951
Feiling, Keith, *The Second Tory Party 1714–1832*, London, 1938
Feiling, Keith, *The Life of Neville Chamberlain*, London, 1946
Finer, Herman, *The Major Governments of Modern Europe*, London, 1960
Finer, S. E., *The Life and Times of Sir Edwin Chadwick*, London, 1952
Finer, S. E. (ed.), *Adversary Politics and Electoral Reform*, London, 1975

Finer, S. E., *The Changing British Party System 1945—1979*, Washington, 1980

Flemming, John, *Inflation*, London, 1976

Ford, J. L., *Monetary Aggregates and Economic Policy*, Birmingham, 1982

Friedman, Milton, *The Optimum Quantity of Money*, London, 1969

Friedman, Milton, *The Counter-Revolution in Monetary Theory*, London, 1970

Friedman, Milton, 'The New Monetarism, Comment', *Lloyds Bank Review*, October 1970

Friedman, Milton, *Monetary Correction*, London, 1974

Friedman, Milton, in *Inflation, Causes, Consequences, Cures*, Institute of Economic Affairs, London, 1974

Friedman, Milton, *Unemployment versus Inflation?*, London, 1975

Friedman, Milton, *From Galbraith to Economic Freedom*, London, 1977

Friedman, Milton, 'Monetarism: a Reply to the Critics', *The Times*, 3 March 1980

Galbraith, J. K., *Economics, Peace and Laughter*, London, 1971

Galbriath, J. K., *Economics and the Public Purpose*, London, 1974

Galbraith, J. K., *The New Industrial State*, 2nd ed., London, 1974

Gamble, Andrew, *The Conservative Nation*, London, 1974

Gash, Norman, *Politics in the Age of Peel*, London, 1953

Gash, Norman, *Mr Secretary Peel*, 1961

Gash, Norman, *Reaction and Reconstruction in British Politics 1832—1852*, London, 1965

Gash, Norman, *Sir Robert Peel*, London, 1972

Gilbert, Martin, *Winston S. Churchill*, vol. 5, *1922—1939*, London, 1976

Gilmour, Ian, *The Body Politic*, London, 1969

Gilmour, Ian, *Inside Right*, London, 1977

Goodhart, Philip, *Referendum*, London, 1971

Goodhart, Philip, *Full-Hearted Consent*, London, 1976

Grant, Wyn, *The Political Economy of Industrial Policy*, London, 1982

Gray, Alexander, *The Socialist Tradition*, London, 1946

Gray, Alexander and Thomson, F. E., *The Development of Economic Doctrine*, London, 1980

Griffiths, Brian, *Inflation*, London, 1976

Grimond, Jo, *The Common Welfare*, London, 1978

Grondona, L. St Clare, *Economic Stability is Attainable*, London, 1975

Group of Thirty, *Rate Policy Reconsidered*, Occasional Paper No. 10, New York, 1982

Guttsman, W. L., *The British Political Elite*, London, 1963

Hahn, Frank, 'Professor Friedman's view on Money', *Economica*, 1971; reprinted in M. J. C. Surrey (ed.), *Macroeconomic Themes*

Hahn, Frank, 'Review of *The Optimum Quantity of Money*', *Economica*,

1971; reprinted in M. J. C. Surrey (ed.), *Macroeconomic Themes*

Hahn, Frank, 'Preposterous Claims of the Monetarists', *The Times*, 28 April 1981

Hailsham, Lord, *The Conservative Case*, rev. ed., London, 1959

Hailsham, Lord, *The Door Wherein I Went*, London, 1975

Hailsham, Lord, *The Dilemma of Democracy*, London, 1978

Halévy, Elie, *The Growth of Philosophic Radicalism*, London, 1928

Halévy, Elie, *A History of the English People in the Nineteenth Century*, 6 vols., London, 1934—47

Halifax, Marquess of, The Works of George Savile, ed. W. Raleigh, London, 1912

Hansard Society, *Report of the Commission on Electoral Reform*, London, 1976

Harris, Nigel, *Competition and the Corporate Society*, London, 1972

Harris, Ralph, and Sewell, Brendon, *British Economic Policy 1970—74, Two Views*, London, 1975

Harrison, Royden, *Before the Socialists*, London, 1965

Harrod, R. F., *The Life of John Maynard Keynes*, London, 1951

Harrod, Roy, *Towards a New Economic Policy*, London, 1967

Hayek, F. A., *The Constitution of Liberty*, London, 1960

Hayek, F. A., *The Road to Serfdom*, London, 1944

Hayek, F. A., *Full Employment at any Price?*, London, 1975

Heilbronner, Robert L., *The Quest for Wealth*, London, 1958

Hibbert, Christopher, *The Rise and Fall of the Medici*, London, 1974

Hicks, Sir John, 'What is Wrong with Monetarism?', *Lloyds Bank Review*, October 1975

Hicks, U. K., *The Finance of British Government, 1920—1936*, London, 1938

Hill, B. W. (ed.), *Edmund Burke on Government, Politics and Society*, London, 1975

Hinde, Wendy, *Castlereagh*, London, 1981

Hirsch, Fred, *Social Limits to Growth*, London, 1977

Hirschman, Albert O., *Exit, Voice and Loyalty*, Cambridge, Mass., 1970

Hirschman, Albert O., *Essays in Trespassing*, Cambridge, 1981

Hobsbawm, E. J., *The Age of Revolution*, London, 1962

Hook, Sidney, *Revolution, Reform and Social Justice*, Oxford, 1976

Howell, David, *Freedom and Capital*, Oxford, 1981

Hume, David, *A Treatise on Human Nature*, 1739—40, Oxford ed., 1888

Hume, David, *Essays, Moral, Political and Literary*, 1741—2, Oxford ed., 1963

Hume, David, *Enquiries Concerning Human Understanding and Concerning the Principles of Morals* (posthumous ed.), 1777, Oxford ed., 1975

Hurd, Douglas, *An End to Promises*, London, 1979

252 *Bibliography*

Hutchinson, George, *The Last Edwardian at No. 10*, London, 1980
Inflation: Causes, Consequences, Cures, Institute of Economic Affairs, London, 1974
Ionescu, G., 'Lenin, the Commune and the State', *Government and Opposition*, Spring 1970
Ionescu, G. (ed.), *The New Politics of European Integration*, London, 1972
Ionescu, G., *Between Sovereignty and Integration*, London, 1974
Ionescu, G., *Centripetal Politics*, London, 1975
Jennings, Sir Ivor, *Cabinet Government*, 3rd ed., Cambridge, 1959
Johnson, Edgar, *Sir Walter Scott*, The Great Unknown, London, 1970
Johnson, Nevil, *In Search of the Constitution*, Oxford, 1977
Jones, Aubrey, *The New Inflation*, London, 1973
Joseph, Sir Keith, *Monetarism is not Enough*, London, 1976
Joseph, Sir Keith, *Stranded on the Middle Ground?*, London, 1976
Joseph, Sir Keith, *Reversing the Trend*, London, 1975
Kahn, Lord, 'Thoughts on the Behaviour of Wages and Monetarism', *Lloyds Bank Review*, January 1976
Kahn, Lord, 'Mr Eltis and the Keynesians', *Lloyds Bank Review*, no. 124, April 1977
Kaldor, Nicholas, *Essays on Economic Policy*, 2 vols., London, 1964
Kaldor, Nicholas, 'The New Monetarism', *Lloyds Bank Review*, July 1970
Kaldor, Nicholas, 'The Irrelevance of Equilibrium Economics', *Economic Journal*, vol. 82, 1972
Kaldor, Nicholas, *The Scourge of Monetarism*, Oxford, 1982
Kapo, Remi, *A Savage Culture – Racism – a Black British View*, London, 1981
Kavanagh, D., (ed.), *The Politics of the Labour Party*, London, 1982
Kennedy, A. L., *Salisbury 1830–1903*, London, 1953
Key, V. O., *Public Opinion and American Democracy*, New York, 1961
Key, V. O., *Politics, Parties and Pressure Groups*, 5th ed., New York, 1964
Keynes, Geoffrey (ed.), *The Complete Writings of William Blake*, London, 1957
Keynes, J. M., *A Tract on Monetary Reform*, London, 1923
Keynes, J. M., *The Economic Consequences of Mr Churchill*, London, 1925
Keynes, J. M., *A Treatise on Money*, London, 1930
Keynes, J. M., *Essays in Persuasion*, London, 1931
Keynes, J. M., *The General Theory of Employment, Interest and Money*, London, 1936
Keynes, Milo (ed.), *Essays on John Maynard Keynes*, Cambridge, 1975
King, Anthony (ed.), *Why is Britain Becoming Harder to Govern?*, London, 1976
Kirk, Russell, *The Conservative Mind*, London, 1954

Kogan, David, and Kogan, Maurice, *The Battle for the Labour Party*, London, 1982

Labour's Programme 1982

Lakeman, Enid, *How Democracies Vote*, London, 1974

Lawson, Nigel, *The New Conservatism*, London, 1980

Layard, Richard, *Unemployment in Britain: Causes and Cures*, London, 1981

Layard, Richard, *Is Incomes Policy the Answer to Unemployment?*, Discussion Paper No. 99, Centre for Labour Economics, London, 1981

Layard, Richard, *A New Deal for the Unemployed*, Working Paper No. 295, Centre for Labour Economics, London, 1981

Letwin, S. R., *The Pursuit of Certainty*, London, 1965

Lever, Harold, and Edwards, George, *Banking on Britain*, London, 1981

Lichtheim, George, *A Short History of Socialism*, London, 1975

Lloyd George, David, *War Memoirs*, 2 vols., London, 1938

Lockhart, John Gibson, *Life of Scott*, Edinburgh, 1837

Macoby, S. (ed.), *The Radical Tradition*, London, 1952

Maccunn, John, *Six Radical Thinkers*, London, 1907

Maccunn, John, *The Political Philosophy of Edmund Burke*, London, 1913

Macdonald, J. F., *The State and the Trade Unions*, London, 1960

McDowell, R. B., *British Conservatism 1832–1914*, London, 1952

Mack, Mary P., *Jeremy Bentham*, London, 1962

McKenzie, Robert, *British Political Parties*, 2nd ed., London, 1963

Mackintosh, John P., *The Devolution of Power*, London, 1968

Mackintosh, John P., *Parliament and Social Democracy*, London, 1982

Mack Smith, Denis, *Italy*, Ann Arbor, 1959

Mack Smith, Denis, *Mussolini*, London, 1981

Macmillan, Harold, *The Middle Way*, 2nd ed., London, 1966

Macmillan, Harold, *The Past Masters*, London, 1975

Macpherson, C. B., *The Real World of Democracy*, London, 1966

Maitland, F. W., *The Constitutional History of England*, Cambridge, 1908

Malthus, Rev. T. R., *Principles of Political Economy*, 2nd ed., 1836

Marshall, A. *Principles of Economics* (7th ed.), London, 1916

Marwick, Arthur, *British Society since 1945*, London, 1982

Marx, Karl, *The Civil War in France*, Marxist-Leninist Library ed., London, 1933

Marx, Karl and Engels, F., *Selected Works*, 2 vols. Moscow, 1950

Matthews, Professor R. C. O., 'Why has Britain had Full Employment since the War?' *Economic Journal*, September 1968

Meade, J. F., *Wage-Fixing*, vol. 1, *Stagflation*, London, 1982

Merrill, Giles, *World out of Work*, London, 1982

Middlemas, Keith, *Politics in Industrial Society*, London, 1979

Middlemas, Keith, and Barnes, John, *Stanley Baldwin*, London, 1969

Miliband, Ralph, *Parliamentary Socialism*, London, 1961

Mill, J. S., *Principles of Political Economy*, London, 1920

Mill, James, *An Essay on Government*, Cambridge ed., 1937

Minford, Patrick, 'A Return to Sound Money', *Banker*, July 1979

Minford, Patrick, and Peel, David, 'Is the Government's Economic Strategy on Course?', *Lloyds Bank Review*, April 1981

Mises, Ludwig von, *A Critique of Interventionism*, New York, 1977

Mitchell, Broadus, *Alexander Hamilton*, London, 1976

Moggridge, D. E., *Keynes*, 2nd ed., London, 1980

Moneypenny, W. F., and Buckle, G. F., *The Life of Benjamin Disraeli*, 6 vols., London, 1914–20.

Montaigne, Michael, Lord of, *Essays*, Temple Classics ed., 1898

Montesquieu, Charles Louis de Secondat de, *De l'Esprit des Lois*, 1748

Moorman, Mary, *William Wordsworth*, 2 vols., London, 1968

Mosse, George L., *The Culture of Western Europe*, London, 1963

Mossner, E. C., *Life of David Hume*, London, 1954

Mowat, C. L., *Britain Between the Wars 1918–1940*, London, 1955

Nisbet, Robert, *Twilight of Authority*, London, 1976

Norris, W. K., 'Differentials in Pay', *Lloyds Bank Review*, October 1975

Norton, Philip, *The Constitution in Flux*, Oxford, 1982

Norton, Philip, and Aughey, Arthur, *Conservatives and Conservatism*, London, 1981

Oakeshott, Michael, *Rationalism in Politics*, London, 1962

Orwell, George, *The Road to Wigan Pier*, London, 1937

O'Sullivan, Noel, *Conservatism*, London, 1976

Outhwaite, Brian, *Inflation in Tudor and Early Stuart England*, 2nd ed., London, 1982

Parkin, M., 'Where is Britain's Inflation Going?', *Lloyds Bank Review*, July 1975

Parliament through Seven Centuries, London, 1962

Patten, Christopher, *The Tory Case*, London, 1983

Peacock, Alan, *The Economic Analysis of Government*, Oxford, 1979

Pelling, H., *The Challenge of Socialism*, London, 1954

Pelling, H., *A Short History of the Labour Party*, London, 1961

Pelling, H., *A History of British Trade Unionism*, London, 1963

Perkin, Harold, *The Origins of Modern English Society*, London, 1969

Pinto-Duschinsky, M., *The Political Thought of Lord Salisbury 1854–1868*, London, 1967

Pinto-Duschinsky, Michael, *British Political Finance 1830–1980*, Washington and London, 1981

Plamenatz, John, *The English Utilitarians*, London, 1949

Plender, John, *That's the Way the Money Goes*, London, 1982

Pliatsky, Leo, *Getting and Spending*, Oxford, 1982
Pollard, Sidney, *The Wasting of the British Economy*, London, 1982
Popper, K. R., *The Open Society and its Enemies*, 2 vols., London, 1945
Popper, K. R., *Conjectures and Refutations*, London, 1963
Popper, K. R., *Unended Quest*, London, 1976
Preece, R., 'The Political Economy of Edmund Burke', *Modern Age*, Summer 1980
Procacci, Giuliano, *History of the Italian People*, London, 1973
Quinton, Anthony, *The Politics of Imperfection*, London, 1978
Rees-Mogg, William, *The Reigning Error*, London, 1974
Rees-Mogg, William, 'How a 9.4 per cent Excess Money Supply gave Britain 9.4 per cent Inflation', *The Times*, 13 July 1976
Ricardo, David, *The Principles of Political Economy and Taxation*, ed. Donald Winch, London, 1977
Richardson, Gordon, *Reflections on the Conduct of Monetary Policy*, London, 1978
Ridley, F., and Blondel, J., *Public Administration in France*, London, 1964
Robbins, Lord, *Political Economy, Past and Present*, London, 1976
Roberts, B. C., *Trade Unions in a Free Society*, 2nd ed., London, 1962
Roberts, J. M., *The Pelican History of the World*, London, 1980
Robinson, Joan, *Economic Philosophy*, London, 1962
Rodgers, William, *The Politics of Change*, London, 1982
Rogaly, Joe, *Parliament for the People*, London, 1976
Rolo, P. J. V., *George Canning*, London, 1965
Rousseau, J. J., *Social Contract*, World's Classics ed.
Rubin, Isaac Ilyich, *A History of Economic Thought*, London, 1979
Runciman, W. G., *Social Science and Political Theory*, Cambridge, 1963
Runciman, W. G., *Relative Deprivation and Social Justice*, London, 1966
Ruskin, John, *Unto this Last*, London, 1906
Ruskin, John, *The Stones of Venice*, 3 vols., Everyman ed., London, 1935
St John-Stevas, Norman (ed.), *The Collected Works of Bagehot*, 12 vols., London 1974–
St John-Stevas, Norman, 'Tory Philosophy', *Three Banks Review*, June 1982
Schenk, A. G., *The Aftermath of the Napoleonic Wars*, London, 1947
Schonfield, Andrew, *British Economic Policy since the War*, London, 1958
Schonfield, Andrew, *Modern Capitalism*, London, 1965
Schumpeter, Joseph A., *Capitalism, Socialism and Democracy*, 3rd ed., London, 1950
Schumpeter, Joseph A., *History of Economic Analysis*, London, 1956
Scott, Maurice, *Can We Get Back to Full Employment?*, London, 1978
Scruton, Roger, *The Meaning of Conservatism*, London, 1980
Seabrook, Jeremy, *Unemployment*, London, 1982

Seldon, Arthur, (ed.), *Crisis '75...?*, London, 1975

Seldon, Arthur, *Charge*, London, 1977

Shaw, G. B., *Man and Superman*, 1903

Shaw, G. K., *Macro-Economic Policy*, 3rd ed., London, 1980

Sieyès, Abbé, *What is the Third Estate?*, London, 1963

Sinfield, Adrian, *What Unemployment Means*, London, 1981

Skidelsky, R., *Politicians and the Slump*, London, 1967

Skidelsky, R. (ed.), *The End of the Keynesian Era*, London, 1977

Smith, Adam, *The Wealth of Nations*, Everyman ed., London, 1954

Smith, D. J., *Unemployment and Racial Minorities*, Policy Studies Institute, London, 1981

Smith, Paul (ed.), *Lord Salisbury on Politics*, Cambridge, 1972

Southey, C. C., *Life and Correspondence of Robert Southey*, 6 vols., London, 1849–50

Southey, R., *Colloquies*, 2 vols., 1829

Southey, R., *Essays, Moral and Political*, 2 vols., 1832

Southgate, Donald (ed.), *The Conservative Leadership 1832–1932*, London, 1974

Steiner, George, *Tolstoy or Dostoevsky*, London, 1960

Stewart, Michael, *Keynes and After*, 2nd ed., London, 1972

Surrey, M. J. C. (ed.), *Macroeconomic Themes*, Oxford, 1976

Talmon, J. L., *The Origins of Totalitarian Democracy*, London, 1952

Tamames, Ramon, *La República, La Era de Franco*, 8th ed., Madrid, 1980

Tapsell, Peter, *Monetarism in Practice*, Cairo, 1981

Taylor, A. J. P., *English History 1914–1945*, London, 1965

Thomas, D. M., *The White Hotel*, London, 1981

Thornton, A. P., *The Habit of Authority*, London, 1966

Tobin, James, 'Money and Income; Post Hoc Ergo Propter Hoc?', *Quarterly Journal of Economics*, vol. 84, no. 2, May 1970

Tobin, James, *Asset Accumulation and Economic Activity*, Oxford, 1981

Tobin, James, 'The Monetarist Counter-Revolution Today – an Appraisal', *Economic Journal*, March 1981

Tobin, James, 'Inflation and Unemployment', *American Economic Review*, vol. 62, 1972

Trevelyan, G. M., *The Life of John Bright*, London, 1913

Troyat, Henri, *Tolstoy*, New York, 1967

Truman, David B., *The Governmental Process*, New York, 1951

Tylecote, Andrew, *The Causes of the Present Inflation*, London, 1981

Tyrrell, R. Emmett Jr (ed.), *The Future that Doesn't Work*, New York, 1977

Ulam, Adam B., *Lenin and the Bolsheviks*, Fontana ed., London, 1969

Usher, Dan, *The Economic Prerequisite to Democracy*, Oxford, 1981

Viereck, Peter, *Conservatism Revisited*, London, 1950

Vile, M. J. C., *Constitutionalism and the Separation of Powers*, London, 1967

Wadhwani, S. B., *Wage Inflation in the UK*, London School of Economics, Centre for Labour Economics, March 1982

Waldegrave, William, *The Binding of Leviathan*, London, 1978

Walker, Alan (ed.), *The Poverty of Taxation*, London, 1982

Walker, Peter, *The Ascent of Britain*, London, 1977

Walters, A. A., *Money in Boom and Slump*, London, 1969

Wand, J. W. C., *The Four Great Heresies*, London, 1955

White, R. J. (ed.), *The Conservative Tradition*, London, 1950

White, T. H., *The Age of Scandal*, London, 1962

Wiener, Martin J., *English Culture and the Decline of the Industrial Spirit 1850–1980*, Cambridge, 1981

Wigham, Eric, *Strikes and the Government, 1893–1974*, London, 1976

Wilson, Harold, *The Labour Government 1964–1970*, Pelican ed., Harmondsworth, 1974

Woodward, Sir Llewellyn, *The Age of Reform 1815–1870*, 2nd ed., London, 1962

Wootton, Graham, *Pressure Politics in Contemporary Britain*, Lexington, Mass., 1978

Index